JEREMY HOWARD-WILLIAMS

SMALL BOAT SAILS

Previously published
as *Dinghy Sails* and
Racing Dinghy Sails

INTERNATIONAL MARINE
PUBLISHING COMPANY
Camden, Maine

Published by International Marine Publishing Co., a division of Highmark Publishing Ltd., 21 Elm Street, Camden, Maine 04843

Published simultaneously in Great Britain by Adlard Coles, William Collins Sons & Co Ltd, London

Printed and bound in Great Britain

10 9 8 7 6 5 4 3 2 1

Library of Congress Cataloging-in-Publication Data
Howard-Williams, Jeremy, 1922–
  Small boat sails.
  Includes index.
  1. Sails. 2. Sailboats. I. Title.
  VM532.H63 1988   623.8'62   87-22796

ISBN 0-87742-964-2

CONTENTS

ACKNOWLEDGEMENTS

In preparation of a book of this nature, there are bound to be many who help by provision of technical advice, photographs, drawings or facilities. I am grateful to all who were kind in this way, and most of them have been acknowledged at the appropriate point in the text. The following were particularly helpful: Tony Marchaj (theory), MacAllister Elliott & Partners (sail rigs), David Thomas (light displacement cruiser/racers), Ian Henry (board sails), W. G. Lucas & Son (sailmaking), Bruce Banks Sails (sailmaking), my son Christopher (the Jeanneau *Fun*), ICI Films and ICI Fibres (sailcloth and sail care), Dimension Sailcloth (sailcloth) and Des Sleightholme and Mike Collins (who each did some of the drawings).

Many proprietary names and trademarks have passed into the language over the years, and they have often assumed the status of everyday terms. Where such words have been knowingly used in this book, the first mention and the index entry have been marked by the symbol ®. Unwitting inclusion of further unidentified trademarks does not imply that they have necessarily acquired a general significance in the legal sense; I apologise for not marking them appropriately, as I do for any incorrect attribution I may have made.

INTRODUCTION TO THE THIRD EDITION

In 1965 Adlard Coles asked me to write a book about sails for the publishing company which bore his name, and I was briefed to produce 'the most complete work on the subject in the English language'. The result was *Sails*, which was certainly the first comprehensive work on the subject since the days of cotton; it has over 400 pages of closely argued text, covering almost every aspect of the subject, and has been regularly revised over eight separate printings, just going into its 6th edition. When it first came out, many owners were inclined to take their sails for granted, and even racing crews were content to 'set and forget'. But I like to think that *Sails* helped to generate a healthy curiosity about the sailing yacht's motive power; at any rate, there was soon a demand for something similar but aimed more closely at racing dinghies, and without the rather lengthy technicalities supported by half the Greek alphabet.

The result was *Racing Dinghy Sails*. This was later expanded to include those dinghies which potter about, as well as the racing fraternity, plus a bit of DIY sailmaking, so in 1978 the second edition was retitled *Dinghy Sails*. Sailboards have now been included and, because they need to be handled like dinghies, it seems reasonable that light displacement keelboat cruiser/racers should also be added. I don't include in this new edition such day-sailing keelboats as the Dragon or Soling, because they are displacement boats and are catered for in *Sails*, to which I refer those readers who are keen to learn more about such technicalities as cloth construction, the mathematics of lift and drag, design and rating, the Chinese rig, etc.

I have kept this smaller work relatively simple, but I hope it will help to explain something of the importance of sails. They are the power unit of a sailing boat, which wouldn't get very far without them. It pays to understand them.

Warsash 1987   J. H-W

1 THEORY

No serious examination of sails, their behaviour, and the proper use of them would be complete without a study of the basic aerodynamics associated with the problem.

Approaches to Sail Shape

There are three different approaches to sail shape, only the last of which is the principal concern of this chapter.

Naval architect
A naval architect draws the outline shape of the sails he proposes for the hull he has designed. He must balance the various water and air pressures involved, must study efficiency of rig, and must consider the relevant class or rating rules. I call this *sail outline design*.

Sailmaker
It is the sailmaker's job to give the sails the right characteristics for the conditions in question (strength of wind, boat shape, and type of spars and rigging). This should include selection of cloth, depth and position of camber or belly, and the degree of control to be exercised over the final shape when in use on the boat. I call this *sail flow design*.

Owner
Finally, it is up to you, the owner, to set, trim, and look after your sails so that you get the most efficiency from them through correct shape and angle to the wind. This is *sail handling* in its widest sense.

The job of a sail is to turn the energy of the wind into thrust acting on the boat (which has been so shaped to turn that thrust into forward movement).

Aerodynamics

There are five facts which should be known before this chapter goes any further:

1. When airflow patterns are illustrated, the direction and relative speed of the air are shown by the direction and spacing of the lines (called streamlines) which depict the flow: the closer they are together, the faster the flow, and vice versa[1].

2. When a force acting on a sail is drawn, its power and the direction in which it acts are represented by the length and direction of the arrow. A long arrow means plenty of power, while a shorter one shows weakness. These terms are relative, that is to say that both forces might be called weak by aircraft engine standards, or strong by those of a fly. It is the *relative* power which is illustrated: an arrow twice as long as another represents a force twice as strong[2].

3. Pressure in a fluid (and air is a fluid) drops as its speed of motion increases; it rises as the speed decreases (this is the famous Bernoulli's Law, which you may hear quoted by the pundits)[3].

4. When fast-moving air (which is at low pressure, as described by Bernoulli's Law) becomes turbulent, as in the stall, it immediately reverts to its original atmospheric pressure[4].

5. A sharp pressure difference between neighbouring masses of air can only exist if there is some sort of barrier between those masses, such as an aerofoil, a sail, or even a mass of turbulent air (e.g. in the stall).

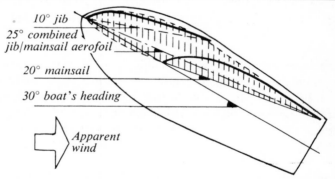

Fig. 1.1 *Apparent Wind Angles*   This figure shows the different wind angles relative to different base lines of a boat when beating to windward; the angle made with the boat's heading doesn't vary much from 30° under the more usual close-hauled conditions. The sails, however, can be at finer wind angles, particularly the jib, depending on the angle at which they are sheeted relative to the boat. In the drawing, both mainsail and jib are as wide as they normally ever go when close hauled (10° and 20° to the fore-and-aft line of the boat for mainsail and jib respectively). The shaded portion shows the approximate area of an aerofoil covering both jib and mainsail, and which is at an angle of 25° under these conditions. A sail's chord angle (to the boat centreline) thus equals the angle of the apparent wind to the boat's heading (say, 30° when close-hauled), minus the angle of incidence of that particular sail to the mean apparent wind (i.e. not the localized apparent wind, which may be altered due to upwash).

Plate 1.1 *The Wind Tunnel – 1*   A jib under test by ICI Fibres to evaluate sail shape and cloth distortion; the tallies reveal airflow, and the triangles allow distortion to be measured. (*Yendell*)

Airflow Direction

As most of you will know, a boat beating to windward will sail at an angle of about 45° to the true wind. The forward speed of the boat has the effect of making the apparent wind felt on board come from farther ahead. The difference is usually about 15° so, for our purposes, we can assume that the apparent wind angle when close hauled is 30° to the boat's heading. But the sails make an angle of anything from 5° to 20° with the fore-and-aft line of the boat, depending on the sail itself, the weather, and the boat, so they are this much closer to the wind individually. But this is not all. We shall see shortly how the jib and mainsail must always be considered as one aerofoil. If you look at Fig. 1.1, you will see how a wind of 30° to the boat is at an angle of 10° to the jib, 20° to the mainsail, and 25° to the combined jib/mainsail aerofoil of the typical boat shown in the drawing.

Figure 1.2 shows the general direction and speed of air flowing round an aerofoil placed at an angle of 25° to the main flow. The aerofoil has caused a change in direction of about 10° to the stream-

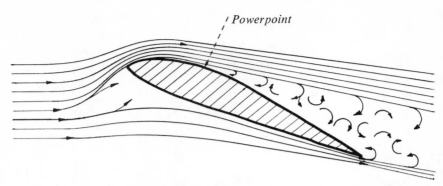

Fig. 1.2 *Airflow Pattern Round an Aerofoil*   An aerofoil at 25° to the wind.
The air is at its lowest pressure on the upper (or leeward) surface just forward of
the position of maximum camber (an unwieldy description, which I have
simplified by coining the word powerpoint); the closeness of the streamlines
near this point reveals their high speed. They break away from the surface just
aft of the powerpoint, turbulence sets in, and pressure returns to normal.

lines at its trailing edge, and the action of forcing this direction
change will result in an equal and opposite reaction (Newton's Law),
which takes the form of thrust on the aerofoil.

Figure 1.3 shows the same conditions around a single sail, shaped
like the aerofoil. Note how the streamlines break away from the lee
side of the single sail at about the *powerpoint*; this is the start of the
stall, and leeward air pressure reverts to normal in the turbulence aft
of this point. I use the word *powerpoint* to describe the position of
maximum camber, because the full phrase is rather cumbersome and
I feel that it's about time there was a single word to describe this
important aspect of sail shape. Powerpoint seems to me to convey the
meaning well, so I shall use it throughout the rest of this book.

In order to delay collapse of the leading edge of the combined
aerofoil as the sails start to lift when the boat sails closer to the wind,
there are sound reasons for having the genoa luff made of a fairly stiff
material; this helps the aerofoil maintain its shape in much the same
way as full length battens help the mainsail. Class rules may have
something to say about this, so take care before you rush off to try it.
Most rules prohibit any sailcloth which will not fold into conventional sailbags (the IYRU requires sails to be 'flexible and capable of
being folded flat in any direction without damaging the fibres'[11]; it
also permits *reinforcement* for stiffening purposes only at each
corner and at cunningham and reefing eyes); many rules go on to
stipulate maximum and minimum cloth weights for different sails;
but there are some classes which do not have an *upper* weight limit
for their sailcloth. These would benefit from having a panel of heavy

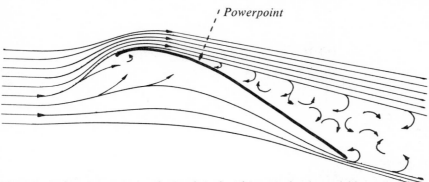

Powerpoint

Fig. 1.3 *Airflow Pattern Round a Single Sail* This typical sail was deliberately drawn a similar shape to the aerofoil in Fig. 1.2. The powerpoint is about one-third aft from the luff. Well-spaced streamlines to windward mean (relatively) slow airspeed and high pressure; the opposite holds good where they are close together. The flow to leeward is turbulent and inefficient over the after two-thirds of the sail, showing that the stall has set in.

weave (up to $7\frac{1}{2}$–$8\frac{1}{2}$ oz/US yard, or 300–350 gm/m²) let into the genoa luff, extending 8–10% towards the leech; this maintains its stiffness better than a heavily resinated cloth, which soon cracks and loses its fillers in use. Note that this panel should form an integral part of the sail, and not be sewn on as a second layer or it would contravene the IYRU rule regarding reinforcement.

Pressure Reduction

There is a difference between the pressures of the air passing above and below an aerofoil, or to leeward and windward of a sail. Mainly because of the way it deflects to leeward from some distance in front of the luff of the sail (the upwash), there is more air trying to pass to leeward then to windward. Because it is incompressible at the speeds we are considering, the air to leeward must travel more quickly than that to windward, if its greater volume is to cover the same straight line distance in the same period as the lesser volume[5]. This in turn means lower pressure to leeward (Bernoulli's Law) and a tendency for the sail to move from windward to leeward (from high to low pressure); in a word, lift.

Pressure Increase

This pressure reduction to leeward is helped by an increase in pressure to windward – for similar, but opposite, reasons. The speed différence is heightened by friction on the surface of the sail, which

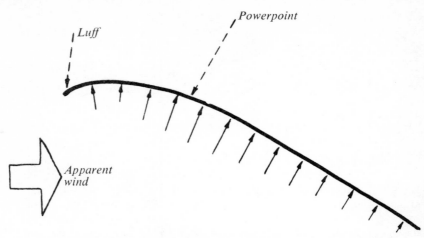

Fig. 1.4 *Impact Effect*   The force of the wind striking a sail acts at right angles to the surface. There is some turbulence just aft of the mast, so impact there is reduced; friction slows the wind in immediate contact with the surface as it travels across the sail, so impact is also reduced towards the leech. Maximum impact effect is experienced near the powerpoint.

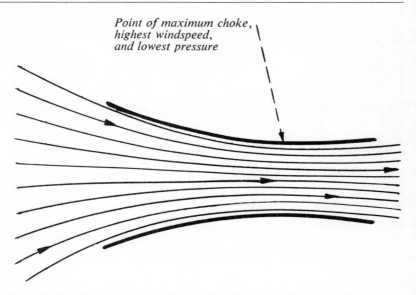

Fig. 1.5 *The Venturi*   A typical venturi, such as is used in the working section of a wind tunnel to increase airspeed locally above that of the main stream. This smooths out the flow and reduces the pressure as the speed increases, and has its application where a mainsail is placed behind a jib, as we shall see in the next figures.

slows down the air to windward more than that to leeward. The slow-speed air to windward will therefore have a higher pressure than normal, and this can be seen in the spacing of the streamlines in Fig. 1.3.

Impact Effect

This pressure difference is also heightened by impact effect. The force of wind striking any surface acts at right angles to that surface, regardless of the direction of the wind. Figure 1.4 shows a typical distribution of this force along the chord of a sail; the longer the arrow the greater the force. The values alter because of local speed variation caused by the aerofoil shape and by the build-up of friction, which slows down the air as it gets towards the leech.

The Slot

A venturi is a funnel through which air passes. If it is the right size and shape, it improves the airflow by increasing its speed, lowering its pressure and ironing out turbulence.

A normal venturi is shaped as shown in Fig. 1.5, but the gap

Plate 1.2 *The Wind Tunnel – 2* The author making minor adjustments to the model crab claw sail, during testing by MacAlister Elliott & Partners at Southampton University wind tunnel. The work bench being temporarily used as a sail loft beside the low speed section ($12' \times 15'$ or 3.5 m $\times 4.5$ m) is more usually given over to racing cars undergoing test in the neighbouring subsonic section ($6.5' \times 8'$ or 2 m $\times 2.5$ m). (*Author*)

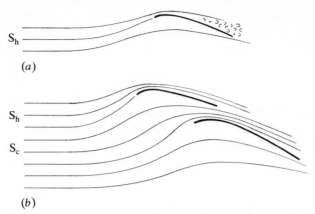

S_h

(a)

S_h

S_c

(b)

Fig. 1.6 *The Slot*   When a second sail is added *downstream* in the airflow (b), the original so-called stagnation streamline impinging on the leading edge of the headsail (S_h in a) is diverted further to leeward, and a new stagnation streamline is set up for the combined aerofoil (S_c in b). This increased flow of air round the headsail luff delays the stall and lowers pressure to leeward. Contrary to much popular belief, it *slows* the wind speed in part of the slot (immediately to windward of the headsail luff), because airflow has been diverted from that point, round the front of the headsail[5].

between a mainsail and a jib can also have a similar effect on airflow. This gap is known as the slot, and its shape is of special importance.

The conventional way of discussing the slot between two sails is to consider the effect which the addition of a *jib* has, when it is added in front of the mainsail. I suggest that we do this largely because the mainsail is usually hoisted first, and the jib is added afterwards. We should, however, be thinking the other way round: what effect does a *mainsail* have when it added behind the jib?

Figure 1.6 (a) shows typical streamlines flowing round a jib on its own. When a second sail is added downstream in the flow system, we get the situation in Fig. 1.6 (b). Note how more air is now diverted from windward to flow round the luff of the jib (there are now two streamlines passing to leeward instead of one); this is called upwash. It means that the airflow to leeward of the combined jib/mainsail aerofoil is even faster than that in the lee of the jib alone; pressure is lower in that area and lift greater. It also means that the headsail has a wider local apparent wind angle than the mainsail, so it can be trimmed to a wider angle relative to the boat's centreline (to give more driving force).

This extra airflow passing to leeward is at the expense of that to windward. An interesting point arising from all this is that, contrary to popular belief, airflow can be considered to *slow down* in the slot[5] (in fact, it depends how you consider the measurement – it is slower immediately to windward of the jib luff, but faster than normal to leeward of the mainsail luff; even here, it is not so fast as it would be if the mainsail had no jib in front of it, because some of its flow has gone to provide the jib's upwash).

Wind tunnel tests have shown that the leech of the jib should come at least as far aft as the powerpoint of the mainsail, for best advantage to be obtained from the slot[6]. Anything less than this disperses the effect of the slot like a venturi which is too wide, and Fig. 1.7 shows a slot which is too open. If, on the other hand, the jib comes

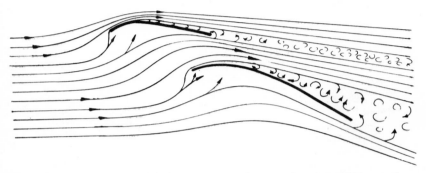

Fig. 1.7 *Slot too Open* This slot is too open, because there is neither enough overlap (the leech of the jib should reach nearly to the mainsail powerpoint for best efficiency), nor are the two sails close enough together. Full venturi effect is not obtained because the two sails revert to being individual aerofoils and thus cease to be mutually supporting; the wind speed is allowed to dissipate, and the airflow breaks away from the lee of each sail independently, near its powerpoint.

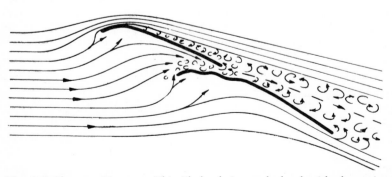

Fig. 1.8 *Slot too Narrow* This jib leech is nearly level with the mainsail powerpoint, but it is too close to that sail. Air cannot get through quickly enough to revitalise the leeward flow, and turbulence builds up in the slot. The whole leeward airstream is badly disturbed.

too close to the mainsail, blockage and turbulence occur (Fig. 1.8) and the mainsail will be backwinded. (This often cannot be avoided in the stronger winds, even with the best-shaped sails and venturi, because so much air is trying to force its way through the slot.) This will also happen if the leech of the jib curls, either from too much belly (Fig. 1.9) or from a curled leech tabling (Fig. 1.10). For best efficiency, the airflow at the exit to the slot should be parallel to the lee side of the mainsail[7].

/ *Jib powerpoint*
/

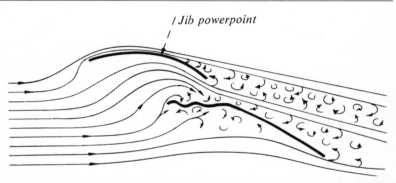

Fig. 1.9 *Backwinding – 1*   The flow of this jib has moved aft over a period of time, through the action of the wind stretching the cloth; the powerpoint is over halfway back from the luff, and the sail is said to have a bellied leech. The airflow off such a jib is directed into the lee of the mainsail, which is backwinded, causing turbulent conditions.

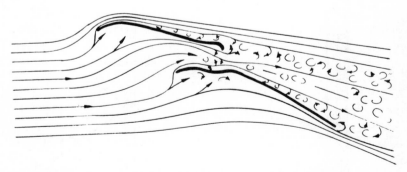

Fig. 1.10 *Backwinding – 2*   This jib has a flat run-off to the wind until the last three or four inches, where the cloth has stretched while the tabling or selvedge at the very edge has held fast. This is the cupped, or 'question mark' leech, and the wind is sharply turned and braked with resulting turbulence and backwinding of the mainsail.

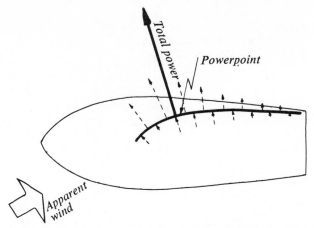

Fig. 1.11 *Total Force* The sum of the windward pressure forces and the leeward suction forces (dotted arrows) can be shown by one (heavy line) arrow. This shows the strength and direction of the total force by its own length and the way it is pointing. When a boat is close hauled, this direction will usually be aft of a line at right angles to the wind, and forward of right angles to the boom. It acts through a point known as the centre of effort, which moves about according to wind strength and sail trim, but is usually slightly forward of the powerpoint.

Total Power

A composite picture of these various forces is given in Fig. 1.11, where pressure reduction (to leeward) and the sum of pressure increase and impact effect (to windward) are shown by the dotted arrows. For convenience, these forces are usually indicated by a single arrow giving the strength and direction of the total power, which can be said to act through one point on the sail known as the centre of effort; this total power is shown by the solid arrow.

This principle of total power holds good for any normal wing section or aerofoil, and the centre of effort usually ranges a little either side of a point about a quarter of the way back from the front of such an aerofoil, its movement depending on aerofoil shape, angle of attack, and wind strength. Where a mainsail is hoisted behind a jib, it is important to remember that the two sails combined act as one aerofoil with a slot through it to improve the airflow. The total power of both sails still acts through a point one quarter back from the front of this combined aerofoil – that is to say through the jib.

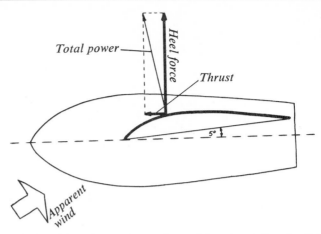

Fig. 1.12 *Thrust and Heeling Forces*   The total force in a sail can be divided for theoretical purposes into two forces acting at right angles to each other (heavy line arrows) in a parallelogram of forces. In a boat sailing to windward the heeling force is usually about four times the force thrusting the boat forward.

Plate 1.3 *Lift*   This Sea Panther demonstrates the literal meaning of the term lift. Note the centrally placed flow and compare Fig. 2.8 (*b*). (*David Eberlin*)

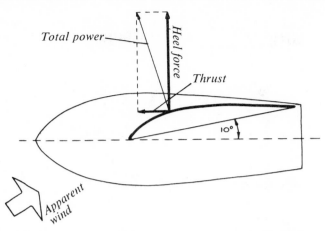

Fig. 1.13 *Effect of Sail Angle on Thrust* Forward thrust varies, for the same total thrust, according to the chord angle the sail makes with the boat. If the boom is eased from its position in Fig. 1.12, even by as little as 5°, thrust will immediately be increased by a half, and heeling force slightly decreased. Wind tunnel experiments have shown that the jib is even more sensitive to these changes of angle than the mainsail.

Resolving the Forces

You will see in Fig. 1.12 how the total power arrow (thin) is pointing at an angle to the direction of movement of the boat, as it was in Fig. 1.11. If this total power is resolved mathematically into forward and sideways thrusts (thick arrows), we can then see how much is available to push the boat forward and how much is trying to heel it or drive it sideways. Under close-hauled conditions the forces trying to heel the boat are usually about four times stronger than those driving her forward.

Figure 1.13 shows the dramatic effect which easing the sheet has on forward thrust (providing the sail stays full). An increase in the boom angle of no more than 5° adds 50 per cent to forward thrust, and reduces the heeling force a little as well. To increase forward thrust by the same amount without altering the boom angle would mean finding enough extra wind from somewhere to increase the total power in the sail by 50 per cent, and this in turn would increase the heeling force by the same amount.

Sail Outline Design

I shall finish this chapter with a few words about the naval architect's view of sail design. A while back, Tony Marchaj and I joined MacAlister Elliott & Partners, the marine consultants of Lymington

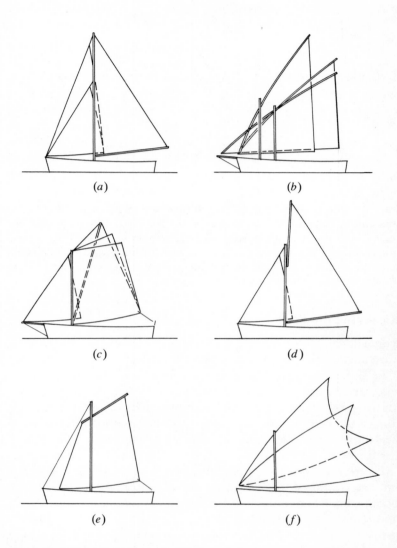

Fig. 1.14 *Sailplans Compared*   Wind tunnel tests were carried out on six different sailplans, all to the same basic area, together with some individual variations, in order to establish relative efficiency[8].

   (a) Bermudan mainsail, with and without two sizes of jib.
   (b) Three different shapes of lateen sail.
   (c) Three different spritsails, with and without a jib.
   (d) Gunter rig, with and without a jib.
   (e) Dipping lug in balanced form.
   (f) Crab claw sail set at different angles of sweep.

in Hampshire, to do some wind tunnel work on behalf of the Overseas Development Administration[8]. It may be of interest to summarise broadly our findings as to the relative efficiency of the six different rigs of the same area which were tested; Fig. 1.14.

1. *Bermudan.* For all-round efficiency, the bermudan rig is not necessarily the best outline shape which it has long been generally considered. This is largely because of its sharp taper ratio towards the head which is an inefficient planform, due to the energy it loses through trailing vortex, or induced, drag; an elliptical shape creates less induced drag (cf. the Spitfire's wing). We showed that up to 15 per cent area could be chopped off at the head with little effect on thrust – even with the unused part of the mast still in place. A board sail, with its bent mast and upper leech extended by full-length battens (Figs 11.3, 11.8), is more aerodynamically efficient than a sharply tapered conventional bermudan mainsail.

2. *Lateen.* Lateens of three different aspect ratios were tested. The

Plate 1.4 *The Crab Claw Sail* A fibreglass West Wight Scow at Lymington carries a crab claw sail of the same area as the standard Scow lugsail shown in Plate 10.3. Full size tests were carried out to check the wind tunnel results. (*MacAlister Elliott & Partners*)

low AR (i.e. with marked sweep-back) was the worst of all; results were somewhat better as AR increased, until a nearly vertical yard gave an efficiency which approached that of the bermudan plus headsail.

3. *Sprit*. Three different aspect ratio spritsails were tested. Spread of results was not wide, and all three were inferior to the best lateen, except down wind (30° and less, off dead astern), when they were slightly better than the bermudan. Addition of a headsail improved efficiency until the wind went aft of the beam when, like the bermudan, it reduced it when related to total area.

4. *Gunter*. When close-hauled, the gunter gave results not unlike the bermudan sail, but was at its best off the wind.

5. *Dipping Lug*. The dipping lugsail was consistently slightly inferior to the gunter and, except when close-hauled, to the sprit.

6. *Crab Claw*. The so-called crab claw sail, much seen in Polynesia, gave such excellent results that a further series of tests was run in order to establish further data regarding optimum shape. It was at least 25 per cent better than most other rigs, being particularly efficient on a broad reach (it was 100 per cent better than the admittedly poor low AR lateen). The crab claw's poorest points of sailing were close-hauled, and with the wind a few degrees either side of dead aft (even here, it showed remarkable potential). Its efficiency can be largely explained through better attached flow due to its ability to shed its tip vortices cleanly.

2 SAIL FLOW DESIGN

I said in the chapter on theory that sail flow design (the decision on how much belly or flow to give a sail and where to put it) is the sphere of the sailmaker, and I implied that it need not concern the owner. This is only true in that you, the owner, can do little to influence the method of achieving a particular shape; you will, however, be better able to get the best from your sails if you know how and why they are made the way they are.

Tailored Flow

One way of building flow into a sail is by adding extra cloth in a convex curve to the luff, in what is called round, so that fullness is increased. Figure 2.1 (*a*) shows a mainsail sewn together and lying on the loft floor before it has had the rope or tape added (which tends to wrinkle the sail and distort the fair curves on the luff and foot). When the sail is roped and then set on straight spars, the round on the luff

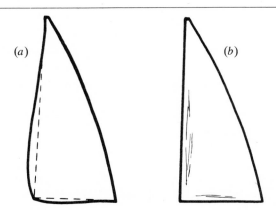

Fig. 2.1 *Tailored Flow*   (*a*) Flow is built into a sail by adding extra cloth in what is called 'round' at the luff and foot. (*b*) When the sail is set on straight spars, the extra cloth at luff and foot is forced back into the sail in the form of fullness.

Plate 2.1 *Computer Design*   Modern sailmakers use a computer not only to store data for quick retrieval, but also to aid design. Here, Peter Lucas calls up details of panel shape at his Portsmouth loft. (*Author*)

and foot will be for.ed back into the sail in the form of fullness, as shown in Fig. 2.1 (*b*).

Broad Seam

If the sailmaker wants to control the position of this fullness, he will taper the cloths or put in darts in much the same way that a dressmaker controls the shape of the dress she is making. This tapering of cloths is called broad seam, although there are many words for it, the darts or gussets being variously called seam, nips, or pies among other names.

Mainsail

The broad seam put into mainsails of three different cuts, either where two cloths join or as darts specially put in because there is no suitable join in the right place, is shown in Fig. 2.2. Where the mast has a bend or sag in it, the sail has to be cut to suit. If the mast curves under tension from the kicking strap and mainsheet, the mainsail must be cut with extra round to the luff to allow the mast to bow forward; any further luff round for fullness must be added on top of this allowance, as can be seen from Fig. 2.3.

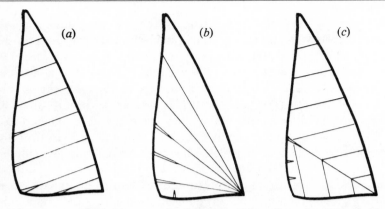

Fig. 2.2 *Broad Seam*   Position of tailored flow in a sail can be controlled by tapering the panels from which the sail is made, just as a dressmaker controls the shape of a dress by gussets and tucks. The horizontal cut (*a*) lends itself to this treatment but, where seams are not conveniently placed for this shaping, two half-width cloths may be put in – as shown in the foot of (*a*), or special darts may be inserted, as in the foot of the radial-cut sail in (*b*) or the luff of the mitre-cut sail in (*c*).

Fig. 2.3 *Allowance for Mast Bend*   If a mast bends in action, it will quickly absorb all the luff round designed to give fullness to a sail which has been made for a straight mast. The sail must have extra round built into the luff, according to the amount and position of bend in the mast. This drawing shows in dotted outline the luff of a sail made for a straight mast (shown by long and short dashes) and, in the thin continuous line, the further round needed to accept the curve of the mast (thick line) as drawn, if it is to keep any fullness at all when it bends. If enough cloth is not added for this bend, or if the mast bends more than the sailmaker has been told, then the sail won't fit, and creases will appear from the clew to the point on the luff where the sail is most lacking in extra round.

Jib

All forestays sag to a certain extent. The degree of sag often depends on the amount of aft tension which can be applied to the mast head – either through adjustable backstay or runners, or else by means of the mainsheet (see Chapter 6, *Rigging and Tuning*). A sagging forestay makes a jib too full for good windward work, unless the sail has been cut to make allowance for it. This means that the luff should be cut with slightly less hollow than the line it will take up when set, so that there is effectively a small amount of round to give just the right fullness to the sail; see Fig. 2.4. The sailmaker will make an intelligent guess at the amount of sag he has to allow, but if yours is abnormally large or small you should tell him. Many owners say, 'We've got a powerful backstay adjuster, so the forestay's as straight as a die'. They then complain that the boat won't point properly, but a ruler laid along the jib luff in a photograph might surprise them.

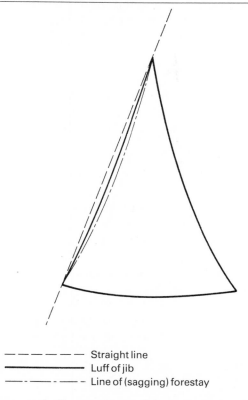

— — — — — — Straight line
———————— Luff of jib
—·——·——·— Line of (sagging) forestay

Fig. 2.4 *Allowance for Forestay Sag*   All forestays sag to some extent, so a jib should be cut to allow for it. If the sail's luff is given slightly less hollow than the forestay is expected to sag, there will be a small amount of surplus cloth in the sail to give it some draft when under the influence of the wind. See also Fig. 9.3.

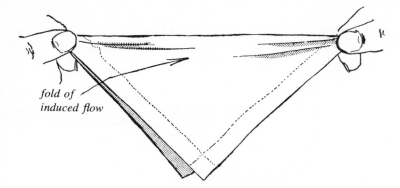

fold of
induced flow

Fig. 2.5 *Demonstration of Induced Flow*   Fold a clean handkerchief corner to corner, and pull the other two corners away from each other. This will put tension at 45° to the bias of the cloth, and will bring a fold of induced flow along the 'luff' of the handkerchief. The harder you pull, the deeper will be the fold, and the two loose corners will rise as the 'leech' is drawn towards the 'luff'.

Induced Flow

Film laminate cloth may give a fast sail, but it has a number of drawbacks (not least of which is expense), so it has been banned by many dinghies and some of the light displacement classes; I shall deal first with all-woven fabrics.

We shall see in Chapter 3 how synthetic sailcloth is constructed and how the weave distorts, particularly when a loading is placed on the bias. Use of the word 'stretch' in connection with sailcloth is misleading; 'distort' is a better word and, while efforts are made to cut this down, some distortion is useful to the sailmaker providing it is not too much and he knows where and how it will appear. By laying his cloths so that lines of tension either come on the threadline or on the bias, he can control the development of flow in different parts of the sail.

The action of pulling the luff of a mainsail until it stretches beyond the length it was made does not make the sail any bigger. If it increases in one measurement it must decrease in another. In this case it is the cross measurement at half height which reduces as the leech roach is pulled towards the mast. The harder you pull, the more the leech will come across, and you will pile up extra cloth just behind the luff, where it will lie in a fold. This shows the flow in the sail, and it will be blown aft again by the action of the wind. If the wind is strong enough to blow this flow well aft to an inefficient position near the leech of the sail, a harder pull on the halyard will draw it forward again. The same holds good to a lesser extent along the foot of a mainsail. You can illustrate this by pulling a handkerchief folded cornerways, as shown in Fig. 2.5; as you pull harder, so will flow appear as a fold near the 'luff' of the handkerchief, while the free-hanging corners draw in towards the fold, thus reducing the cross measurement.

(a)

(b)

Plate 2.2 *Induced Flow* A handkerchief is folded diagonally corner to corner and held without tension (*a*). When the two hands are pulled apart (*b*), the weave distorts and the two free-hanging corners rise as cloth is drawn towards the 'luff', where flow is evidenced by the fold. (*Author*)

An important factor in any sailcloth which is woven, is its ability to recover its original shape after it has been distorted either through loadings applied by sail controls, or else through wind power. If even the best cloth is subjected to stresses which are too high for it, it will distort out of shape never to recover (this is even more true of film laminates, and is somewhat similar to metal which reaches its yield point). This movement of flow, therefore, needs to be controlled. So that this does not occur, a rope or tape is sewn along the edge of the sail with tension carefully graded to allow just the right development of this *induced flow*, as I call it.

Jibs

During the first half of this century, jibs were made with wire in the luff to take the strain put upon it by the halyard. This meant that induced flow had to be arbitrarily fixed in each particular sail by the sailmaker, who made the luff of the sail shorter than the wire and then pulled the sail until he had what he felt was the correct tension, whereupon it was fixed to the wire for all time by a seizing. Thousands of jibs are made in this way still, and very good they are too, but the benefit of being able to control the luff tension in a jib in the same way as a mainsail has given rise to the adjustable or stretchy luff jib, which I prefer to call by the more positive name of *control luff jib*.

It is usual for a dinghy jib to be made with a wire, rather than a tape or rope, in the luff. A conventional jib may be seized all the way along the wire, and the sail is given pre-set flow in the luff as described above. A control luff jib is either seized at the head only, or else seized at both ends of the wire and the luff merely sleeved on to the wire so that it 'floats'; an eye is worked into the luff near the tack. The flow is controlled by varying the tension on the luff by pulling down on the eye, which is virtually a cunningham hole (of which more anon).

The object of altering the tension on the luff of any sail is to vary the amount of induced flow: the more you pull, the more flow will appear at the forward part of the sail. We have already seen that this cannot come from nowhere and in fact comes from the leech as it is drawn forward. This means that less excess cloth is available at the aft end of the sail to be distributed around as flow, so the sail flattens aft.

Thus, when increasing wind drives the flow from the luff towards the leech, it can be drawn forward again by increasing the tension on the control luff.

Camber

A full sail is needed for light weather and a flat one for heavy weather. This is a rule which needs qualification. What is full and what is flat? What about light weather which becomes heavy? Isn't some fullness required in heavy weather; if so, where, and how much? Whereabouts should fullness be in a sail?

How full?

One of the troubles which besets a sailmaker is this question of fullness. What one man thinks is flat may be only medium to another; what is medium to one may be full to someone else. Unless some sort of yardstick is used, you are likely to end with the wrong answer. When ordering new sails, the best way is to compare your

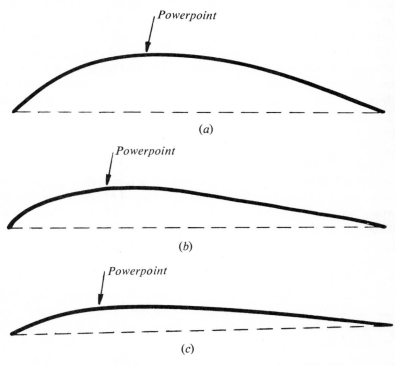

Fig. 2.6 *How Full is Full?* The curves in this drawing show the shapes produced by depths of flow at the powerpoint of 17 per cent or 1 in 6 (*a*), 11 per cent or 1 in 9 (*b*), and 7½ per cent or 1 in 13½ (*c*) of the cross measurement; these are typical shapes for light, medium, and heavy weather mainsails respectively. Note how the powerpoint is moved gradually forward as the sail becomes flatter. The shapes are those which the sail should take up when the wind is blowing into it.

needs with another suit for the same class by the same sailmaker, who can then refer to his records and make the new sails flatter or fuller as required. For the purposes of this book we can say that a full mainsail is one which has a depth of belly anything from 15 to 20 per cent (1 in 5 to 6½) of the distance from luff to leech at the point in question (chord). A flat one has a belly of about 5 to 10 per cent (1 in 10 to 20), while the medium sail comes somewhere in between, overlapping rather more at the full end of the scale than at the flat end; see Fig. 2.6. Light displacement boats racing under the JOG and IOR are not allowed to change mainsails during a race; they should be careful to have a mainsail which will not be too full for Force 5 or 6 – it can always be given extra draft in light winds by easing the clew outhaul. Headsails, while usually restricted in number in the cruiser/racer classes, can be changed to suit the prevailing conditions.

Light winds
If a suit of very full sails is hoisted in light weather, it should do well while the light winds hold. In most waters, however, one of two things usually happens: either the wind dies away, or else it freshens to a medium strength or more. In the first case it won't matter what sails you have, for you probably won't finish the course; in the second case your boat will be knocked down as too much heeling force builds up, as described in Chapter 1. Ultra-light weather sails lose more races than they win.

Heavy weather
Of greater importance is heavy weather. Gone are the days of really flat sails, made so that the wind could slide off without heeling the boat too much – it also slid off without driving it very much either. Nowadays bendy masts allow fullness to be taken out of the sail (Chapter 6) as the wind gets up, and the head in particular can be feathered to reduce heel effect aloft, where it hurts most. Sliding seats and trapezes allow crews to hang out farther, thus balancing the boat better so wind need not be spilled so much. You will want a fair amount of drive, and there should be anything up to a 10 per cent belly immediately over the boom; this gives power low down where it is most wanted.

Mainsail fullness – where?
A boat which has both mainsail and jib should have a mainsail with the powerpoint between a third and a half of the way from the luff towards the leech *when the sail is under the influence of the wind*. This means that a heavy weather sail should start with its flow right forward, for it will blow aft in strong winds; a medium weather sail should allow for some movement of flow, which should therefore be

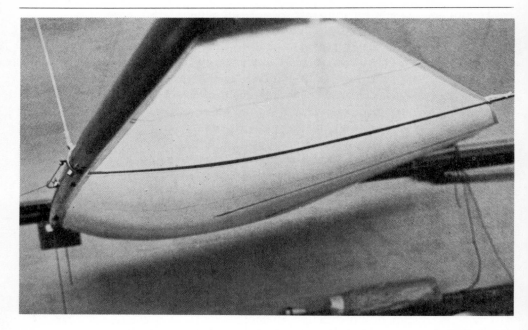

Plate 2.3 *Bendy Mast Test Rig*   This horizontal test rig, at the loft of Bruce Banks Sails near Southampton, enables the sailmaker to examine all parts of a mainsail when its mast is bent. (*Yachting World*)

just about at the one-third point; flow in a light weather mainsail (if you *must* have one) can be tailored to the halfway position, for there should never be enough wind to blow it anywhere else. Figures 2.7 (*a*), (*b*) and (*c*) refer.

Una or cat rig
A boat with only one sail, like a Contender or a sailboard, doesn't have the benefit of a jib. This means that the air will separate from the lee side of the sail at the powerpoint, because there is no slot effect to delay this breaking away. In order to keep the air in contact with the sail as long as possible, so that low pressure to leeward can cover a greater area, this powerpoint is well aft – at least halfway towards the leech. If it were put any farther back, the shape of the aerofoil would be reversed and the leech would act as a brake when beating to windward. Figures 2.8 (*a*), (*b*) and (*c*) show the reasoning behind this.

Jib fullness – where?
The function of the jib when close-hauled is to combine with the mainsail and carry the main driving force of an efficient slot. We have

already seen that, for best efficiency to windward, airflow at the exit of the slot should be parallel to the lee side of the mainsail. This not only means a jib leech which doesn't curl, but also one which has a flat run for quite a way into the sail; if there is a belly or too much camber in the leech, there will be a danger of backwinding the main, particularly as the wind increases. For high pointing in light conditions, the powerpoint should be at about 45–50 per cent of the chord aft of the luff, particularly in the head; this will give a fine entry aloft and enable the streamlines to adhere to the leeward camber (the need for flat sails in *very* light winds is discussed in *Sails*[9]). In strong conditions, the powerpoint should be further forward (35–40 per cent) – particularly low down in the sail; the fact that the boat will need to be sailed slightly more free, means that the air flows freely onto the deeper entry, separation is delayed, and a smaller proportion of power is converted into heeling moment (the total heeling moment is, of course, greater because the total force is greater).

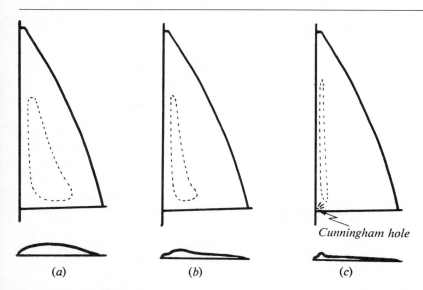

(a)   (b)   (c)

Fig. 2.7 *Fullness with the Boat at Rest* These curves show the shape of the mainsails drawn in the previous figure, while they are at rest without the full action of the wind blowing into them. In light weather there will not be enough wind to change the shape of (a) so it should not be hoisted hard enough to draw any of the flow forward; medium weather will cause a slight shift in flow towards the leech, so enough tension is put on the luff to cause the beginnings of a fold to appear (b); the flow which has been induced in the form of a fold up the luff of sail (c) will be blown well aft by heavy weather, so not only should there be plenty of tension on the halyard, but a cunningham hole should be pulled down if one is fitted.

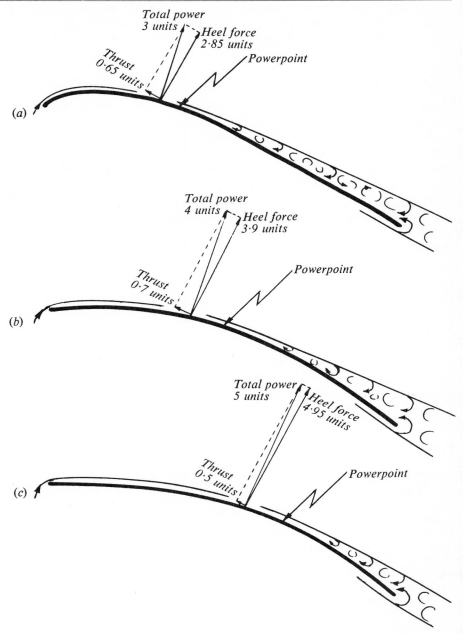

Fig. 2.8 *Powerpoint Position in Cat Rig*   Where a mainsail operates without a jib to smooth out the airflow to leeward, turbulence sets in just aft of the powerpoint. In a cat-rigged boat such as the Finn, therefore, it is logical to have the powerpoint rather further aft than usual, in order to delay airflow separation and thus get more of the sail doing useful work. Sail (*a*) is a conventional sloop's

Lower pointing might actually mean that you make better speed to windward. See also Chapter 9, under *Genoa Tune*, for further discussion specifically related to light displacement keelboats.

Spinnakers

The stresses in a spinnaker run radially from the corners. It is logical, therefore, to lay the cloths so that these too run radially from the corners if we want to restrict distortion with its concomitant bellying of the sail. The concept of the starcut spinnaker, as originated by Bruce Banks Sails in the sixties[10], is nothing more revolutionary than that (but it took the right man to bring it out and develop it). It was a short step to introduce some horizontal panels across the middle of the sail, in order to help spread the load and the sail in this important area; this is the tri-radial. And then to revert to horizontal cloths for the whole of the lower half (this is the radial head spinnaker), on the grounds that the foot also needs to spread and, in any event, the tri-radial uses a lot of both time and cloth (the starcut is even more prodigal) and is thus expensive. In general terms, therefore, we have two principal spinnaker cuts for boats larger than dinghies (which are usually best served by an all-horizontal cut); see Fig. 8.2.

Radial head

The radial head cut absorbs the loadings from the head, and generally offers a good all-round sail. The horizontal panels in the lower half mean that a moderately deep belly develops for running, but it can be kept flat enough to be fairly stable and to reach, when the

---

mainsail with the powerpoint one-third aft. Its total force, without the help of its jib, measures 3 units, and the forward thrust is 0.65 units. The powerpoint in the cat-rig sail at (*b*) has been put further aft to the midway position, with the result that the total force in the sail is increased by about one-third to nearly 4 units for the same conditions, because separation of the airflow from the lee side of the sail is delayed by shifting the powerpoint aft, thus more of the sail is doing useful work. Although the direction of this force is angled slightly further aft, thus reducing the proportion available as forward thrust, the actual driving power is increased by about 10 per cent over sail (*a*) to 0.7 units; but note that the heel force has also gone up by rather more.

   If we now take the powerpoint even further aft in order to make more of the sail work to increase the total force still more, the direction of this force is by now angled so far aft that the forward thrust component is reduced to 0.5 units, or 25 per cent below that of sail (*a*); in addition, the heel force is by now nearly double that of sail (*a*).

   In practice it is found that sail (*b*), with its powerpoint at the midway position, is best for cat-rigged boats.

apparent wind is on the beam in light conditions. Because the apparent wind strength increases on the reach, however, the radial head spinnaker quickly develops fullness from the lower corners, so that a boat becomes overpowered. As a general sail, it should be the first purchase on a racing boat, and the only one on a cruiser.

Tri-radial

A tri-radial spinnaker is usually cut with less fullness aloft in the first place, and it remains flatter because the warp threads of the cloth are more nearly aligned with the lines of stress at all three corners; there will be less cloth distortion and thus less extra belly caused by gusts. This means that its trim should be slightly different – the pole should be kept lower than with a radial head sail, and the sheet lead brought forward, so that the tri-radial can develop some flow[10]; when the apparent wind angle drops below 80°, the pole should be progressively raised to flatten the head and accept the finer wind angle. The tri-radial is thus a specialist reaching sail; because of this, and the fact that it is more expensive than a radial head cut, it is usually the second spinnaker in the locker of a racing boat.

Size

The proportions of a spinnaker for a dinghy or a light displacement fractional rig cruiser are about right; masthead rigs tend to have spinnakers with slightly too tall an aspect ratio for the best all-round stability. For light weather, sheer size is not the answer because even the lightest cloth will fall in, if there is too much of it and not enough wind to hold it up. Proper shape, with fairly narrow shoulders for less bulk, is more important than extra area for a light weather spinnaker. The same can be said for a close reaching spinnaker for the higher wind strengths – too much area aloft will give too much heeling moment, while a narrow sail (say, $1.65 \times J$, as opposed to the normal $1.8 \times J$; see Fig. 9.1) will open the slot and, indeed, often allow a No 2 genoa or spinnaker staysail to be set inside it. There can be no hard and fast rule, because these proportions often result in a narrow sail best suited to heavy weather reaching only, but which would be somewhat unstable down wind – much depends on the relationship of I to J (fractional rig v. masthead again).

It is important that the tapes on the luffs/leeches are strong enough, do not shrink, and even stretch a little with the cloth. If they cause the edges of the sail to curl (possibly from the cloth stretching slightly while the tapes do not), you will get an inefficient shape, particularly on a reach (Fig. 13.4).

If you want extra area in your spinnaker, one way it can often be safely added is by means of a skirt at the foot. This is extra round built on to the foot and is sometimes allowed by the rules. It has the

Plate 2.4 *Flow Check on a Jib* A jib needs no special rig to show its shape. This one has been stretched on the luff by a tackle in the Portsmouth loft of W. G. Lucas & Son, and the clew pulled out to one side. Gravity then makes the sail take up its basic flow. (*Author*)

advantage that it does not risk getting a deep belly (often called a 'Roman nose'), so the airflow remains virtually undisturbed; equally the additional weight of cloth doesn't have to be lifted so high by the wind, so it is more likely to set properly in light airs. If your boat is a slow mover downwind in Force 2, it's worth talking it over with your sailmaker.

3 SAILMAKING – PRINCIPLES

It is the object of this chapter to tell you something of what happens in a loft when a sail is made. It is not possible to cover the subject fully in one chapter, but a background knowledge will be useful in looking after your sails. We shall see in Chapters 4 and 5 the practical aspects of home sailmaking.

Sailcloth

As most sailing people know, there are two principal kinds of cloth used for sails (three if you count cotton, which I don't propose to cover); these are synthetic film laminate, and all-woven polyester. Although it is the newer material, I shall deal with the former first,

Plate 3.1 *Film Laminates – 1*   Inter-ply uni-directional laminates by Dimension Sailcloth embody uncrimped Kevlar on Dacron yarns (for warp strength) between a polyester substrate (for seamability and tear strength) and film (for bias control). The twenty pence pieces are roughly 0.8 in (20 mm) across, and provide a scale. (*Author*)

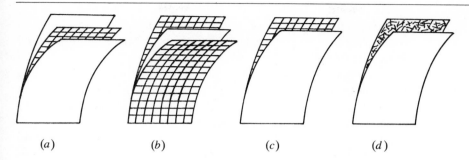

(a) (b) (c) (d)

Fig. 3.1 *Film Laminates*   To prevent tears developing, Mylar and Melinex film is bonded to a polyester or nylon woven reinforcement substrate. Initial experiments saw two $\frac{1}{4}$ mil films of Mylar either side of 2 oz spinnaker nylon (a). This suffered from distortion of the outside layer when the cloth was folded (the so-called I-beam effect), so that delamination occurred. When the more rigid film was sandwiched between two layers of flexible woven substrate (b), the reduced compression effect, coupled with improved adhesives, countered this problem; more flexible film also helped. Modern laminate sailcloth, however, is more likely to be a construction of film one side and woven cloth the other (c), which gives a flexible end-product with little compression effect; thickness and weight can vary widely to suit the requirement. Sometimes the reinforcement is formed by a random-laid scrim cloth (d), thus producing a sail which is not woven at all. Any of these constructions may be further reinforced by a series of unwoven (Kevlar) yarns inserted between the layer of film and the substrate, in the direction – warp or weft – which it is desired to emphasise. The possible combinations of film with woven, knitted, twisted and/or uni-directional un-woven (and therefore uncrimped) yarns, not to mention random-laid scrim or chopped strand mat, are many.

and then the latter at somewhat greater length – a woven cloth complicates life by distorting when loaded off the threadline (on the bias, therefore) and, if its qualities are thoroughly understood, they can easily be transferred to film laminates where they apply.

Film Laminate

Film laminate sailcloth is often referred to as Mylar® (which, in fact, is a registered trademark of the duPont de Nemours Company of the USA) or Melinex® (a similar registration of ICI in the UK). It was developed as a result of the never-ending quest for a sailcloth with a high modulus of elasticity in all directions and a low porosity. Polyester film has both these qualities (it stretches marginally more than woven polyester sailcloth which is loaded on the threadline, but far less in all other directions because it has no threadline itself and thus no bias, so it is uniform in its reaction; porosity is zero). But film will tear easily once a hole is started, so it needs reinforcement. This is achieved by bonding it to a light substrate, usually of woven polyester but sometimes of nylon and sometimes of a random-laid scrim, to give it tear strength; it may also be further reinforced by uni-directional Kevlar® threads (see Fig. 3.1).

When used for sailcloth, the thickness of film is measured in thousandths of an inch (mils) – usually in the range 0.5–3.0 mils; the substrate(s) vary between 1.0–3.5 oz/US yard (which is 25–125 gm/m²). The result is a cloth which is light and smooth, and which has virtually no stretch at all until, like metal, it reaches its yield point; it then distorts out of shape never to recover. It is thus important to know the maximum apparent wind speed for each and every film laminate sail (more important, to mark it on the clew and see that everyone respects it).

This unyielding form brings with it, of course, the need for a sail to be tailored in the loft to its required shape, so that it sets the way it should look as soon as it is hoisted. If too much, or indeed, too little, tension is put on the halyard, the camber doesn't move, but the sail suffers from over-stress or point loading along the luff (with danger of minor delamination at best, or permanent deformation at worst). The only way to change the shape of a film laminate sail is to alter the line of the luff – to give more or less sag in the forestay, or more or less bend in the mast; see Chapter 6 under *Bendy Spars* and Chapter 9 under *Genoa Tune – Forestay Sag*.

Film laminate is an expensive cloth, which has a harsh handle (though continuing attempts are being made to produce a softer finish); it also suffers from UV degradation if exposed to prolonged sunlight or industrial smoke. The closely spaced holes made by a sewing machine are a further source of weakness; any regular perforations encourage material to 'tear along the dotted line'. Where the line of stress is at right angles to a seam, cloths may suffer from slippage as the stitch holes enlarge, thus spoiling the tailored shape of the sail; adhesive should be used in the sewing process. Seams which run parallel to the load line don't suffer from this problem but, if the overlap is too wide, the doubled area acts like two-ply and is liable to stand proud, because it moves less (the solution is to make these seams narrow, with only one row of stitching, but incorporating adhesive tape to give the necessary strength).

Kevlar®

Some film laminates are reinforced by Kevlar, an extremely strong low-stretch aramid fibre produced by duPont. It suffers from fatigue failure, however, and should not be used without the back-up reinforcement of woven polyester or some form of scrim. It also tends to aggravate the seam slippage problem referred to above, because it imparts so much load into the seam when the stress is at right angles.

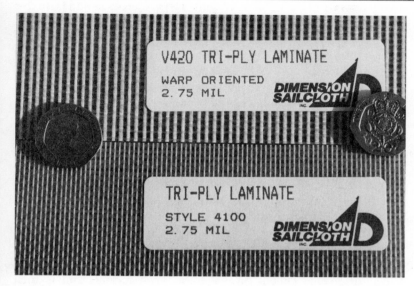

Plate 3.2 *Film Laminates – 2*   Two Tri-Ply® laminates of 2.75 mil film using reinforcement of different constructions. The upper cloth is warp-orientated, and the lower is weft- or fill-orientated; there is film-to-film adhesion between the substrate yarns. The twenty pence pieces are roughly 0.8 in (20 mm) across, and provide a scale. (*Author*)

A fair number of classes prohibit the use of film laminates. Paradoxically, this is an indication of a plus mark for the cloth, since the ban is usually imposed because owners who are able to afford the expense of original purchase and regular replacement have a speed advantage over their rivals. The cloth is undoubtedly fast.

Woven Polyester

All-woven polyester cloth is often referred to as Terylene® (a registered trademark of ICI Fibres of the UK) or Dacron® (a similar registration of duPont); it is called by other trade names according to who makes it (though a lot of the original licences have now run out and a free market has developed). The thread is made to the same chemical formula, originally invented in England during World War II; any difference in the finished cloth lies in the way the thread is woven and then subsequently treated during the finishing process.

Terylene, Dacron, or whatever you like to call it, is virtually immune from the effects of water and from a wide variety of chemicals, although it can suffer if bits of dirt or salt work their way into the weave and then chafe the threads; in addition, mildew can form on it if damp and dirt are also present (as it can on glass under similar circumstances); finally, prolonged sunlight or industrial smoke (constant exposure for a year or so) can weaken the material to the point where it will tear like paper. When woven into cloth it is strong, doesn't stretch a lot, doesn't soak up water, and can be woven close enough to be smooth and pretty airtight. The ideal sailcloth, you might say – and you wouldn't be far wrong.

A good deal depends on the way the threads are woven into cloth. If they are slackly arranged on the loom and not banged up tightly together at each pass of the shuttle, the resulting weave will be loose, porous, and stretchy. The aim is a firm cloth, which is woven under great tension with the weft, or cross threads, banged close up together as it builds up on the warp, or lengthwise, threads.

Even the highest tension on the most modern looms cannot get the weave tight enough to be all right without further treatment. Therefore cloth straight from the loom goes through a finishing stage. During this, it is scoured and dried, may have chemical or resin fillers added to reduce stretch or make the cloth harder, and is then heat-relaxed to shrink and settle the material, thus helping the individual threads to lock together. Addition of resins can turn a slack cloth into one which has a pleasing appearance for a time, but they break down in use and become detached from the cloth, to run off with rain or spray in a milky liquid, or else the surface deteriorates into typical marble crazing as the filler cracks. This process of build-up and break-down can be likened to starching a shirt or blouse.

Improved weaving techniques, originally pioneered by Ted Hood of America, led the way to achieving sailcloth which is so closely woven under great tension that little or no added chemicals are needed, and the only finishing process is heat relaxation. This is the ideal, for there are then no fillers to break down and the cloth does not deteriorate so much with use; such a cloth is also much softer to the touch than one which is heavily resinated. Its main drawbacks are that it is more difficult to sew without puckers, and light sails are liable to wrinkles; therefore cloth destined for the sails we are considering has a hardener added. The sailcloth with which we are mainly concerned thus has some kind of chemical added in the finishing stage and is none the worse for it. Technical advances in recent years have been such that these chemicals stick to the weave much better, and there is so little of them that only a small proportion of cloth is below standard in this respect.

Research in England by ICI Fibres Ltd has revealed more about the way in which synthetic cloth stretches when it is made into sails. This in turn indicates a requirement for different cloth construction, depending on how it is going to be used. Stretch in the head of a

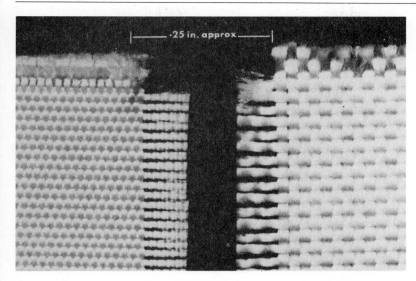

·25 in. approx

Plate 3.3 *Woven Cloth*   Two all-woven polyester sailcloths of similar weight, but using yarns of different decitex counts (the metric method of measuring what used to be known as denier). The cloth on the left uses a low decitex yarn, giving what is known as a fine sett but having a high cover factor (yarn concentration in the weave); the one on the right has high decitex threads at a low sett and cover factor. (*Yachting World*)

horizontally cut mainsail, for instance, is partly across the cloth, whereas it is more along the run of the warp nearer the foot: this points to cloths of different warp and weft construction being needed for the top and bottom of a mainsail. A mitre cut jib, on the other hand, stretches more across the cloth than along it, so a relatively heavy weft construction is advisable. Variation of cut (radial, vertical, spider-web, etc.) will alter the direction of local stresses in the cloth and will change the requirement.

Apart from these considerations, it is sometimes a good idea to use a stiff cloth for the upper half of a mainsail to help support a large roach, while the foot is made of softer material to encourage the development of flow.

All this, of course, goes on outside your control. What can you do about cloth? Tests which you can make to prove the quality of sailcloth which you are being offered are twofold.

Stretch
Pull a sample between your hands at an angle of 45° to the weave (the angle of least resistance to stretch). You will produce a small fold in the material (induced flow), depending on the strength you use and

the quality of the cloth. This fold should recover when you stop pulling, and the more it recovers the better the cloth. You will become a better judge with practice, so compare one or two cloths before pronouncing judgement.

Fillers
Crumple a sample of cloth and then rub it back and forth between your hands as though washing it. You will soon see if there is a lot of loose filling in the material, for it will craze and possibly even flake off if it is bad.

One of the most important factors in sailcloth, as I implied above, is its resistance to stretch (in the jargon of today it is said to need a

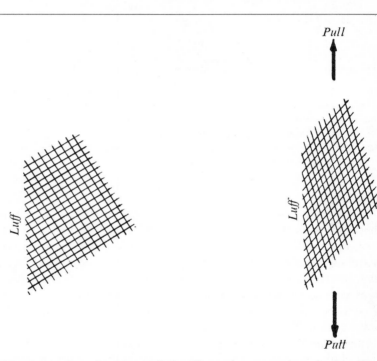

Fig. 3.2 *Bias Stretch* Woven cloth will stretch at an angle to the threadlines, because the little squares formed by the weave will distort into little diamonds; if the pull is along the threadline, either warp or weft, no such distortion takes place and stretch is almost eliminated. For this reason most sails have cloths at the leech (where stretch would be bad) laid so that the threadline runs in the same direction as the pull – along the leech. This usually results in the cloth meeting the luff on the bias, where movement of the weave can be used to induce flow in the sail. Note how stretching the luff brings the leech across, thus reducing the cross measurement. This shows that you can't get something for nothing, i.e. the sail doesn't get any bigger when the luff and foot are stretched – it merely distorts the original area to a different shape.

high modulus of extensibility). Any woven material will stretch if tension is applied on the bias (at an angle to the threadline), and sailcloth is no exception. Indeed some stretch can be useful, as we have already seen in the previous chapter: it enables the sailmaker to influence the amount and position of flow in the sail. Bias stretch shows movement of the weave. As pull is exerted at an angle to the threadlines, so the little squares formed by the weave distort into little diamonds (Fig. 3.2). This causes the material to get longer in the direction of pull, but as it does not get any bigger the extra length has to come from somewhere, and the cloth shrinks across the line of the pull. Translated into terms of a sail, a pull on the luff acting at an angle to the threadline (which usually meets the luff at an angle) causes the luff to grow longer but the leech to pull over towards the luff, thus reducing the cross measurement of the sail.

'Plated' cloth

Sometimes a sailmaker will recommend a particularly heavy cloth (200 to 250 gm/m²) which has a hard finish, where a boat has a sail plan which will profit from this. An example is the British Merlin Rocket, which can get more area aloft if a stiff cloth is used to help hold out a top batten which becomes almost a free-standing gaff. In this case the sail relies almost entirely on tailored flow for its shape, because the cloth won't stretch as easily as a soft material and so won't form the fold up the luff which is induced flow. So-called plated cloth has two main drawbacks: creasing and insensitivity. Extra care has to be taken to stop the heavy finish from cracking and creasing, and so making the sail inefficient. Also, a jib made of hard cloth will not give advance warning of the stall by quivering up the luff as the boat points too high; this can be overcome by tell-tales sewn into the luff of the jib, if you are one of those who can work to windward while using them without getting hypnotised!

Cloth weight

In England sailcloth is measured by the number of ounces it weighs to each square yard. In America the width of cloth to be measured is fixed at 28½ in (an Old English standard for broadcloth) and the ounces in every yard of this rather narrower material are weighed; this results in a figure lower by some 20 per cent than in England for exactly the same cloth. When grading a particular piece of cloth, therefore, you have to weigh more actual material under the British system than you do under the American, and this is well illustrated in Fig. 3.3. Countries using the metric system weigh the number of grammes per square metre, and this is the method I use in this book because it can only mean one thing. I have given a comparative scale for all three systems in Fig. 3.4, and you can see that a normal dinghy

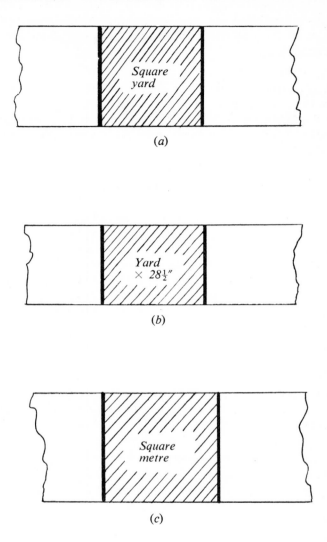

(a)

(b)

(c)

Fig. 3.3 *Cloth Weight Measurement*   Imagine two rolls of sailcloth, one of which is 36 in wide and the other $28\frac{1}{2}$ in wide. If a yard length of each of these otherwise identical cloths is cut off and weighed, the wider cloth will have a larger area (a) and will tip the scales at a greater weight than the narrow strip (b). Sailcloth in Great Britain is weighed in yard lengths of 36 in wide material (36×36 in); in USA the standard is a yard length of $28\frac{1}{2}$ in wide material (36×$28\frac{1}{2}$); $28\frac{1}{2}$ in is an Old English broadcloth standard somehow inherited by the Americans from the days of Robin Hood. There is thus less material to be weighed in America, and the apparent difference between the two systems when describing the same cloth is about 20 per cent.

The metric system measures grammes per square metre (c).

weight of material for a mainsail and jib of 4½ ounces per square yard (oz/yd²) in England, is equivalent to just over 3½ ounces per American yard (oz/yd × 28½ in) and 150 grammes per square metre (gm/m²) on the Continent.

Mainsail Cuts

A sailmaker has to be careful how he lays the cloths of his sail. Tension directly on the line of the threads – either lengthwise (warp)

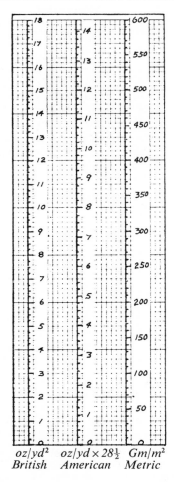

oz/yd²   oz/yd × 28½   Gm/m²
British   *American*   *Metric*

Fig. 3.4 *Cloth Weight Conversion Table* In America sailcloth is graded by the number of ounces in a yard of cloth 28½ in wide (oz/yd×28½); in Great Britain it is ounces per square yard (oz/yd²); countries using the metric system weigh the number of grammes in a square metre (gm/m²). This table converts from one system to another at a glance.

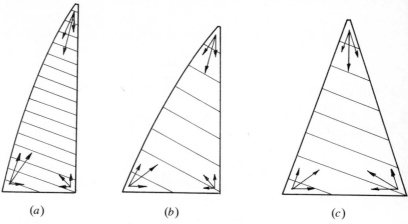

(a) (b) (c)

Fig. 3.5 *Sail Stresses*   The stresses in a mainsail of high aspect ratio (a) are largely up and down the leech; in a horizontally cut sail, the resultant loading is thus on the line of the weft or fill, which should be suitably stout. A low aspect ratio mainsail (b) also has fairly high leech stresses, but there is also a significant bias loading, particularly in the lower part of the sail, so that weft and bias distortion are more nearly equal. A low aspect genoa (c) has loadings which are more equally distributed throughout the sail, so a square construction is called for (with equal emphasis on both warp and weft), in order to withstand distortion in all directions. Film laminate sails usually have a woven substrate, which needs to be considered in a similar, if reduced, manner.

Fig. 3.6 *Mitre cut Mainsail*   A mitre cut mainsail has the same advantages as a horizontal cut, plus the fact that more cloths strike the foot, so that broad seam can be better incorporated to tailor the flow. The drawback of this cut is that the mitre itself, being double thickness, may be rather hard and slow to stretch. If this happens, it can stop the clew drawing aft, to the detriment of flow development.

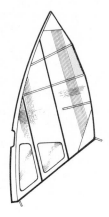

Fig. 3.7 *Vertical Cut Mainsail*   An all-woven mainsail of this cut suffers from changing bias at the leech, as the curve of the roach cuts across the warp threadlines; this applies to sailboards, dinghies and small cruiser/racers alike. In the board sail shown, the leech may be reinforced by a narrow panel of film laminate, but many dinghy class rules prohibit this.

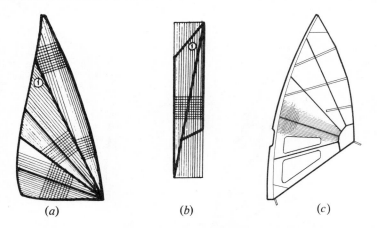

(a)   *(b)*   *(c)*

Fig. 3.8 *Radial cut Mainsail*   As with the vertical cut, a radical or sunray all-woven mainsail suffers from varying bias distortion along the leech. In addition, luff bias reduces from a large angle aloft to zero as the tack is approached (and, in the case of the board sail in (c), starts to increase again as the boom is passed). The main advantage claimed is a better absorption of the stresses which radiate from the clew. But the disadvantage of uneven distortion, both at luff and leech, would seem to me to outweigh this gain, especially if the panels have been economically cut two to a cloth as in (b), because one seam will be on the selvedge and the next on the bias. There is rather more drama than design in this cut, unless the sail is made of Mylar.

of crosswise (weft) – will not result in much stretch, as no distortion of the little squares formed by the weave will occur. As soon as the angle of pull comes off the threadline, even by as little as 1° or 2°, stretch starts to take place and must be allowed for.

This explains why a mainsail is usually made with cloths running at right angles to the leech, so that pull in this unsupported area will be kept on the line of the weft or cross threads. With a conventional horizontal cut, cloths meet the luff at an angle, ready to receive the tension of the main halyard on the bias and to produce a fold along the lines of that tension if it is great enough; this is one way of inducing flow in a sail and we have already seen the use made of it.

Both the horizontal and mitre cut mainsail respond to the above theory (Figs 3.5 and 3.6). Other cuts are vertical (Fig. 3.7) and radial (Fig. 3.8), neither of which would appear to have much resistance to stretch in the unsupported leech, particularly where a curved leech means a constantly changing bias angle. A way of overcoming this latter problem is to fit small panels in the leech, with the threadline (usually weft) parallel with the leech as shown in Fig. 3.9.

To overcome the drawback of lack of stretch in the lower luff, due to the low bias angle of radial sails in that area, some sailmakers combine it with the vertical cut to produce a semi-radial cut. This is claimed to give most of the advantages and few of the disadvantages

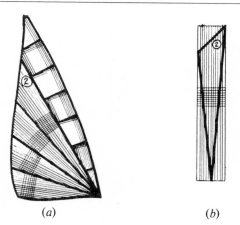

(a)   (b)

Fig. 3.9 *Radial Cross-cut Mainsail*   This version of the radial cut has short lengths of cloth laid at the leech as for a horizontally cut sail, to bring the threadline on to the line of the pull round the curve of the roach. In addition, the radial panels are cut with the warp threadline running down the middle, and not along one side as a selvedge. Both sides of the panel, therefore, have similar bias and similar stretch characteristics; all radial seams will thus stretch the same. This is more expensive on cloth, as only one panel can be taken from each length of material.

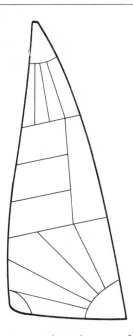

Fig. 3.10 *Film Laminate Cuts*   The substrate of Mylar/Melinex is usually woven and, being light, suffers from detectable distortion off the threadline. We saw in Chapter 3 that the film part of the composite stretches very slightly more than woven polyester which is loaded on the threadline – so it does have a slight give, and this shows when the substrate is stressed on the bias. In addition, stresses across a seam may lead to unwanted slippage of one cloth over another. For both these reasons, the sailmaker tries to arrange for seams to follow the stress lines broadly identified in Fig. 3.5 and, since in practice these are even more numerous and varied, we often get a similar display of panels. In recent years, however, there seems to have been a sensible return to orthodoxy, so that film laminate sails are beginning to look simpler rather than more complicated.

of both cuts, but the sail now seems to be unduly complicated for woven cloth, and I still suspect the leech. Film laminate, on the other hand, seems to know no laws, and cloths run in whatever directions the sailmaker thinks will provide the best resistance to lines of loading (or, I sometimes suspect, the best talking point among potential customers). In broad terms, Mylar or Melinex seams are basically orientated along the stress lines shown in Fig. 3.5, with variations to suit the particular theories of the sailmaker concerned. We thus get radial heads with vertical cloths slashed across by reinforcing panels, or radial clews, or zig-zag leeches; you name it, if someone thinks it will work, it's been tried (but there appear to be signs of a welcome return to sanity in recent seasons); see Fig. 3.10.

Jib Cuts

Where cut is concerned, the same basic rules as for mainsails apply to jibs. The big difference in the case of the jib is that the sail has two unsupported edges (leech and foot), so it is important to have the weave lined up on both these sides if stretch is to be eliminated; this leads to the mitre cut which we all know (Fig. 3.11). The drawback of this cut lies in the mitre itself. It is thicker than the rest of the sail, and so tends to stop the full development of stretch along its line.

Plate 3.4 *Vertical Cut Genoa*   The loadings in a large genoa are high and if, as here, the leech is well hollowed, a vertical cut all-woven sail will offer varying leech threadline angles, with attendant danger of cloth distortion; film laminates can suffer similar problems. In this case, the leech panel has been divided by a series of horizontal seams rocked round the angle of the leech, in order to reduce bias angle (North Sails' leech-cut). Control is enhanced, and the sailmaker has seams he can adjust if trouble does arise. (*Chris Howard-Williams*)

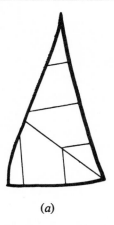
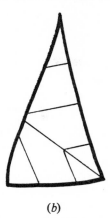

(a)   (b)

Fig. 3.11 *Mitre Cut Jib*   Standard mitre cut jibs have the weft threads parallel with both leech and foot, to keep down stretch in these highly stressed areas unsupported by rope, tape, or wire. The mitre, apart from being just another seam to offer the risk of wrinkles, is extra thick and so resists stretch; it can produce a hard line of unstretched material.

Synthetic cloth, however, has enabled sailmakers to allow the foot a certain amount of bias, so that it will stretch a little (*b*). This helps the mitre to stretch, lets the clew draw aft and allows the flow of the sail to develop, thus giving a flat run-off to the leech.

Fig. 3.12 *Horizontal Cut Jib*   There is no mitre in a horizontal jib and this means that not only is there less work involved in making the sail (thus keeping the price down) but there is less doubled cloth to stop the clew drawing aft to flatten the leech. As I have said before, stretch along the threadline (as opposed to on the bias) is almost nil in sailcloth. Between warp and weft, there is slightly less stretch on the former because the threads across the cloth are under less tension than those lengthways (due to the mechanics of weaving), resulting in crimp which tends to straighten.

Fig. 3.13 *Vertical Cut Jib*   The vertical jib is another way of getting simplicity of cut. The leech is uncluttered with seams and, if this is heat-sealed instead of having a tabling, it is remarkably clean and free from curl.

Fig. 3.14 *Spider-Web Jib*   This cut reduces the size of each piece of cloth in the sail. The result is that stretch anywhere in the sail is kept to a minimum, so that the cut is best suited to large jibs with specially heavy loadings; it is not recommended for dinghy jibs as it restricts development of flow in small sails. Disadvantages are that there are several different bias angles at the luff, so stretch will be uneven; also the doubled cloth at each mitre will stop the clew drawing aft to flatten the leech in all but the largest sails.

In order to let the clew draw aft and thus flatten the leech, it is a good idea to let the foot of the sail stretch a bit. This means that the cloths should leave the foot at an angle (anything from 2° to 15°), and the mitre cut sail sometimes has the foot cloths deliberately offset a bit as in Fig. 3.11(*b*).

Other cuts which take advantage of the fact that the cloths in the foot don't nowadays have to be on the threadline are the horizontal and the vertical (Figs 3.12 and 3.13). They both do away with the

Plate 3.5 *Warp Orientation*   Bruce Banks Sails, ever innovators (remember the Starcut spinnaker?), were one of the first to commit themselves to warp-orientated laminates and vertically moulded sail designs. As these laminates became more highly engineered with the use of Kevlar, it became more advantageous to emulate the 'panel rocking' of fill-orientated crosscut sails, which created a curve in the threadline up the leech. The only way this could be done in vertically moulded sails was to introduce a few transverse seams purely to control threadline direction (see Plate 3.4); this explains the chessboard pattern for which Banks coined the name 'Checkmate' in 1984. Greater and greater threadline orientation has progressively overtaken the simplicity of the original Checkmate concept, but the principle remains unaltered. The light patches in *Chia Chia*'s Melinex genoa are reinforcement; those in the mainsail show where the Mylar leech panels have been alternately reversed, when being laid aft of the Melinex luff and bunt. Note also the reinforcing tape on the genoa foot seams. (*Bruce Banks Sails*)

Fig. 3.15 *Radial or Sunray Jib*   This type of jib suffers from the same disadvantages of changing and different bias stretch as a radial mainsail. A jib's leech, however, is usually straighter than a mainsail's, so threadline problems in this area are less. But a jib relies for its flow more than a mainsail on stretching the luff, so the different bias angles in this area will bring even more problems than in a mainsail.

restricting influence of the mitre, are simple to make and result in good sails. The vertical cut jib is possibly superior to the horizontal for dinghies because it has a seam-free leech, which is more important to keep flat than the foot. If the leech is cut fairly straight (i.e. without hollow) and heat-sealed instead of having a tabling, then the chances of a curling leech with this cut are few.

Another cut is the spider-web (Fig. 3.14), but the object of this is to keep down stretch in any part of the sail by reducing the run of the cloth before it comes up against a seam. It is therefore more suited to large sails where the stresses are great, and is not suitable for small boats where cloth lengths are never very great anyway.

The radial cut jib (Fig. 3.15) is the last with which we need concern ourselves. It suffers from the same problems as a radial mainsail, with the particular disadvantage of different bias angles at each panel in the luff, which means different stretch and thus different amounts of induced flow up the luff. You may also get uneven stretching between individual panels in the sail unless the cloths are cut to their wedge shape by trimming equally from each side, as shown in Fig. 3.9 for the mainsail.

Putting Together

It is no good having a good sail perfectly designed and cut if the machinist who puts it all together can't sew carefully and consistently. A seam which wanders off line, even for a few inches, will start wrinkles at best, and cause hard spots and major creases at worst.

The sewing machine is a crucial link in the chain of sailmaking, and a good operator is worth almost as much to a sailmaker as is a good hand worker for finishing off the sail with cringles, casing, slides and eyelets. Use of double-sided sticky tape has, however, removed much of the danger of wandering seams (the panels are aligned and stuck together on the loft floor, before being taken to the sewing machine); this tends to clog the needle, particularly if the sewing machine is a domestic one, so have a silicone spray such as Ambersil *Formula 6*® or BP *Adsil D.1*® handy.

Tablings

The unsupported edges of a sail (the leech of a mainsail, leech and foot of a jib) are subject to stresses due to the pull of sheets, wind pressure, and boom weight. Such an edge, in dressmaking, has a hem to reinforce it, and it can also have one in sailmaking, where it is called a tabling.

The width and weight of tabling on a sail can make a big difference to the set of a sail: a narrow tabling might allow too much stretch to the leech; a wider one is stronger and stops the leech stretching at the very edge but, if the sail just forward of the tabling stretches, you get a cupped or question mark leech (Fig. 3.16). The sailmaker will decide the width and strength of tabling according to the task of the sail, and then lay his cloths at a corresponding angle to the leech so that it stretches just the right amount: narrow tabling and no bias angle for a light sail; wider tabling and a bit of bias (say 1° or 2°) to allow it to stretch a bit, tabling and all, for a general-purpose sail. It's a good idea to do away with the tabling altogether at the leech of some racing jibs, and to seal it with a hot soldering iron in order to

Fig. 3.16 *Cupped Leech* If the leech tabling is too wide and strong, it may stretch less than the sail just inside, or forward, of it, which will result in a hollow or cup just at the leech, in the shape of a question mark. This causes backwinding and 'motorboating', which is such a destroyer of morale, and is a good reason for heat-sealing the leech without any tabling at all, where day sailing on inland or coastal waters only is involved.

fuse the threads together on the raw edge to stop them fraying. This gives a clean run-off to the air, and so means a better airflow along the lee side of the mainsail. Such a jib has a shorter life than one with a tabling because, not only does the sail tend to fray at the leech (it can be resealed but the process cannot go on indefinitely), but the unreinforced leech is vulnerable to mishandling and is quick to stretch out of shape. It is not, moreover, a practice which should be encouraged for boats which sail offshore, because a torn jib leech in a Force 7 or 8 at night can lead to trouble on a lee shore.

Luff Rope or Tape

A mainsail or jib used with a foil has to have a rope on the luff to enable it to slide up the groove. Sometimes this rope has a second job whereby it controls development of induced flow in the luff of the sail, while in other sails the luff is controlled by a Terylene or Dacron tape and the rope is fed inside this tape, where it acts as a safety precaution to prevent overstretching.

The advantage of having a tape on the luff is that the sailmaker is dealing with similar materials both for the sail and for the luff control. In addition there are no seams in a tape, as there are in a tabling, to chafe on the groove and pick up splinters from wooden spars.

Ancillary Items

Your sailmaker will be the best one to help you finalise your decision on ancillary items and extras. He will certainly have his own ways and reasons for doing many of the tasks set out below, and will be pleased to talk them over with you. If his ideas are not what you are expecting, he will take a deal of persuading that your way (or mine, for that matter) is better than the one he has been following successfully for a good many years. You would be unwise to try to talk him into a new technique without being prepared for the worst consequences.

Headboard

For years dinghies used to have wooden headboards sewn through holes in the board into pockets at the head of the mainsail. These proved too cumbersome and heavy aloft so were abandoned in favour of alloy, but the system of hand-sewing through holes in the board was a constant source of creases in synthetic cloth. There are now several ways of stiffening the head of a mainsail including sewing through an alloy or plastic board as before, slipping the board into a pocket where it remains loose and free from stitching actually through it, or riveting the board on one or both sides of the sail outside the cloth. The aim is to keep creasing and weight to a minimum.

Window

A window in a sail is allowed by most rules nowadays and is a first-class extra if it is put in right. Even if it only reveals one boat on starboard tack during its lifetime, it will have repaid its original cost. Being made of a material which bends but does not distort or stretch, it should be placed in a fairly flat part of the sail, otherwise it will have to try to take up complex multiple curves and will thus make creases. It should also be sewn on to the sail before the cloth is cut away, so that it lies evenly over the area and does not pull at one corner after the canvas is cut away. If you have any fixed ideas of window position, it is best to order a new sail without one, try it out afloat, and then mark the sail exactly where you want it to go. Most class rules limit the size of windows, and many prohibit them being nearer to the leech or foot than a certain distance (usually, like the

(a)   (b)

Plate 3.6 *Zipped Shelf* I carried out some model tests on a zipped shelf for a 14′ International dinghy in the Ratsey & Lapthorn wind tunnel at Cowes back in 1964 (a), and then tried the full size sail on our test rig (b) and afloat. There was a five per cent gain in thrust when the shelf was unzipped on a reach. (*Ratsey & Lapthorn*)

IYRU *Sail Measurement Instructions*[11], about 6 in); this is to stop extra thick windows being fitted to act as battens supporting a large free roach area.

Zippers

A zipper may be fitted along the foot of a mainsail to close off extra fullness in the sail, either in the form of a slab reef or a shelf (which is really only an extreme form of the same thing). Both are useful additions to thrust when reaching and running (I did some wind-tunnel tests in the shelf foot as fitted to an International 14 ft dinghy, and unzipping it on a reach with everything else unaltered produced 5 per cent more forward thrust) and they can also help windward work when unzipped in light weather. The idea of closing the zipper is to flatten the sail for windward work in anything but the lightest winds (Fig. 3.17). Similar zippers may be fitted up the luff, but they are usually more trouble than they are worth for it is often impossible to reach the slider if it jams. Some rules ban zippers – the IOR doesn't allow mainsails to be reefed or flattened along the luff (other than by roller furling)[12], so the effect is the same up the mast. It is not practical to fit a zipper after a sail has been made because the extra cloth which it controls is not built into the foot; if you want one, therefore, it should be specified when a new sail is ordered.

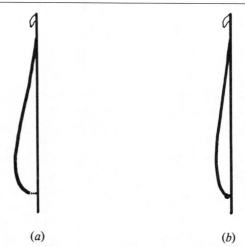

(*a*)   (*b*)

Fig. 3.17 *Zipped Shelf* These two drawings show the principle of the shelf foot, which can be closed off by means of a zipper to make the sail into a more normal shape (*b*). The shelf is unzipped when the boat comes off the wind (*a*), increasing forward thrust by as much as 5 per cent. Depending on its depth, it may also be unzipped when close hauled in very light weather.

     Care should be taken to see that the sail is not too flat when the zipper is closed, because it is just over the boom that fullness is most useful.

Cunningham hole
I shall go into greater detail on cunningham holes in the chapter on trim. It is enough here to say that one can very easily be put in after the sail is made, and its cheapness and efficiency make it a Best Buy.

Battens
Battens may be made of wood, plastic or fibreglass. Their job is to help spread and support the roach, usually at the leech of a mainsail, although some jibs have them in either leech or foot. They should be stiff enough to stop the roach from flapping, but should bend enough to take up the natural curve of the sail. This means that the inner end should be thinner than the leech end and a top mainsail batten should bend rather more than the rest; plastic is often chosen for the top batten for this reason. If a batten goes right across to the luff of the sail, its length, tension when in the pocket, and amount of bend must all be right if it is to set properly. If only the top batten is full length it should lie in its pocket with very little tension because, if it is held in hard enough to force it into a curve, it may refuse to bend the other way when you change tacks in light winds. Full-length battens lower down the sail don't give this trouble so much and their tension can be varied to control the amount of flow in the sail. It is to enable you to vary this tension that full-length battens usually tie into the sail, rather than slip into pockets with a pre-set elastic tensioner at the inner end.

Full-length battens
Full-length battens take some of the inefficiency out of a mainsail when going to windward. The sail becomes more allied to a solid aerofoil, because it does not lift so much under the influence of backwinding by the jib; this means that laminar flow is maintained over a greater area. The powerpoint should be about one-third aft near the head, becoming halfway near the foot. To achieve a full camber in light winds, push the battens in hard; use less pressure in strong winds so the sail is flatter. Test for stiffness by standing each batten vertically on a set of scales and pushing on its upper end until it takes up roughly the correct shape. The scales should read between 3–6 lb; any batten needing more than about 10 lb is far too stiff. Curvature can also be changed by use of the leech line, although this seems to have most effect in the top third of the sail only. Be careful not to overdo this, because a hooked leech will have a braking effect at the high speeds enjoyed by some fully battened multihulls. See also Chapter 11, *Sailboards – Battens*, for fuller discussion of the problems those specific sails have to meet in their full-length battens.

Jib foot round

Some rules do not control the amount of round on the foot of the jib and this can offer a way of increasing area by a significant amount. Even a narrow jib with a short foot can have up to 10 to 12 in of round built on to it if a stiff cloth is used (Mylar) or a drawstring is fitted to help hold it in shape. This certainly pays off when reaching and it can also be made to set when beating to windward if the boat is sailed right; see description of power sailing in Chapter 7.

4 SAILMAKING – PREPARATION

Home sailmaking need not be the prerogative of the talented few. All that is needed is determination, care, the right equipment (much of which may already be in the house or workshop), and guidance. You will have to provide the first three of these ingredients, while this book is designed to give you the fourth, albeit somewhat sketchily. In these days of spiralling costs, the result can be economical as well as satisfying.

It will be manifestly impossible to give full details on all aspects of sailmaking for all kinds of sails, in the confined space of a few thousand words; I shall accordingly content myself with stating broad principles, starting with the preparation and then going on to some practical work. You will be credited with a certain basic competence, so that we can dispense with the more elementary detail and so new skills can be acquired if you are pointed in the right direction and given the background knowledge, from which you can expand your ability from more comprehensive source material.

Equipment

Apart from a suitable workspace (and we shall discuss this when we come to cutting and sewing in Chapter 5), you will need certain basic equipment.

Knife or scissors

A sharp knife or pair of scissors is usually to be found in most homes. The knife need not be large and may be of the kitchen type or a pocket knife; scissors should be the medium or large dressmaking variety and must be sharp.

Sealing iron

If you do not already own an electric soldering iron with a fairly fine blade ($\frac{1}{8}$ in bent rod is as good as the special knife blade variety), now is the time to buy one if you are going to use synthetic cloth for your sails; it will be invaluable for heat-sealing raw edges of cloth and rope ends to prevent fraying.

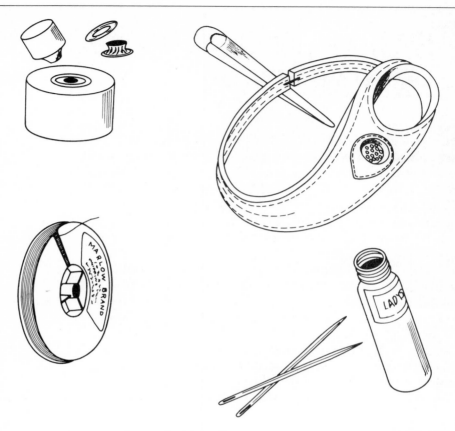

Fig. 4.1 *Sailmaking Tools*   The eyelet punch and die can normally be found in camping shops if not in chandleries; the Swedish splicing tool behind the sailmaker's palm has a groove which makes tucking strands much easier; hand seaming twine comes on reels ready waxed; wrap your needles in a piece of lightly oiled cloth and store in a plastic bottle to keep away rust.

Sewing palm

A sailmaker's sewing palm is not difficult to get used to, particularly if you start with some rough work; you will probably be a bit clumsy at first, so get a bit of practice on some spare cloth before you start to use it for real. Make sure that you don't buy a roping palm which, having a deeper set needle guard to take the longer needle used for roping (it is a size or two larger), will make it hard to hold the shorter sewing needles when they are back against the guard. You can usually tell a roping palm by its built-up thumb protection. Palms are available for left-handed workers if you look hard enough.

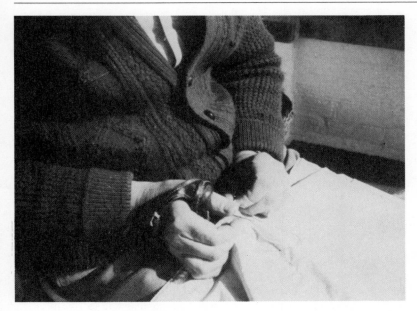

Plate 4.1 *The Sailmaker's Palm*   A sailmaker's sewing palm is not difficult to get used to. Practise on an old sail or piece of spare canvas before you tackle the real thing – even then, you would be wise to turn your favourite racing sail over to the professionals, unless it is only a question of replacing a couple of stitches. (*Author*)

Needles

Sailmakers' needles are sized according to the British wire gauge. This ensures continuation of the illogical reasoning which bedevils all sailmaking, such as making a hole with a number 13 cutter for a number 2 eyelet to be clenched with a number 4 punch; or sewing a 4 oz cloth with a 2 lb (number 1) thread using a number 18 needle. It is all part of a conspiracy to shroud the sailmaker's craft in mumbo jumbo so that the layman shall not learn too much, too quickly. You should get enough practice so that you do not have to use a needle which is too big for the task, just because you are not able to control the smaller, correct, size. Too large a needle will make large holes with the danger of wrinkles; too small a needle will result in uneven workmanship and worse wrinkles. You should get by on dinghy sails with sizes 17 and 18, plus a domestic needle for use on your spinnaker. Dull the point of one of your 17s and keep it for roping; it will then more easily pass between the lay of the rope without picking up part of a strand. If you find a 17 too small, don't go larger than a 16 whatever you do, for a 15 would be too big and clumsy for most small sails (except for roping).

Plate 4.2 *The Sewing Machine – 1* Seaming at the Southampton loft of Alpha Sails. This Pfaff® machine is set up for mainsail or jib cloth (or light cover work); anything really heavy is joined on an Adler® kept for the task, and a twin-needle Pfaff is used for medium work. It is more efficient to maintain specific machines for specific cloth weights, rather than to change needles and thread, because of the time required to set up a machine from zero for a new task. (*Author*)

Plate 4.3 *The Sewing Machine – 2* This 3-step zig-zag Singer® with pull-feed, is what Alpha Sails use for most of their spinnakers. The 3-step process sews three stitches at 45° to the seam line, then three more at 45° the other way, and so on, back and forth. The correct tensions for each particular job are important if missed or broken stitches are to be avoided, and the operator must spend a couple of minutes fine-tuning the machine for each new job, using a piece of scrap canvas. (*Author*)

Sewing machine

If you already own a domestic sewing machine, it will almost certainly be suitable for any work involving three or four thicknesses of dinghy sails, particularly if it is grandma's old trusty rather than a lightweight modern gadget. It is best if the machine can sew a cross-stitch, or zig-zag as it is also called. This allows the canvas to work slightly when sailing, without putting too great a strain on the stitching. Make sure that the tension is adjusted so that the stitches link together inside the cloth rather than above or below, where they can be broken by chafe.

Spikes or prickers

If you are lucky enough to have a wooden floor into which you can stick prickers or spikes, you should buy half a dozen cheap screwdrivers and sharpen them to a point; these will be useful for holding the individual cloths rigidly on the full size pattern. If you cannot make holes in the floor, get hold of some 4–5 lb weights to do the same job.

Plate 4.4 *Sail Prickers*   Whether cutting out on a table (as here, in Alpha's loft) or on the floor, prickers or sharpened screwdrivers are useful for holding the cloths in place. If the floor cannot, or must not, be pierced, then use weights. (*Author*)

Tape measure
A metal tape measure will give much more accurate measurements than a linen one, which will stretch slightly. If close accuracy to quarter of an inch is not essential, use a linen tape, because it can then double as the tape which is laid on the floor in a curve to give a guide to the exact shape to draw in chalk for the luff, leech and foot.

Chalk and string
The sail will need to be drawn in chalk full size on the floor. The basic triangle is marked in string stretched between prickers, and the round to the luff and foot, and the roach or hollow to the leech are shown by a tape laid in relation to the straight line of the string. If a straight leech is wanted, for instance, the string is rubbed with chalk then pulled up in the middle and allowed to snap back against the floor; the chalk will fall off the string and mark a neat line.

Fid
A fid is an oversize marlin spike, and is used when making eyes or cringles; it is a specialist item usually made of hard wood or lignum vitae. It is not essential.

Bench hook
Like the fid, this is a specialist item (which can be made quite easily at home) and, if the truth were told, equally unessential. But both items make life a good deal easier so they are worth acquiring at the start. The bench hook is stuck into the cloth to be tied away to one side; this keeps tension on the work and makes sewing easier and neater.

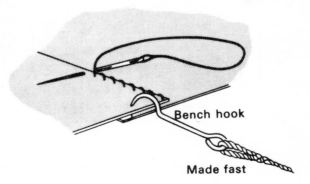

Fig. 4.2 *The Bench Hook*   A bench hook goes into one end of the work and is tied by a line away to one side. One hand then tensions the cloth against the pull of the bench hook, while the other does the sewing; the result is much steadier work. The stitch shown here is the flat seaming, or tabling, stitch.

Hammer
The hammer from your workshop will do, but a hide hammer is easier on the sail and can be bought from many government surplus stores.

Rubbing iron
Old time professional sailmakers always kept their own specialist tool for the task of creasing the canvas where required. The back of your pocket knife, the blunt edge of your scissors or even your own thumb will do as good a job.

Materials

Canvas
All sailcloth is canvas, be it cotton or synthetic. Some people feel that cotton is an easier medium to work in, and thus is a better material for the amateur sailmaker. Compared with polyester cloth (Terylene, Dacron, or whatever trade name it may enjoy in its country of origin – it's called Lavsan in Russia, would you believe?), the advantages of cotton are that it is cheaper (if you can find it these days), more forgiving when it comes to small creases (which tend to disappear as the cloth stretches), less subject to chafe on its stitching because the thread beds into the cloth and is thus partly protected, and rather easier to manipulate due to being less slippery. The advantages of synthetic cloth are that it does not stretch anything like cotton (which has to be carefully evaluated for stretch), paradoxically Terylene and Dacron sails remain bigger than cotton ones of a similar starting size, precisely because the former stretch less (cloth stretch is a misnomer, it distorts and draws material from another part of the sail as it elongates on the bias; cotton shrinks in use). Synthetics can be heat-sealed along a raw edge, thus avoiding much tedious hemming with attendant extra thicknesses to pass under the arm of the sewing machine, they are also smoother giving faster sails, and finally they are almost immune from rot and the action of domestic chemicals – an important factor in any sail's life (but they are weakened by sunlight). Film laminate is very much a specialist material, not suited to the amateur sailmaker; it needs great care and knowledge in shaping, handling, and sewing, even in deciding seam width, as we saw in Chapter 3, so that any mistakes will ruin the result. My recommendation is to go for all-woven polyester every time.

Twine
Hand seaming twine should be compatible with the cloth used: cotton for cotton and synthetic for synthetic (and this can mean Terylene or Dacron when making a spinnaker from nylon cloth). For

any hand sewing on dinghy mainsails and jibs, use a 2 lb or 4 lb (No 1 or 2) twine, which should be waxed to help hold the twist together and to give protection; there are ready-waxed twines on the market, otherwise a block of beeswax is required. For machine work, use a medium polyester thread, which may also be used for any hand sewing on the spinnaker.

Rope, tape and wire
Pre-stretched Terylene rope is the best for the amateur sailmaker (Italian hemp for cotton sails). Dacron or Terylene tape may be used on the luff of all sails, either with or without rope or wire; but be careful to get a stout webbing if the tape is to take the full weight of the sail (i.e. it will be fitted direct with slides or hanks). A wire luff jib is somewhat complicated to make (a rope or tape being easier to fit and form into eyes at tack and head); if you use wire, it should be galvanised and cased in a plastic cover, or else stainless steel (which may react with synthetic cloth and cause stains if it, too, is not cased in plastic).

Slides, hooks and snaphooks
The appropriate accessories for the type of boat must be considered. Stainless steel is usually best but, failing this, plastic or bronze avoid

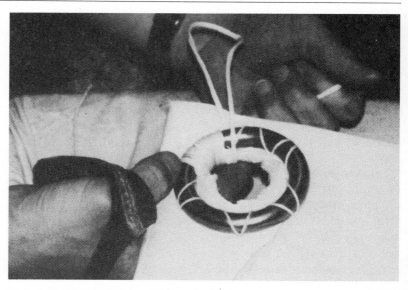

Plate 4.5 *A Worked Ring*   The DIY sailmaker will always work a clew eye by hand. One which is hammered in over a die will not be strong enough, and a hydraulic press (see *Sails* Chapter 6) is, of course, far too expensive for the amateur. (*Author*)

corrosion. Don't use bronze or brass next to bare galvanised wire or it will quickly remove the galvanising through electrolytic action.

Eyes, rings and thimbles
The same applies to these as to slides and the like, with the difference that plastic (principally nylon) may be used up to much larger sizes for eyelets and thimbles. Shops selling camping gear often stock eyelet sets complete with punch and die, to enable rings to be punched straight into canvas. The result is weak, and should only be used for those eyelets which are not going to take a lot of strain (close spaced slide or hank eyelets on small sails); in addition they are usually made of brass which will quickly corrode in salt water. A hand-sewn solid ring with the stitching protected by a bronze liner is best. To fit the liner a special punch and die must be bought for the size in question, and these are often only available from a specialist supplier (your sailmaker may be able to help).

Anti-chafe leather
The professional sailmaker will often protect points of likely chafe with hide or 'green' leather; examples are the clews or headboards of mainsails, the luff rope in way of slides especially if these are shackled on, or the clews of jibs. If you can get hide, soak it in water for half an hour before use in order to soften it for sewing. But a small piece of sailcloth will do almost as good a job, and there are also slide attachments incorporating a plastic protective piece as standard.

Design

We saw in Chapter 2 the general principles of design. Let us now examine in some detail specific measurements for cruising sails for an average dinghy of 12–15 ft (3.5–4.5 m) length.

Mainsails
A bermudan mainsail for a general purpose dinghy using a straight mast and boom needs $2\frac{1}{2}$ in (6 cm) of luff round placed about one-third up from the tack for heavy weather use, or 4 in (10 cm) of round for light weather; in both cases the round should taper gradually to the tack in a convex curve, and to a point about two-thirds of the way to the head, from where it takes up a straight or even a slightly hollow path to the top of the sail in order to keep this part flat. Sails intended for bendy masts must have this round added to the allowance made to accommodate the mast bend. Foot round needs to be about one inch less, again tapering to a point short of the clew to keep the leech flat; see Fig. 2.1.

Plate 4.6 *Broad Seam*   This Enterprise jib, awaiting rubbing down on Alpha's table, shows evidence of flow where the tapered seams have been joined together. (*Author*)

Broad seam

Under 16 ft (5 m) on the luff, a mainsail does not need broad seam. Above this figure, broad seam roughly equal to the amount of luff round may be incorporated in the ratio 3 : 2 : 1 at the tack; the first seam up; the second seam up (except that sails under 19 ft (6 m) on the luff need only have broad seam at the tack itself). Mainsails with more than 3 in (8 cm) of foot round should have ¾ in (2 cm) broad seam halfway along the boom, which means that the bottom panel usually has to be split or else a dart put in. The taper caused by broad seam should be taken to a point about one-third of the way towards the leech.

Jibs

Jibs normally need to be cut fairly flat, particularly in the head (they can always be given extra draft by easing the sheet). In the days of cotton and the early synthetics, a jib used to be given some round in the lower luff; modern materials are more stable, however, and the luff is usually pulled harder, so that the sail is now cut straight or slightly hollow along this edge for efficient windward work. A jib with a rope or tape luff is much easier to stow than one with a wire, besides being easier to make and more controllable as to flow, so my advice is to go for the former.

Roach

There is a good deal to be said for cutting a cruising mainsail with a straight leech and, what is more, for doing away with a headboard and merely using a stout ring at the top. Not only is this easier to make (the cloths can be laid vertically, that is parallel to the leech), but it does away with the hassle of battens and also the possibility of breaking the headboard at sea. This advice is possibly more suited to trailer boats and daysailing keel boats so, if you want a roach for better looks, then battens are necessary to make it stand, and they will support one-third of their length in the form of roach outside the straight line joining head to clew. Jib leeches, on the other hand, are best cut hollow, allowing 1 in (2.5 cm) inside the straight line for every 5 ft (1.5m) of leech length; maximum hollow should be about halfway along the leech.

Cloth

The average dinghy will not stray far from a cloth weight of 150 gm/m², whether for cruiser or racing; a particularly heavy large dinghy such as those used for open water fishing might go up to 200 gm/m². A light displacement cruiser/racer of some 22–24 ft (7–7.5 m) LOA will have a mainsail and working jib of 190–225 gm/m², a genoa of 150–175 gm/m² and, if engaged in open water cruising, may well go as heavy as 250 gm/m² for its working sails (certainly for storm canvas). Choose a material without too much resin finish if you want ease of handling.

Sailplan

The size and shape of the sails you make may already be determined for you by an existing sailplan. If you are launching into racing sails (a bold step for the first time amateur) you must, of course, read the class rules carefully because there is always some small print governing certain dimensions, which may control cross measurements, eyelet position, size and placing of windows[11], or even the size and shape of insignia and numbers (the IYRU also has a few words to say on this last matter[13]). If you have to draw up your own sailplan, you should study some books on the subject of centres of effort and lateral resistance (I recommend *Small Craft Conversion* by John Lewis, published by Adlard Coles Ltd).

If you are proposing to adopt different sail sizes for a boat which already possesses a sailplan (perhaps to make a heavy weather jib instead of a standard working jib), then you would be wise to relate

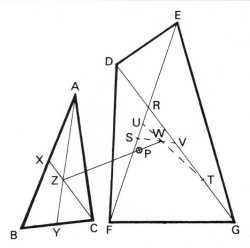

Fig. 4.3 *The Sailplan Centre of Effort*   I have used a gaff mainsail in order to
show how this more complicated area is resolved; a bermudan mainsail resolves
like the jib.

AX=BX	GT=DR	SU=RU
BY=CY	FS=ER	RV=TV

C of E jib is Z, and mainsail is W. The combined C of E is P, which lies along WZ
in proportion to sail areas of jib and mainsail. This can be worked out as follows
(all units are feet or square feet)

$$\frac{\text{jib area}}{\text{total area}} \times WZ = WP$$

Alternatively draw a line to represent the jib area to any convenient scale,
vertically upwards from W, and another to represent the mainsail area to the
same scale, vertically downwards from Z. The line joining the ends of these two
lines will cut WZ at the combined C of E.

your own proposed areas and centres of effort to those of the naval
architect who designed the boat, so that the proper balance is maintained and you don't find that you have got too much weather helm
with your smaller headsail, even with a reef in the mainsail. At all
events, you need to draw a scale plan of the boat in side elevation,
showing the mast with accurate rake, the sheer, the underwater
outline (with centre of lateral resistance when the plate is down), and
the sheeting angles.

When you have the plan finished, scale carefully the sails you have
drawn and mark on the plan their sizes to the nearest inch.

Drawing Out

Now is the time for you to draw in full size the sail you propose making; ideally you need a large floor space. This may mean clearing the living room, so you (or your spouse) just have to face up to facts: if you want to make a sail, you must first make room. I say 'ideally' because you can in theory draw the sail carefully to a large scale, mark in each cloth with the overlap on its neighbour, and then cut to the scaled measurements – but rather you than I for the first attempt.

Let us therefore assume that you are tackling a 13 ft (4 m) luff jib, and that you have cleared the living room (including the carpet); you now have a wooden floor which will take chalk.

'Hang on,' I hear you cry. 'You made ominous remarks earlier on about spikes or prickers. My wife may be prepared to move out of the lounge for a few weeks, but she won't stand idly by while the parquet is peppered with holes.'

All is by no means lost. Thumb tacks do a good job of holding down the cloth in the cutting out stage, while plastic-headed map pins are even better, and both these hardly make a mark. Alternatively you can collect half a dozen 4–5 lb weights (which don't do quite such a good job) to hold the cloth in place while cutting.

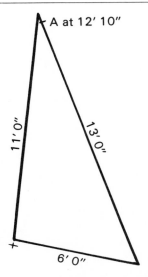

Fig. 4.4 *Scaling Cut Sizes*   Cut the jib short on the luff 1 in per 6 ft, so mark the plan of our jib, 2 in short at the head with a line A. Dinghy jibs need no allowance for stretch on leech and foot, so scale 11 ft down from point A and scribe an arc, then 6 ft back from the tack; where the two arcs intersect will be the clew as cut and before the sail is stretched.

Jib

First take the scaled-down sailplan with the finished sizes marked on it. It is conventional to draw both scale and full-size plans looking at the starboard side of the sail, but this is not essential. Draw on the scaled plan an allowance for stretch on the luff in the ratio of 1 in (2.5 cm) for every 6 ft (2 m) of luff, so if the luff is 13 ft (4 m), scale 12 ft 10 in (3.975 m) up from the tack (which is our datum point); make a mark (A on Fig. 4.4) across the luff. A dinghy jib needs no allowance for stretch on either foot or leech, so scale off the full length from tack and point A so that the two arcs cut each other just below the clew (if your cloth is particularly soft and stretchy and the clew position is critical, take 1 in extra off all three sides).

Decide your leech hollow as we saw earlier (1 in (2.5 cm) hollow for every 5 ft (1.5 m), so probably 2½ in (6 cm) total hollow in our case); there is no round or hollow to the luff; allow 1 in (2.5 cm) round to the foot for every 3 ft (1 m). Annotate the plan with the actual measurements.

Place a chalk cross on the floor at an appropriate spot to mark the tack. Measure the other two corners as just scaled on the plan and then push a spike or thumb tack into the floor at each corner. Take the string and stretch it round this triangle, keeping it tight and half-hitching it at each corner. Measure the hollow at the mid-point

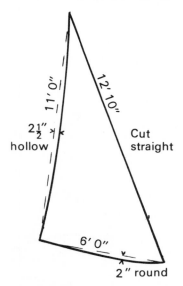

Fig. 4.5 *Full Size Drawing* Mark out the basic triangle as determined in Fig. 4.4, then draw the actual line of luff, leech and foot, allowing for any hollow or round.

of the leech and mark it on the floor; do the same for the foot round one-third from the tack.

The next step is to chalk the actual line of the three edges of the sail. You may either use a thin wooden batten to bend to the line required, holding it in place with thumb tacks or weights, or else you can 'throw' a linen tape. The latter should be pinned at one end (the head or tack) and then laid carefully on the floor to pass through the various marks, being adjusted by eye until it lies in a fair curve (you will see that, far from being thrown, this is carefully and meticulously adjusted); if you have a linen tape measure it will serve for this task very well. Draw on the floor in chalk the line of the batten or tape as shown in Fig.4.5.

Finally, draw a dotted line all round the sail at a distance equal to the tabling you propose giving; let us say 1 in (2 cm) on the leech and foot and, if the luff is to have a tabling from sailcloth and not from tape or webbing (and later I shall recommend the latter), $1\frac{1}{2}$ in (4 cm) on the luff. If you propose turning the edges of the tabling and sail under to stop fraying, rather than heat-sealing them, the extra distance has to be allowed for at this stage.

5 SAILMAKING – PRACTICAL

Cutting Out

You now need to take your courage in both hands and cut cloth. We shall be using the horizontal cut for simplicity, so start with the foot cloth and lay it at right angles from the leech, in such a way that it is used most economically (unless the clew is a right angle, there will be a wedge-shaped piece to cut to waste along the foot); pin the leech end in position. Ensure that you have allowed slightly over the tabling line (to allow for any creep of one cloth on another in the sewing process), cut the cloth from the bolt using a pair of scissors or a knife with the sharp part of the blade uppermost, and then pin the

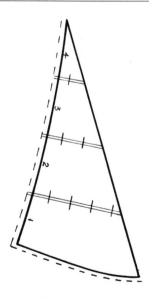

Fig. 5.1 *Cutting Out*   Each cloth is pinned carefully in position while the next one is cut, pinned and marked. The two cloths are then struck up with match marks, or stuck together using double-sided sticky tape. Allowance must be made not only for tablings, but also for any creep which may occur in the sewing process if you do not use sticky tape – say an inch at each end.

Plate 5.1 *Cutting Out*   A Mirror spinnaker being cut out on the table at Alpha Sails, Southampton. The outline of a number of permanent patterns can also be seen. (*Author*)

panel at the luff end. Mark the leech with a figure 1.

Leave the spikes or thumb tacks in each end of the first panel and lay the cloth again, working from luff to leech this time. You therefore need to turn the bolt round (but not over) so that the slanting edge which you cut at the luff lies nicely along the luff again. Lay it so that the overlap for the seam is correct (about $\frac{1}{8}$ in for every ounce of cloth weight, so $\frac{3}{8}$ in or $\frac{1}{2}$ in for the average dinghy; this is 1 mm per 10 gm/m², so 1.5 cm in this case), and pin in place. Mark the cloth at the leech with a 2, flip number one cloth on to the top of the second one and draw the seam overlap the full length of the latter, then 'strike up' the two cloths by putting match marks across them both at intervals of about a foot (if you are not using double-sided sticky tape, these will be used as progress guides when sewing, to see that one cloth does not creep up on the next).

Turn the bolt round again, so that the square edge runs along the leech, pin it in place, and proceed to cut the third cloth in a similar manner (but working from leech to luff this time). Unless the leech has an exaggerated hollow, you should lay each cloth so that it strikes the straight line joining the head to clew at right angles; this will give a weft which follows the line of the leech in the middle, but which has a small amount of bias near the head and clew so that these parts of the sail may develop slightly. If you decide that a large amount of hollow (a heavy weather jib might have extra leech hollow to form a larger slot and to reduce sail area) requires that the cloths should be tripped round in order to keep the weft more nearly parallel with the run of the leech, the overlap of one cloth on another will be greater at the leech than at the luff, and you should make sure that you mark this accurately each time (note that this is not broad seam to tighten the leech, because the taper runs the full length of the cloth). You may remove the prickers or pins from each cloth once the next panel has been laid, pinned and marked.

Joining Up

Start with cloths numbered 1 and 2, and sew from leech to luff; cloth number 1 should be on top and to your left with the leech away from you and going first into the machine. This ensures that each new panel is added to the rest of the sail from the right, so that only one cloth has to pass under the arm of the sewing machine. Place the cloths with the correct overlaps as marked and, if your machine has a reverse capability, start a short distance along the seam, before backing up to the leech and then engaging forward gear for the full run.

To keep the match marks level without sticky tape, you will find that you will have to hold back the bottom cloth slightly and see that the top one is helped through the foot of the sewing machine. This is due to the slippery nature of the material, which is being pulled through by the teeth of the feed mechanism underneath the lower cloth but which has no comparable feed for the top cloth. Unless you watch this carefully, the match marks you put on when striking up each pair of cloths will soon get out of phase. At the same time you have to be careful to maintain the correct overlap, because any irregularity will result in tight spots and wrinkles.

All this lining up of panels can be helped if you pin each pair together accurately before sewing, but this is a tedious business which, in any event, may not be possible because the pins get in the way of the mechanism of the sewing machine. Seams may be glued effectively with clear Bostik® sufficiently for sewing, but the glue tends to clog the needle so it must be kept to a narrow band in the middle of the seam; used in this manner it is undoubtedly the best solution for the amateur who is not a skilled machinist. Finally there is double-sided sticky tape which does an excellent job.

Keep close to the outer edge all along the seam from leech to luff, then turn the sail over and sew a second row along the other edge of the seam, working from luff to leech this time. This process is repeated until all cloths are joined together and the assembly starts to look like a sail. It is a good idea to use thread of a contrasting colour

Plate 5.2 *Joining Up – 1* Many lofts arrange their sewing machines in a battery, with one long table serving several machines, as shown in this shot of the Alpha sail loft. (*Author*)

so that broken stitches will show up more easily (but this will also show up uneven sewing as well so, if this worries you, perhaps it is best to stick to the same colour).

Proprietary sealers such as Seamkote® and Duroseam® make an excellent job of protecting the stitching of a sail. Painted on each side of a new sail in turn, the product penetrates and, when dry, binds stitching together to such an extent that it can be chafed completely away on one side but will still hold. Experiments with disc-sanding the surface thread from each side of a seam resulted in the untreated part of the seam falling apart, while the treated part resisted all efforts to separate it. Old sails can only be effectively protected in this manner if all salt is washed right off, even that part of the sewing thread which passes through the cloth.

Rubbing Down

Now comes the time when the sail receives its final shaping. If you have been careful, the original chalked plan will still be on the floor; if not, you have to mark again. Lay the sail on top of it and pricker down each of the three corners, pulling firmly to remove all wrinkles (but not so hard as to stretch the cloth). An alternative is to pricker

Plate 5.3 *Joining Up – 2*   W. G. Lucas & Son prefer to give each machinist his or her own table. (*Author*)

the sail out anywhere on the floor and draw the outline direct on to the sail itself, using a pencil for white cloth and tailor's chalk for coloured material.

Turn up the cloth to the final size and crease along the chalk line. The professional sailmaker will cut off the tabling and move it across to cover the edge without turning it over, so that the threadline continues to run in the same direction as it does in the sail itself. This is a factor only where the threadline is not at a right angle to the edge concerned, however, so we may certainly fold the leech over without cutting it off. Trim carefully with a sealing iron one inch ($2\frac{1}{2}$ cm) outside the crease all down the leech, and it is ready to be turned down and sewn (if you want to tuck the raw edge under again as a hem, then you have to allow a further half inch (12 mm) and crease this as well). It is a good idea to pin the leechline away to the bottom of the fold if you decide to fit one, as this avoids accidental sewing of the cord itself. Leave about a foot (30 cm) unsewn at head and clew, so that the reinforcement patches can be slipped underneath as we shall see shortly.

I suggest that you do the same for the luff and foot, accepting the small wrinkles which will result (but see later, where I shall suggest that the luff be fitted with a tape to hold the wire and act as tabling at the same time). Fit a drawstring into any luff tabling before sewing it down, for use later in pulling through a rope or wire.

Bermudan mainsails

The method of cutting jibs with horizontal panels, just described, suits bermudan mainsails equally well, except that you should only allow for a luff stretch of 1 in per 12 ft (1 cm per 1.5 m), and no stretch at all for dinghies on leech and foot. If a headboard is to be fitted, this should be placed on the full size floor outline so that the leech may be drawn at the correct distance from the luff to accommodate the board. When drawing the leech, any roach which is given to the sail (not more than one-third of the batten length outside the straight line joining head to clew) is best marked in three places: the full roach at the mid-way mark, and half this at the quarter and three-quarter heights. When it comes to rubbing down, mark the batten positions on the sail and make the leech straight from the head to the top batten, between all batten ends, and finally down to the clew (this will help to avoid flutter at the leech). As I said earlier, there is much to be said for doing away with the headboard and fitting a stout eye instead, and for not having any roach at all (when the sail may be cut vertically).

Plate 5.4 *Finishing – 1*   Final hand work on a mainsail. (*Author*)

Broad seam

A mainsail profits more than a jib from tailoring its flow through introduction of broad seam, although it too can be satisfactory for most purposes without it. We saw earlier the amount of seam tightening for the average mainsail. As they are cut out, the cloths need to be overlapped this much extra at the end where the broad seam will be incorporated. The overlap is drawn parallel from the leech to the point where the broad seam will start, from where it broadens out towards the luff. Mark the taper well, and then sew to this wider line when you reach it; if you sew one long taper all the way from the leech, you will not alter the shape of the sail at all. If you want some tailored shape at the luff of a vertical cut sail, you will have to slit the cloth and put in a couple of darts.

Finishing Off

After the sail has been put together and rubbed down to its final shape, the finishing touches have to be put to it. These can be summarised as follows:

1. Reinforcement patches.
2. Luff rope or wire.
3. Eyes, eyelets and headboard.

Plate 5.5 *Finishing – 2*   The luff tape is checked at Alpha's Southampton loft. (*Author*)

4. Batten pockets.
5. Reef points, if any.
6. Slides and hanks or snaphooks.
7. Sail number and insignia.

Reinforcement Patches

If the canvas is to take the strain which will be put on it, head, tack and clew need strengthening because this is where the stresses are concentrated. Shape of patches varies from sailmaker to sailmaker, and some like to have tongues running into the sail roughly bisecting the angle of the corner in question. For our purposes the segment of a circle is simply and easily fitted; use off-cuts from any material which you may have cut to waste. You should aim to fit at least two thicknesses on each side of each corner; three if your machine will sew seven thicknesses (plus one where the tabling runs over the patch, though this short distance can easily be finished by hand). Each patch should extend into the sail less than the one which goes on top of it, and should be a different size from its partner on the other side. Thus, the six-clew patch thicknesses for our sail should each fit snugly along the leech and foot, and the series might start with a 4 in radius for the underpatch to port, 5 in for the underpatch to starboard, 6 in for the port middle patch, 7 in for the one to starboard, 8 in for the top patch to port and 9 in for the top starboard patch. When these have been fitted, complete the sewing of the loose ends of the tabling and the clew is ready for its eye.

Luff Rope or Wire

To continue with our example of the 13 ft jib, there are several ways of finishing off the luff; three out of the four listed below require the rope or wire to be drawn through the tabling by a light line, which should have been fitted rather like a leech line as the tabling was sewn down.

1. A wire measuring 13 ft between the spliced or swaged eyes at each end, with the tack eye worked in and the head of the sail pulled (2 in, or 5 cm, for our particular jib) up to the head eye and seized to it. The luff of the sail may be seized round the wire at intervals along its length, or the wire may be left to float inside the tabling. In any event, the flow of the sail is fixed in the sail loft and cannot be altered once the sail is finished.

2. A 13 ft wire with the head eye worked in and the tack running out of the tabling at the bottom. There is an eye at the tack end of the luff tabling, so that tension can be varied by downward pull on the sail over the wire.

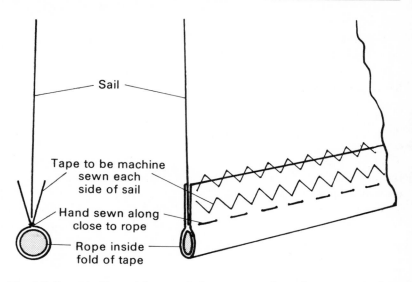

Fig. 5.2 *Rope in Tape*   The rope is free to move along the tape, apart from seizings at head, tack and, in the case of mainsails, clew. This is a simple method of roping for the amateur, with little risk of irregularities.

3. A 12 ft 11 in pre-stretched polyester rope sewn to the outside of the sail all along its length, as with many mainsails.

4. A 12 ft 11 in pre-stretched polyester rope running inside the tabling, with the eyesplice worked in at both head and tack. The rope is free to float inside the tabling, being only attached to the sail at top and bottom.

For our purposes we shall assume case 4 above, and shall put on a tape of webbing luff tabling (sometimes the webbing also does the job of rope or wire, so that hanks are fitted direct to the webbing; in this case, the material has to be specially strong as it has to act as luff wire). It is important to use pre-stretched polyester rope, because anything else will allow the luff to elongate to the point where the cloth may be seriously overstretched. You need to know just how much the rope will pull, so that you can make the correct allowance when deciding how short to cut it; even with pre-stretched rope, I suggest that you should allow a very small amount of give (about half of one per cent). You can check whether you are more or less right by pulling both sail and rope as hard as you can, with the aid of a single part tackle. Strike up the rope and tabling (or tape) if you are going to sew the full length of the rope – but you will get a more even result by leaving it to float inside the tabling. If you find later that you have not made the rope short enough, you can always unpick the head or tack, remake the eyesplice to shorten the distance between the eyes, and remake the sail.

Take a length of 2–3 in (5–8 cm) wide webbing sufficient to pull to 13 ft, fold it round the rope and then sew along the two parts of the webbing as close to the rope as you can get, either by machine or hand. If your machine will not get close enough to the rope, sew in a length of string or cord and pull the rope through later. Rope and webbing combined are now struck up to the raw edge of the luff, with tension on both parts to keep them equally extended (this will mean that the rope and webbing must be gathered an inch or so in the case of our jib). One part of the doubled tape is sewn to each side of the luff so that the webbing forms the tabling. The head and tack eyes must now be worked into the tape, and metal or nylon thimbles inserted.

Mainsails

Where a mainsail luff rope runs in a groove in the mast and boom, it should be enclosed in a fold of the webbing as described above, made fast firmly at the head, tack and clew, and left to float free inside the tabling or webbing. Cut it so that it is 5 or 6 in too long at each end, leaving the tail of the rope sticking out of the tabling at head and

Plate 5.6 *Handwork in the Loft*   A mainsail's luff is nicely accessible when the sail is stretched by means of a tackle, as in this shot of Len Hackett, fifty years with W. G. Lucas apart from Army service in World War II. (*Author*)

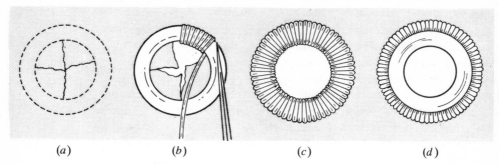

(a)   (b)   (c)   (d)

Fig. 5.3 *Worked Eye* Note how the cloth is not cut right away from the middle of the ring, so that something is left for the thread to grip. Punching in the brass turnover to protect the stitching needs special equipment.

clew. If the sail is then found to need more stretch on the luff to develop its flow but that the rope is acting as a restricting influence (often recognised by a multitude of wrinkles all along the rope), it is a simple matter to ease some more rope into the tabling to give the sail the extra distance to stretch.

Eyes, Eyelets, and Headboard

A handworked eye has far more strength than one punched in by a machine, unless a sailmaker's heavy duty equipment is used for the latter. The drawing shows the various stages of the operation, which requires a special hand punch and die to hammer in the metal liner to protect the stitching. You may decide that a length of thin webbing running from the eye in the direction of maximum tension will be beneficial. This may be sewn in either before or after the thimble or liner is inserted; it should only go in after the thimble, if the shackle or pin which goes through the eye when the sail is in use won't bear on the webbing and thus chafe it through.

Headboard
The best system for the headboard as far as the amateur is concerned (apart from doing away with it altogether) is to rivet two plastic or light alloy boards on opposite sides of the sail, outside the cloth; second best is to allow the headpatch to form a pocket, into which the board is slipped before the final stitches are put in.

Batten Pockets

We have decided not to have any mainsail roach, thus eliminating the bother of battens (nearly a quarter of all mainsail repairs at sea concern battens or their pockets). However, if you must have them, cut the cloth for the pocket so that the threadline runs in the same direction as it does in the sail, and then make the pocket half as wide again as the batten and $\frac{1}{4}$ in to $\frac{1}{2}$ in longer; a sailmaker will usually sew elastic into the inner end so that the batten is forced against the leech of the sail all the time. You should therefore put some reinforcing stitches of heavy twine by hand each side of the entry and at the inner and outer ends.

Reef Points

Reef eyelets should be worked by hand into patches placed on each side of the sail (again, one patch should be slightly larger than its companion on the other side of the sail, so that the stitching goes through different parts of the canvas; put the smaller patch on first for neatness). Traditionally, reef patches are diamond shaped, but

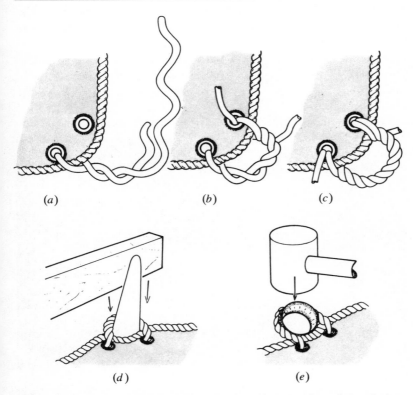

(a)   (b)   (c)

(d)   (e)

Fig. 5.4 *Cringle*   Twist the two ends together in a ratio of 2:1, bring the long end back again to form a three strand rope; splice in the ends. The tricky bit is knocking in the thimble, but it is most satisfactory when you get it right.

there is nothing to stop you having yours circular if you feel that they would be easier to sew. Each reef should aim to reduce sail area by about 20 per cent, and the row of points or eyelets should be fitted with a slight curve down towards the boom so that some flow is left to the sail when they are all tied in. The luff cringle or earring should be a heavy duty ring, hand worked into at least five and preferably seven thicknesses of cloth; the leech cringle may be similar, or may be worked as an external rope cringle (with a metal thimble banged in with a fid and hammer) fastened to a pair of close set hand worked eyes in a heavy patch. I don't propose to pronounce on the relative merits of individual reef points as against a continuous lacing running through eyelets; they both need hand worked eyelets in patches on the sail, and the points have to be added as extras if this is what you want.

Slides and Hanks or Snaphooks

If fitted, slides should preferably be fastened by Terylene or Dacron tape. This neither chafes the sail nor the slide, and is extremely hard wearing. Punched eyelets may be used as attachment points only for very small sails, but any boat larger than about 12–13 ft long should have hand worked eyes; an alternative is to sew the slide right through the rope itself, but this presupposes a rope sewn to the

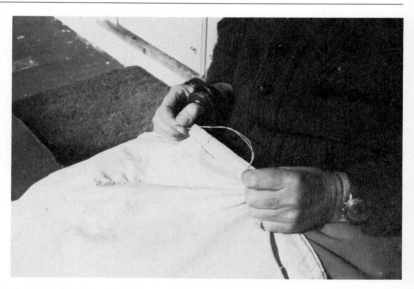

Plate 5.7 *Handwork at Home*   A few reinforcing stitches being put into batten pocket ends during the winter. (*Author*)

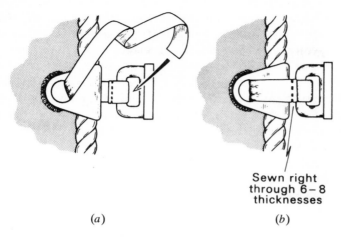

Sewn right
through 6 – 8
thicknesses

(a)   (b)

Fig. 5.5 *Taped Slides* Synthetic tape is strong and resists chafe, yet remains flexible. Protection for the rope is not essential, but it should ideally be cased with sailcloth or, as here, with a plastic liner.

outside of the sail, or you will seize the cloth to the rope when you want it to be free.

The same generalisations go for hanks or snaphooks, which may either be fastened by heavy twine threaded back and forth with the aid of a needle, or else with a leather thong, if you are not using the press or screw-on type.

Sail Number and Insignia

A certain amount of dexterity with the sewing machine is needed before sail numbers can be sewn to lie nice and flat without causing wrinkles. The amateur should invest in sticky back material, and accept the fact that it will come off eventually; it holds better if pressed down with a low heat iron when it is first put on.

Film Laminate

I recognise that some DIY enthusiasts may be tempted to try their hand at sailmaking with Mylar or Melinex, despite my warning in Chapter 4. So the least I can do is to offer a few tips and hints, and disclaim any responsibility for failures (which will be expensive).

Material
Have a word with your local sailmaker – he may have a few yards of film laminate left over from a part-used bolt, which he will sell you as

a remnant. You will have to gauge how trustworthy he is, because there will be a temptation to unload stock which is of poor quality. This temptation should not be too big, because he ought to have been able to return any sub-standard material to the manufacturer.

Shape
We have seen that a film laminate sail needs to have all its shape tailored into it. You will have to pay particular attention, therefore, to the number and size of tapered seams; if you are using double-sided sticky tape, you should be able to stick the cloths and then hold up the result for inspection and any necessary alteration to the broad seam. Don't forget to allow extra round on the luff of any mainsail which will be set on a bendy mast.

Panels
You will have seen photographs of Mylar mainsails with panels running in more directions than a compass needle at the magnetic pole. These are dictated not only by the need to shape the sail, but also by the requirement to avoid as much as possible any stress lines which run along the weft (across the narrow width of the cloth, and thus at right angles to the seams, which would give rise to the seam slippage problem discussed at the start of Chapter 6). Hence some film laminate sails have fan cut head and clew and, indeed, tack.

Seams
I said enough about seams at the start of Chapter 3 to make you realise that there can be problems; Table 1 summarises.

Table 1 Seaming of film laminate cloths.

Stress lines along the seam	Stress lines at right angle to the seam	
All areas	High load areas (at corners)	Lower load areas (mid-sail)
$\frac{1}{4}''$ overlap	$\frac{1}{2}''-\frac{3}{4}''$ overlap	$\frac{1}{2}''-\frac{3}{4}''$ overlap
1 row zig-zag	2 rows zig-zag	2 rows zig-zag
Use adhesive	Taped (with insignia cloth)	No tape

Corner patches
The sailmaker will build up a clew patch, using perhaps half-a-dozen wedge-shaped pieces of Mylar, each of which has its substrate primary threadline aligned with the major predicted loadings; see Fig. 5.6.

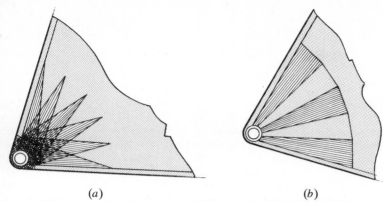

(a)   (b)

Fig. 5.6 *Film Laminate Clew Patch*   Ideally, a film laminate corner reinforcement patch should align the primary threadline of the patch along the projected stress lines of the sail. The so-called poker hand construction in (*a*) is economical and quick, but it can lead to uneven distortion causing hard spots, particularly at the two-ply points at the edge. The radial gores in (*b*) recommended by Dimension Sailcloth are each cut to shape and joined edge to edge, so that problems arising from differing thicknesses are eliminated.

If he puts one fan patch on top of another, the result will be uneven stretch causing hard spots – this is particularly true when Kevlar is used. But we are not trying for perfection first time, so the more usual Terylene practice detailed earlier in this chapter may be followed, using half the number of patches and, indeed, using all-woven cloth of fairly heavy gauge for the patch material (250 gm/m²). This keeps down the amount of stitching, which we have seen is a possible source of trouble, and it also makes a firm base into which the clew or tack eye can be hand worked.

Batten pockets
There is a danger that premature fatigue will be caused in the batten pocket area if it is not properly reinforced, particularly where warp-orientated Kevlar is being used for the sail; this manifests itself by the development of a hard line down the inner ends of the battens after a few hours' use. A precaution is to have two relatively large square Kevlar patches under the inner end of each pocket, one with the primary threadline parallel to the pocket, and one parallel to the sail warp or weft; alternatively, a 'stop-sign' of four Kevlar rectangles may be similarly fitted (see Fig. 5.7). If the problem develops because this kind of reinforcement has not been applied in the first place, cut out the cloth under the batten and replace it with new material, perhaps also fitting a large circle of heavy gauge Mylar under the pocket.

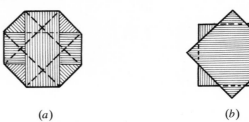

(a)   (b)

Fig. 5.7 *Kevlar Batten Pocket Patch*   Film laminate sails can develop hard
lines in front of the battens after a few hours use, unless proper reinforcement is
added under the pocket ends. Dimension Sailcloth suggest the so-called stop
sign patch (*a*), which consists of four Kevlar rectangles superimposed so that
primary threadlines run across each other. An alternative is the star construction
in (*b*), where two squares are superimposed, with primary threadlines at right
angles (note that the upper square is cut on the bias).

General

The more stitches, the greater the chances of weakening film laminates; don't be too adventurous with your panel layout, therefore.
Use plenty of reinforcement tape in the form of adhesive number
material, sewing over it *after* it has been stuck in place; also use
adhesive on the seams. Have a silicone spray (Ambersil *Formula* 6 or
BP *Adsil D1*®) handy to help the needle work through the adhesive.
Be prepared to write off your handiwork, despite your best
endeavours.

6 RIGGING AND TUNING

Most of what follows in the next two chapters concerns the racing man, but his cruising colleague will do well to pay it attention, for it can be important to get round a headland before the tide turns or to claw off a lee shore in a gale. So speed and ability to point high will interest potterer and racing man alike.

Mast Function

A mast has two jobs. First, it must hold the sails aloft; secondly, it controls the belly of the mainsail. To do the first it needs to be strong enough, with supporting rigging where necessary, to stand up to the pressures it will meet from wind in the sails. To do the second it must be able to bend in a controlled manner so as to flatten the mainsail by the right amount, in the right place, at the right time.

Mast Construction

Mast shape
It is not my intention to go in detail into the construction of masts as such, but they exert a great influence over the airflow round a mainsail and so a few words are needed. A square mast which doesn't rotate and so is always at an angle to the wind creates most turbulence. You may be surprised that a so-called streamlined shape which doesn't rotate also causes a lot of disturbance; if the mast is fixed, a near round section is better (Fig. 6.1). A pear-shaped mast which swivels into the wind is better again, and if it rotates past the dead upwind angle it is better still. One which is wing-shaped is best of all, but these are unwieldy and are liable to be blown over in the marina or dinghy park; they are specialist items with which specialist craft are concerned, and are not allowed by many classes.

Drag
There is a lot of drag put up by shrouds, diamond wires, jumpers, spreaders, and so on. Therefore, a mast which does away with some of these will be a better streamlined shape than one with a lot of wires and struts. Turnbuckles and terminals cause more air eddies than

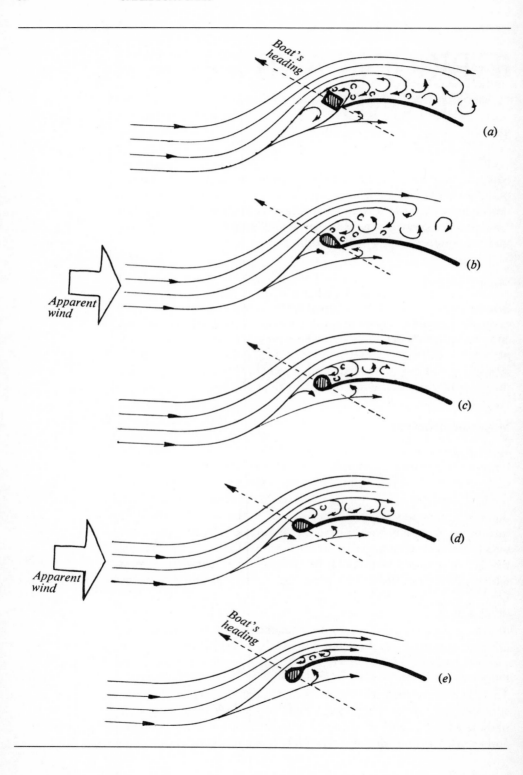

plain wire, so it also pays to bury them inside the mast if possible; otherwise they only add to the amount of unnecessary ironmongery presented to the wind, which should be kept to the minimum safe and efficient level.

Note that I have qualified the safe minimum level by adding the words 'and efficient'. It's nearly as bad to have a mast which is not properly stayed and braced, and so bends wrongly, as it is to have one which breaks.

Bendy Spars

The basic aim of bendy spars is to flatten the mainsail. They also have a number of other effects such as easing the leech and opening the slot, as we shall see shortly.

The main force which bends a mast (and boom) is tension applied by means of the main sheet; the kicking strap can also impart bend on certain occasions, although when it is most needed (when going to windward) you will nearly always find that the mainsheet pulls the boom so far down that the kicking strap hangs loose; the backstay is also a powerful bending control.

Flattening

When a mast bends it bows forward in the middle, thus taking out some of the round built into the luff of the sail to give it fullness. A glance back at Fig. 2.3 will show how this luff round is absorbed by the curve of the mast, thereby flattening the sail. The same process takes place with a bendy boom, as shown in Fig. 6.2, but fullness

---

Fig. 6.1 *Mast Streamline*   A square mast, which is at an angle to the wind, causes a lot of disturbance to the airflow (a). If the sail is attached to the mast by slides running on an open track, there will be a loss of thrust due to the leak of pressure to leeward through the gap between the luff and the mast.

Most racing dinghies have a streamlined mast with a groove for the bolt rope (b); this causes less disturbance and seals the gap between sail and mast. But a non-rotating pear-shaped mast always presents an unstreamlined shape to the airflow except when the boat is head to wind; a round section (c) offers less wind resistance. If class rules allow, and the mast will rotate into wind, disturbance of the air is even lower (d). Because of the way the wind bends to leeward just before it reaches the mast (see upwash in earlier drawings showing general airflow patterns), the mast should be turned some 15° past the direction of apparent wind (e) for best results when close hauled; it can then actively help the airflow take up a smooth path by becoming in effect a mini-wingsail.

Clutter, in the form of wires, spreaders, jumpers, etc., should be kept to a minimum to reduce drag.

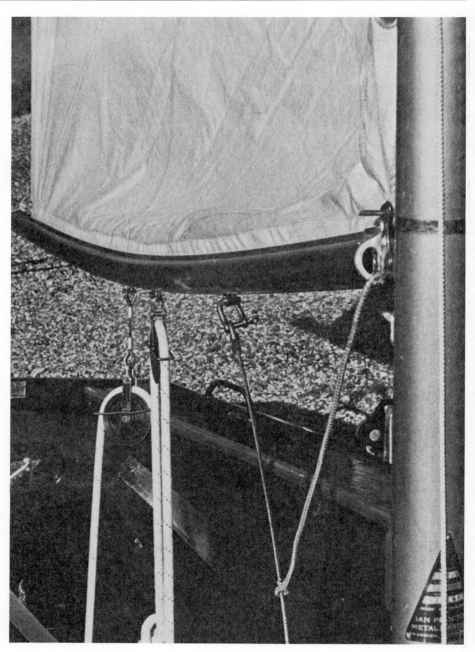

Plate 6.1 *Boom Bend*   A bent boom will take fullness from the foot of the mainsail. Because it is low down where it is constantly under the eye, this is a popular control – but don't overdo it, or you will lose drive where it is most efficient, precisely because it is low in the sailplan. (*Sir John Oakeley*)

Plate 6.2 *Mast Bend*   When the mast is bent as in (*a*), it bows forward at mid-height and takes with it the surplus cloth built into the sail as luff round, thus flattening it. When the mast is allowed to straighten as in (*b*), the extra cloth which then moves aft, gives the sail more camber. (*Author*)

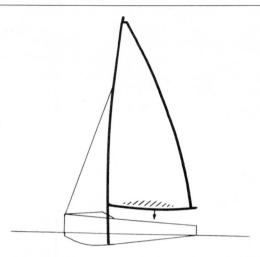

Fig. 6.2 *Boom Bend*   In the same way that a bending mast flattens the sail up the luff, so a bending boom will flatten it along the foot, in the shaded area of this drawing. This does not affect the overall fullness of the sail as much as the bending mast but, as it is low down and in front of their very eyes, it is readily noticeable by the crew; this tends to make it a popular refinement. It is just over the boom, however, that fullness gives best efficiency, for it has little effect on heel so low down, but gives plenty of forward thrust. When you add the fact that a bending boom also tends to make the mainsail leech go slack (which can, however, be cured by use of a cunningham hole), this item is not necessarily an essential part of 'go-fast' equipment.

along the foot gives efficient thrust low down, so the sail shouldn't be flattened too much in this area. You need to start the process near the head, where heel force is greatest and forward thrust least. The sail can then be progressively flattened towards the foot as the wind gets stronger, in order to get rid of power in excess of that which you can control. Figures 6.3 and 6.4 show how a dinghy mainsail can be flattened over various parts of its luff; Fig. 6.5 shows the use of a baby stay on a mini-cruiser to achieve a flatter mainsail – the same effect can be achieved by easing the after lowers on a masthead rig (Fig. 6.6), or by easing the running backstay on a fractional rig which has no baby stay (Fig. 6.7). It pays to spend a bit of time perfecting this on your boat, particularly if you have Mylar sails (whose shape can only be altered in this way).

Leech
As well as altering the fullness of the mainsail, bendy spars affect the leech. When a sheet pulls down on the end of a stiff boom against a stiff mast, tension is added to the leech which gets tighter. When the

pull is applied to the middle of a bendy boom fitted to a bendy mast, the ends of the boom bend up, the mast head comes aft and tension is eased along the whole leech area. The most obvious symptom of this is a crease running from the clew to the inner end of the bottom battens: this can be cured by pulling down on a cunningham hole to increase tension in the sail.

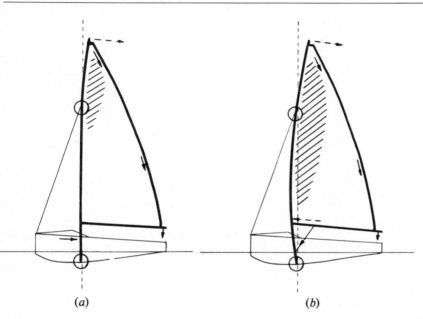

(a)   (b)

Fig. 6.3 *Flattening by Mast Bend*   Most of the forward thrust in a mainsail comes from the lower half of the sail, and most of the heel force from the upper half where sideways moment is greatest. As the wind increases and heels the boat to the point where balance becomes difficult, the mainsail should be flattened progressively from the head down. This feathers the sail, and is shown shaded in the drawings. In this way as little forward thrust as possible is lost, while heel force is reduced according to the crew's ability to keep the boat upright.

A mast is normally anchored at the two points circled in (a) and (b): the heel and the forestay attachment. Depending on the material and section of the mast, and its arrangement of stays, it can be bent by pulling hard down on the main sheet. If a stop is placed in front of the mast at or near deck level, it will not be able to bow forward below the forestay, and bend will be restricted to the mast head only, thus flattening the sail in that area (a). When further flattening is wanted, the stop is removed, or eased, thus allowing the lower half of the mast to bow forward and take cloth out of the middle of the sail (b).

A deck-stepped mast acts all the time like one which goes to the bottom of the boat without a stop to hold the lower half straight. Bend is controlled by tension on the main sheet (and, to a lesser extent, on the kicking strap), and by the arrangement of stays; see Figs 6.5 to 6.8.

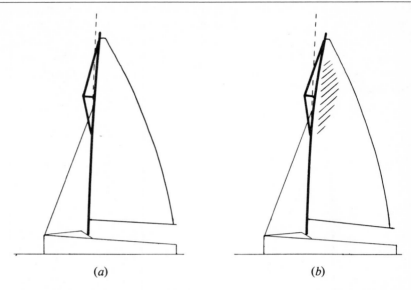

(a)   (b)

Fig. 6.4 *Jumper Stays*   Tight jumper stays as in (a) mean that the mast head is stopped from bending back. When the jumpers are eased off as in (b), the mast head is free to bend more, thereby flattening the sail in the head. More or less the same effect can be produced by chocking the mast at deck level as in Fig. 6.3 (a), without the damaging wind resistance produced by jumpers.

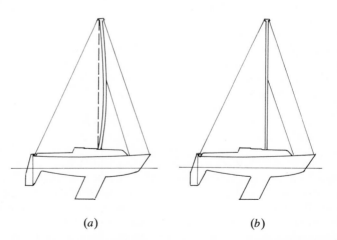

(a)   (b)

Fig. 6.5 *Mainsail Flattening – Babystay*   A spar which is masthead rigged will bend under best control if it is pulled forward at mid-height by a babystay (a). Adjustment of tension on the babystay will prevent the mast bowing aft (b).

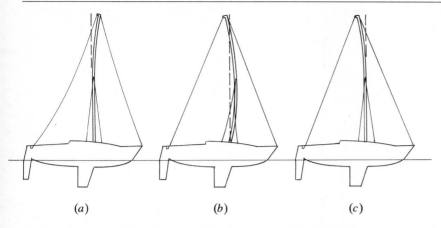

(a)   (b)   (c)

Fig. 6.6 *Mainsail Flattening – Masthead Rig*   If the backstay on a masthead rig is allowed to go slack when close-hauled with little mainsheet tension in light winds, the forestay will sag badly and the boat will not point (*a*). If the backstay is tightened, control of mast bend is effected by the lower shrouds: ease the after lowers and the mast will bend in the middle (*b*); hold them taut, and bend will take place aloft (*c*). The mainsail will flatten accordingly.

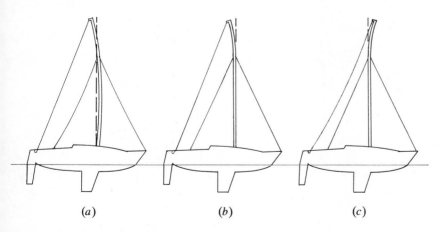

(a)   (b)   (c)

Fig. 6.7 *Mainsail Flattening – Fractional Rig*   To bend the topmast of a fractional rig, the backstay is hardened. The degree to which the resulting bend extends down the mast may be controlled by slackening the running backstays *very slightly*, which increases the extent (*a*); alternatively, they may be held tight to confine the bend to the topmast only (*b*). If the permanent backstay is allowed to go slack on the wind, the mast head will bend forward and cause a lot of creases.

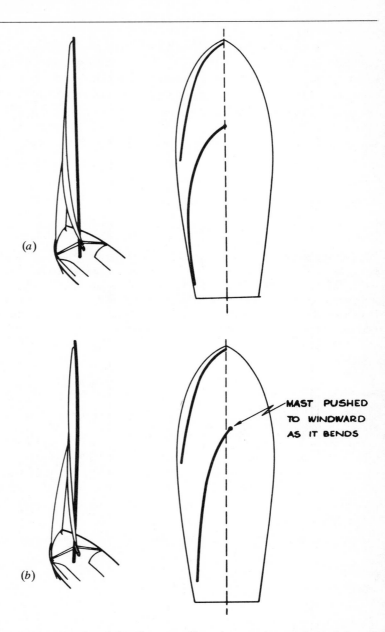

Fig. 6.8 *Mast Bend and the Slot* (*a*) When the mast is straight and the sail therefore has a lot of camber, the slot is fairly narrow because the jib leech is near the lee side of the mainsail at its powerpoint. (*b*) When the mast is bent in order to flatten the sail, the lee of the mainsail is drawn away from the leech of the jib. In addition, the act of bending the mast forces it slightly to windward, thus opening the slot still further. This is fortunate, because it occurs in higher wind speeds, which need a wider slot so that more air can pass through it.

Slot opening
When the mainsail is flattened the slot will get wider as the mainsail powerpoint is drawn away from the jib. In addition, thrust along a boom acting on a bendy mast not only pushes it forward but also to windward, because the boom is angled off to leeward (Fig. 6.8). This causes the mast to bow slightly to windward and carry the mainsail bodily away from the jib, thus also helping to open the slot. A wider slot allows more air to pass through it undisturbed, which is what we want in stronger winds.

Control of Mast Bend

It is not enough for a mast just to bend. You must be able to control the amount and position of bend if you want to make the most of it. This depends on:

1. The material the mast is made of.
2. The shape and thickness of the mast section.
3. The shape of the sail.
4. The controls used to limit bend.

Material
A wooden mast can be made to bend more than a metal one but, size for size, it will not be as strong. If you pay a lot of money for it, you can get one which might be lighter than a metal mast, with a lower centre of gravity (which all helps to make it easier to keep the boat upright when it is blowing hard). But besides being more expensive to maintain, it may be affected by hot sun or water absorption or it may bend in unexpected places and amounts, whereas a metal mast will be more predictable, will go on bending the same way year in and year out, and will possibly have a smaller area to present to the wind. On the whole a metal mast is best for most small boats, while the cruising man may get a cheaper one secondhand in wood.

Section
There are various different sized cross-sections available for metal spars, which all have known bending characteristics; you can thus choose the basic flexibility of your rig fairly accurately. The bend of a wooden mast can be altered by shaving it down where you want more bend. It is unusual for two wooden masts to bend exactly alike, whereas it is possible to be pretty certain how a metal mast of given section will behave under most conditions. Some mast makers sell sleeves to stiffen certain metal sections.

Plate 6.3 *Excess Mast Bend*   This OK dinghy has a sail which does not have enough luff round to cope with its very bendy mast. It shows typical creases running from the clew to the area where cloth is most deficient. (*Yachts & Yachting*)

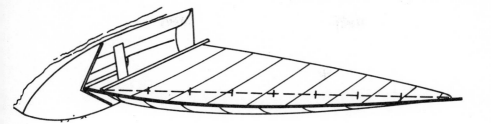

Fig. 6.9 *Measuring Mast Bend – 1*   Hoist a mainsail which will allow the mast to bend the right amount, tighten the kicking strap normally, then lay the boat on her side and haul in the main sheet until the mast is bent as you want it. Stretch a tape measure straight between the tack and the head, and measure the distances (called offsets) from the tape to the mast at 3 ft intervals. Write down the answers or you will forget, and also note whether you start measuring your 3 ft intervals from the head or the tack.

It is important to set a sail which has been made for a bendy mast, or it won't allow a proper curve to be taken up. If you don't have a suitable sail, you can get a fair result by attaching the main halyard to the outer end of the boom to give the right leech length, and then pulling down on the main sheet as before.

Sail

If a sail is cut without much round to the luff, a bendy mast will soon absorb all the spare cloth available, and it will then be stopped from bending any more by the tensions in the sail. The lesson here is that mast and sail must be matched if they are to perform well together. You must tell your sailmaker how much your mast bends before he makes you a new mainsail; he will then cut it to fit. Figure 6.9 shows how to measure the bend on a dinghy mast; you can either do something similar at the marina berth with your J.24, or else try taking offsets with the boat upright (Fig. 6.10).

Controls

You can control the bend in any particular mast in four main ways: mast chocks (a screw crank, or a piston controlled by means of a line working through pulleys or on a drum is more complicated but more effective; a strut is probably best), rigging, main sheet and kicking strap.

Chocks

Every stayed mast has two fixed points through which it must pass at all times: the heel and the hounds. A mast which is stepped in the bottom of the boat (rather than on deck) and which passes through a gate is also restricted in its movement at deck level by the play allowed by the slot in the deck. If a chock or other form of adjustable

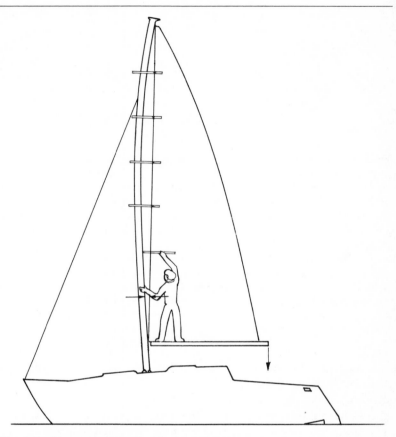

Fig. 6.10 *Measuring Mast Bend – 2*   When measuring for a new suit, borrow a mainsail which allows your mast to bend the correct amount, and hoist it with a graduated offset line attached to the head eye, so that the line is outside the mast groove, if you cannot tilt the boat on its side. Sheet in so that the mast is bent to its maximum correct curve, and then make fast the lower end of the offset line to the tack, so that it makes a straight line from head to tack. If you have no suitable sail at your disposal, proceed with a length of line as suggested in Fig. 6.9. Measure the distance from each graduated station that you can reach, to its nearest point on the aft face of the mast; those which are too high can either be assessed, or else calibrated sticks can be tied to the offset line and manoeuvred until they will give the required offset distances.

control (Fig. 6.11) is used to limit fore and aft travel, mast bend will be limited; sideways bend is usually restricted by the width of the gate. A look back at Fig. 6.3 will show how a mast which is not allowed to bow forward at deck level bends aft from the top only, whereas one which is free to bend as it wishes will bend evenly all the way up. Thus, if you only want to flatten the top of the sail you should stop the mast moving forward in the gate; if you want to

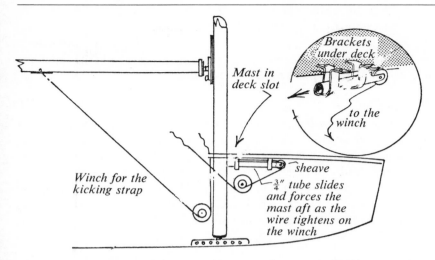

Fig. 6.11 *Control of Mast Bend at Deck Level*   If you use a chock to control mast bend at deck level, you will probably find that you won't alter it a lot while sailing, because you are most likely to want to vary the bend as the wind increases, and it is not always possible to change chocks in heavy weather. The system shown here has the advantage that it is simple to operate, and is therefore more likely to be used. A screw crank, or worm gear, would also do the job, but would take longer to adjust.

Plate 6.4 *Mast Slot*   The size of this Flying Dutchman's mast slot reveals not only the available adjustment fore and aft, but also how much the keel-stepped spar can be bent low down. (*Author*)

flatten the whole sail you should remove the chocks (or allow the crank or piston to go forward) and allow the mast to bow forward at deck level. See the section on power sailing in Chapter 7 for discussion on use of the strut together with variation in sail flow design, to achieve better speed made good to windward.

Jumpers
Jumper stays will also control bend at the top of the mast. Figure 6.4 shows how jumpers which are tight will keep a straight mast head, while slackening them off allows it to bend back. Any unnecessary weight and windage aloft is a handicap you can well do without, however, and you want to think twice before you start making your mast look like a radar aerial; about the only time when jumpers may pay is if there is a lot of unsupported mast above the hounds, such as on the 14 ft International.

Spreaders
In the absence of diamond shrouds, spreaders are chiefly responsible for control of the sideways bend of a given mast section. They achieve this largely through their length, and Figs 6.12, 6.13 and 6.14 show the different effects of spreaders which, with the boat at rest, pull the shrouds inboard, lie evenly on them without tension, and displace them outboard. The actual differences are only measured in half inches, so I have had to exaggerate the drawings. A displacement of about $\frac{1}{2}$ in to 1 in outboard is the most usual arrangement, and spreaders with adjustable ends are worth having.

Main sheet
For a while small boats gave up the single point main sheet attachment in favour of the traveller, which gave them control over leech tension (twist) through the mainsheet, while the traveller allowed the boom to move in and out. More efficient kicking straps can now do the job adequately, so many owners have gone back once again. The cruising man will also not do better than to forego complication and use the traditional single point attachment in the bottom of the boat or on the transom, or else the spread arrangement leading to the boom via a block on each quarter.

Kicking strap or boom vang
The advent of the 20:1 kicking strap, by means of levers and cranks, or else through a bar or strut, means that nowadays the kicker can effectively keep down twist and allow the main sheet to return to its traditional role of moving the boom in and out. The traveller is thus eliminated, to the joy of those who dislike its restricting influence on movement in a small boat. Such a high ratio, however, puts a terrific

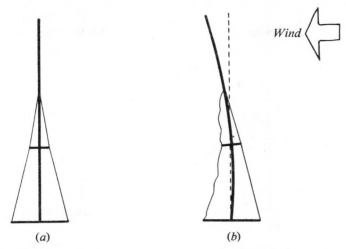

(a)   (b)

Wind

Fig. 6.12 *Lateral Mast Bend – Short Spreaders*   Short spreaders which do not reach as far as the shrouds pull the shrouds inwards when the boat is at rest (*a*). As the lee shroud goes slack when close hauled, the windward spreader pulls the mast to weather at that point (*b*). The amount by which the spreader is short is only an inch or so, and both this and the bend of the mast have been exaggerated in the drawing.

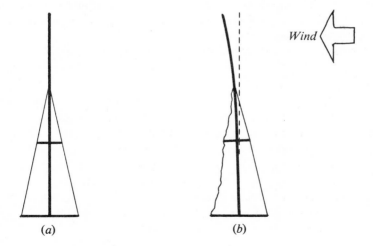

(a)   (b)

Wind

Fig. 6.13 *Lateral Mast Bend – Even Spreaders*   Spreaders which just reach the shrouds, so that they are neither pushed out nor pulled in when the boat is at rest, give fairly good support in light airs (*a*). As the wind increases, the amount of mast movement will depend on how the rigging is set up in the first place: tight shrouds will let the mast bend from the spreaders upwards; slack shrouds will let it lean to leeward as well as bend (*b*). Here again, the amount of bend has been exaggerated in the drawing to make it easier to see what is happening.

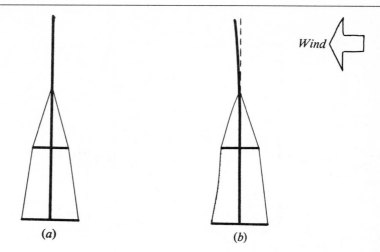

Wind

(a)   (b)

Fig. 6.14 *Lateral Mast Bend – Long Spreaders*   Spreaders which push the shrouds outboard of the straight line by an inch or thereabouts will give most support (*a*). If the rigging is set up hard, the mast will stand up to quite a lot of wind before it bends much to leeward (through the wire stretching), except above the hounds (*b*). The drawing is exaggerated for clarity.

Spreaders where you can adjust the length are useful, because they not only let you tune shroud displacement through a range of 2 or 3 in, but change in mast rake also alters the position of the shrouds in relation to the ends of the spreaders; if you alter mast rake, you must also alter spreader length if you want to keep mast bend the same.

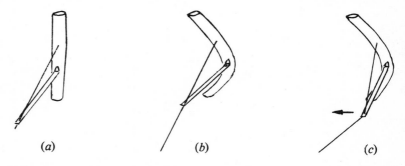

(a)   (b)   (c)

Fig. 6.15 *Fore-and-aft Bend – Swinging and Fixed Spreaders*   When the mast bends out of the straight line (*a*), it causes the spreaders to move forwards at their inner ends in relation to the shrouds; see (*b*) and (*c*). Swinging spreaders (*b*) allow the angle to vary, and thus avoid awkward cross tensions building up in the rigging. Fixed spreaders (*c*) cause the shrouds to be displaced forward of their line, thus setting up a pull aft, which restricts mast bend, because it is pulling the centre of the mast aft against the bend.

Plate 6.5 *The Strut*   A compression strut limits forward movement of the mast at gooseneck level. Bend is controlled by a screw at the base of the strut, which adjusts the length; this operates by an endless line which runs over the wheel and back to the cockpit. (*Rondar Boats*)

load on the boom and gooseneck which, besides being strong, should be firmly joined together, for no friction nut will ever hold under such a strain.

The strut
The strut (Fig. 6.16 (*d*)) is a development of the ram (Fig. 6.11) and transfers to the foredeck the forward force imparted to the boom by the high loading of the kicker. This stops mast bend and allows the kicker to be pulled hard down even in light winds without danger of the mainsail being immediately flattened.

Pylon sheet point
Elimination of the main sheet traveller permits reversion to single point sheeting. Ideally, the main sheet should not have any effect on leech tension, even when pulled hard down – this is left to the kicker. It can be achieved if the lower block in the system is raised nearly to the same level as the block on the boom, so that the pull of the sheet is forward rather than down (Fig. 6.16 (*d*)). Additional load is transmitted along the boom, so use of a strut is important if a straight mast is wanted.

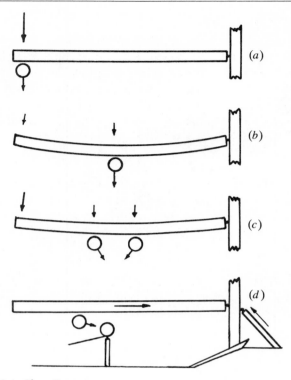

Fig. 6.16 *Main Sheet Leverage*

(*a*) Pull on the outer end of the boom will have most leverage down the leech of the mainsail, and least along the boom. This will bend the mast high up, and leave the boom straight.

(*b*) A centre-boom attachment which leads vertically down splits the pull between bending the mast and the boom.

(*c*) If the attachment is divided and spread over a wide enough distance, the boom will bend less and put more tension on the leech than it will with a single-point central pull. In practice, it is seldom that the two pulleys can be separated enough to make a great deal of difference.

(*d*) If the lower pulley in the system is raised on a pylon nearly to the level of the pulley on the boom, most of the pull will be forward, so that there is little tendency to bend the mast high up as in (*a*) or the boom as in (*b*); if the thrust is cancelled by a strut forward of the gooseneck, the mast will remain straight. This pylon can also, of course, be mounted on the transom for a simple boom-end arrangement more conveniently.

Precautions

Always remember that it is no good having a bendy mast and all the gear if you have forgotten to tell your sailmaker about it. The sail must be tailored to the mast (or vice versa) for good results.

Mast Rake

Another area where rigging can have a marked effect on performance is in mast rake and the change it brings about in the balance of the boat. The naval architect usually designs his boat to have a little weather helm when it is slightly heeled in medium winds (with the centreboard down, if applicable). That is to say, the boat will tend to turn into wind if left to steer herself. This gives what is known as feel to the tiller and also ensures that any inattention by the helmsman means that the boat makes ground to windward rather than loses it to leeward.

To give a boat weather helm it is necessary for the centre of effort of the sails to be behind the centre of lateral resistance of the hull (including keel and rudder). This will have the effect of weathercocking the boat into wind unless the rudder is held slightly over to one

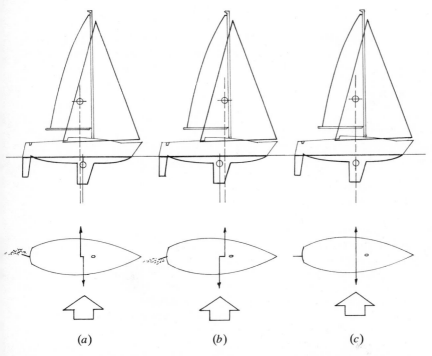

      (a)   (b)   (c)

Fig. 6.17 *Weather Helm – Mast Rake*   If the Centre of Effort (CE) of the sails is aft of the Centre of Lateral Resistance or Plane (CLR), the boat will have a force couple tending to turn into wind (a); the counteracting rudder will slow her down as well as keep her straight. If the mast is raked forward too much, the CE will move forward of the CLR, so that lee helm results (b). The ideal is to have the two in line, so that none of the boat's energy is wasted in keeping her straight (c).

side to counterbalance the tendency. The effect which mast rake has on this carefully balanced system of forces can be seen from Fig. 6.17. Raking aft will increase weather helm and raking forward will decrease it, as the centre of effort is moved in relation to the centre of lateral resistance. Equally, movement of the centre of resistance as a centreboard is pivoted fore and aft has a similar effect; see Fig. 6.18.

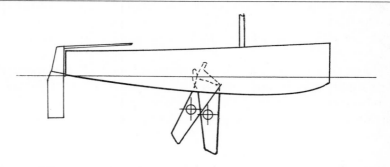

Fig. 6.18 *Weather Helm – Centreboard* A tendency to weather helm usually increases on a reach (for the reasons explained in Fig. 7.6, *Broaching*). A pivoting centreboard enables the CLR to be moved aft as the board is raised, often with beneficial results.

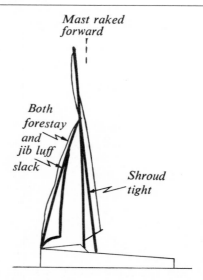

Mast raked forward

Both forestay and jib luff slack

Shroud tight

Fig. 6.19 *Slack Rig – Running* The wind has blown the mast as far forward as the shrouds will let it go. The forestay and jib luff are slack, but the jib doesn't mind a slack luff off the wind unless the boat is on a close reach. In this case, you have either got to accept some jib inefficiency, or else have adjustable shrouds to rake the mast aft and tighten the jib luff (because the main sheet is not tight enough to do the job as it does when beating to windward).

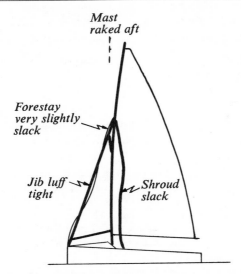

Fig. 6.20 *Slack Rig – Close-Hauled* When beating to windward, the mast is pulled back by tension on the main sheet, until it is as far aft as the jib luff will let it go (or, if it is shorter – and it shouldn't be – the forestay). The resulting loose shrouds will allow the mast to lean to leeward, unless you have some sort of adjustment to take up the slack in the weather shroud.

Slack Rig

It is a fact that most boats go better to windward with the mast raked aft and better downwind with it raked forward. These opposing requirements can both be met if the rigging of the boat is slack enough to allow the mast to move back and forth. Figure 6.19 shows the mast allowed to rake forward until checked by the main shrouds. This results in a slack forestay, but the jib is not interfered with in its performance under these conditions; indeed, it can use the extra fullness which such a slack stay gives it. In many cases the jib is lowered and a spinnaker hoisted instead.

Figure 6.20 shows the same dinghy beating to windward. Tension on the main sheet (transmitted through the mainsail leech) has pulled the mast back until it can go no farther due to the limit imposed by the jib luff, which is therefore pulled nice and straight, as required for close-hauled work. Both shrouds are relatively slack, so the one to windward will have to be tightened by means of an adjustment lever.

Slack rigging and adjustable shrouds are not suited to all conditions. River sailing places greater importance on the anticipation of wind shifts and less on looking into the boat to fiddle with gear for what, in any event, may only be a short leg of the course. Equally, estuary sailing makes it of doubtful value because the slam of a boat in a seaway will soon upset a mast which is not fairly tightly rigged. Nevertheless, there are plenty of occasions when it pays off and its correct setting and adjustment is one of the basic aspects of tuning.

Backstay Tension

In Chapter 9 (*Forestay sag*), I expand on changing genoa camber by altering backstay tension. It is enough here to say that this is one of the only ways of altering the fullness in a Mylar jib, and you should try various tensions and note the effect on the draft in your headsails.

Table 2   Backstay tension and its effect. The ideal camber of all-woven sails is not reached through forestay sag alone; jib halyard and cunningham should be played, to redress the somewhat unfavourable shift of powerpoint position caused through sag alone.

Conditions	Backstay	Genoa Fullness	Effect
Close-hauled; strong winds	Tight	50%; fine entry (flatter sail)	Higher pointing, less heel
Close-hauled; light winds	Slightly eased	35%; round entry (fuller sail)	Lower pointing, more power
Down wind	Eased	N/A (spinnaker)	Fuller main

Jib Halyard

It is no use tuning your boat to achieve the mast rake and movement you want if you spoil it all by hoisting your jib as hard as it will go, thus pulling the mast right forward against the stops. A jib luff tighter than the forestay will stop the mast raking aft as much as the forestay would otherwise let it; one which is slacker than the forestay means that the jib luff will hang away from the stay in loops when you are close-hauled, which is inefficient. Ideally, you should hoist the jib every time so that the wire luff is *just* tighter than the forestay when beating to windward, as drawn in Fig. 6.20. This means that the weight will come on the jib when the mast is pulled hard aft in the close-hauled condition, so that then the luff is good and taut. Equally, you will not hold the mast too far forward by overhauling on the halyard. To ensure that this desirable state of affairs is exactly right each time the jib is hoisted you should use a non-stretch wire halyard with an eye spliced in the end to fit a tensioning lever hook on the mast when the sail is up.

If you have woven headsails with control luffs, however, the jib

Plate 6.6 *Jib Halyard Lever*   The wire halyard comes up to the adjustable halyard hook, so that the same tension is applied each time the sail is hoisted. (*Author*)

halyard has an important function. Strong winds blow the power-point aft towards the leech in any woven sail, and it is application of extra tension on the luff which draws it forward again, flattens the leech, and gives a rounder entry more suited to the slightly larger angle off which is required in these conditions. This extra tension is provided by pulling harder either on the halyard or the cunningham. Hard winds mean hard tension; light winds mean light tension.

Jib Sheet Leads

A final point of tuning which should receive careful attention from the racing man is the position of the jib sheet; sometimes this is fixed by the class rules, but often there is a choice.

As seen from above, the jib sheet should make an angle of 12° to 20° with the centreline of the boat (Fig. 6.21). But see Chapter 7 for discussion of the merits of sheeting sails well into the middle of the boat by means of Barber haulers, particularly for racing boats going to windward in smooth waters under light conditions.

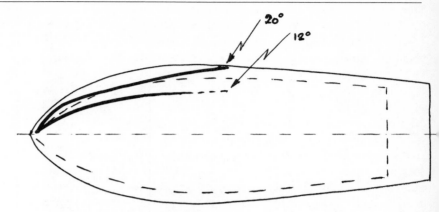

Fig. 6.21 *Jibsheet Angle – 1*   When viewed from above, the jib should usually make an angle somewhere between 12° and 20° from the centreline of the boat. The smallest of these angles is usually only used by slim, tender boats sailing on smooth waters (although there are exceptions, such as racing scows like the Fireball, which sometimes go down to 12° to 13° even on open water); the largest value is common on bluff, sturdy dinghies sailing habitually on open waters.

When measuring the angle on your deck, remember that 1 in of sideways movement across the boat, 5 ft back from the jib tack, is 1°.

Boat shape

A slim, tender, racing boat can usually afford to have its jib sheeted to a narrower angle than a boat which is bluff bowed and fairly beamy. This is because the former will normally be more responsive to the tiller and can change direction quickly enough to take advantage of the higher pointing which the finer angle offers. A more chunky boat needs to be driven along harder; you could say that there needs to be more brute force and less finesse. Boats of the scow type seem to like the narrow end of the range, even keeping their jibs sheeted fairly hard on a reach.

Jib shape

A tall narrow jib will have its leech some way from the lee of the mainsail, however close the sheeting angle. This means that a wide angle would be wrong for such a sail because it would open the slot too much. On the other hand, a wide low-cut genoa will backwind the mainsail easily and its leech needs to be kept as far away from it as possible, so it should have a wider sheeting angle.

Sailing conditions

Rough water and blustery winds mean that the slot should be wide enough to pass a lot of air or there will be a poor flow due to blockage and turbulence: the sheeting angle should be wide. In addition, a boat should normally be driven fairly free under these conditions and a wide jib angle helps this requirement. Conversely, smooth water and light winds mean that a narrow sheeting angle can be used to its full advantage.

Fore and aft position
Viewed from abeam, the sheet of a medium-shaped jib (i.e. one not cut with a foot particularly low like a genoa, nor particularly high like a cutter's jib) should prolong forward approximately along the line which bisects the clew of the sail; this bisector is sometimes shown by the mitre. A lower sail should have a lead farther aft, and a higher one should have it farther forward (Fig. 6.22), but see the next chapter for refinements for the racing man.

Active Tuning

Even if you don't achieve anything spectacular by tuning, you certainly get to know your boat and this in itself must result in better

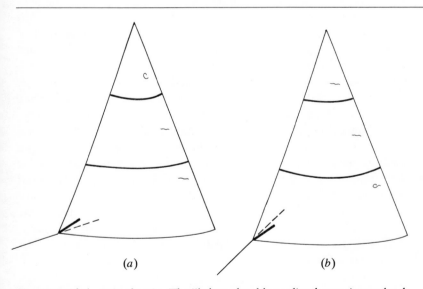

(a)   (b)

Fig. 6.22 *Jibsheet Angle – 2* The jibsheet should equalise the tension on leech and foot; the short foot of a working jib needs less tension (and thus a more forward sheet lead) than the relatively longer foot of a genoa (where the lead should be more aft). Tune so that all tell-tales break simultaneously as the boat luffs above close-hauled (see also Chapter 9). If the top tell-tale breaks first (a), there is not enough downward tension to close the leech and reduce twist; the reverse is the case with (b). The shape stripes at one and two thirds height reveal the camber in the sail.

performance. Don't forget, it's only a few seconds improvement that we are seeking, so don't expect startling results.

The best way to set about tuning is to decide first where you want to step your mast, how much bend and rake you want to allow it, and how slack or tight you are going to have your rigging.

These factors all vary from one boat to the next, let alone between classes. Short of being an expert in the matter you will probably decide what you want by talking to other owners and by examining boats which are known to be fast. Remember that one factor often has a crucial bearing on another, so it is no good doing only half of what the fleet leader does and still expecting the same results. A bendy mast needs a sail cut to suit; a whippy topmast needs slack jumpers, or none at all, if it is to be allowed to bend and make the sail flat in the head; slack rigging requires shroud adjusters; a mast well forward in the boat will probably need a good deal of rake aft to bring the centre of effort back, or else a centreboard which is well forward to adjust the centre of lateral resistance so that there is no danger of lee helm.

Having fixed these, the next thing is to go sailing in the conditions you are tuning for. Get a friend to sail alongside you in a boat of similar performance, preferably one of the same class and rigged in the same way as your own. Now settle down on a beat to windward and see who is going faster. The slower boat should try alterations until she catches up or passes the other (if this never happens, cast a critical eye over the whole rig to see whether some major component is below standard: sails, rudder, centreboard, or surface finish). Then try another alteration and see its effect, each taking it in turn to try something different and, if it proves successful, the other boat making the same alteration. It is important only to try one alteration at a time, or you won't know what is causing any improvement (or deterioration, as the case may be). It is also wise to write down what you are doing so that you will know exactly what to undo if it is not successful, or what to do to the other boat if it works (how many turns of the turnbuckle, how many holes in the adjustment plate, etc.). This is a slow process of trial and error which brings best results to the methodical and persevering owner.

7 TRIM

Trim is different from tune in that tune is the basic arrangement and setting up of the hull, mast and rigging, and is best done before the boat ever puts to sea, while trim is active adjustment of the sails during sailing.

Light displacement cruiser/racers will almost certainly only have one mainsail (it is usually against the rules to take more than one afloat at any one time when racing, e.g. the IOR[14]), but they may have a restricted choice of headsails — usually limited in quantity according to class. Their problems are dealt with in Chapter 9, this one being devoted largely to dinghies; there is bound to be some duplication, but each type of owner should be able to learn something from reading both chapters. For racing dinghies, however, trim does start ashore with the choice of the right sails: heavy weather or general purpose. But the object of the various controls we have just been looking at is to make one sail able to suit a wide range of wind strengths. We shall now look at some more ways of doing the same thing, and by the end of this chapter I think you will agree that one sail can cover many conditions if the right controls are properly used. The expense of the controls is more than offset by the saving on sails.

If there is a choice of sails it is more likely to be between old and new. In any event, you must now hoist them. The mainsail will usually be made fast to the halyard at the head by a shackle and to the boom at the tack by a pin; if the tack is fastened by a shackle, a common fault is to have one which is too short in the jaws so that the tack eye has to be forced over on to its side in order for it to squeeze into the small space available. This causes distortion of the sail and can lead to creases, and can also mean delay in getting afloat as you struggle with it. For some reason the right shackles seem hard to come by, but it's worth persevering with such a basic requirement until you get what you want.

It is important to see that the clew is properly fastened. A great many small boats use a lashing at the mainsail clew and while this is cheap, positive, and allows choice of tension, it is almost impossible to adjust while sailing for it takes both hands and all your concentration just when these are most needed to keep the boat going properly. If you do have this arrangement it is likely that your boom is a wooden one of several seasons' standing with a worn groove, so it is important to see that the sail can't pull out of the boom: take a couple of turns round the boom as well as out to its end when you tie the clew lashing.

It is better to have a snug groove and to shackle an outhaul wire direct to the clew so that it can be controlled while sailing. There are various ways of making this outhaul wire adjustable in use, it being better to have a length of rope operating through a system of pulleys inside the boom and coming out near the mast (so it can be adjusted by the crew whatever the boom angle), rather than a handle working on a worm gear at the outer end of the boom (which can only be reached when the sail and boom are close hauled, under stress, near the centreline of the boat, and only then by the helmsman standing up and facing aft).

Main Halyard

At the sizes we are considering, a mainsail should always hoist to the same place (the upper black band), whether it is made of film laminate or all-woven polyester. It is better to have a main halyard which hooks on to a lug or hook on the mast or perhaps engages a lock aloft when the sail is right up to its upper black band than to have a rope halyard which might stretch and let the sail down, or even a wire halyard with a rope tail on to a cleat, which will never get the sail up to the same place twice. A hook or a lock is positive and easy and leaves adjustment of tension on the luff to the cunningham hole, or to the gooseneck slide, which can be raised and lowered on the mast to suit the weather.

A woven mainsail should always be hoisted with regard to the strength of the wind it is going to meet. We are trying to achieve a sail which will have its powerpoint at or around half the way back from the luff *when it is under the influence of the wind.* We have already seen how tension on the luff of a sail made of woven cloth draws its belly forward and how action of the wind blows it aft again, so we should hoist hard enough to put the flow in a position from where it will move to the halfway point when under way. The next five sections refer to woven polyester sails.

Light airs

In light airs there should be practically no tension on the luff at all (with the gooseneck as much as 2 to 3 in short of the fully stretched position if the sail is an old one or normally on the flat side) so that the sail naturally takes up the nice camber the sailmaker has built into it. The wind will not be strong enough to alter the shape of the sail, so it should start off properly cambered, ready to turn the softest breeze into motive power (Fig. 2.7 (*a*)).

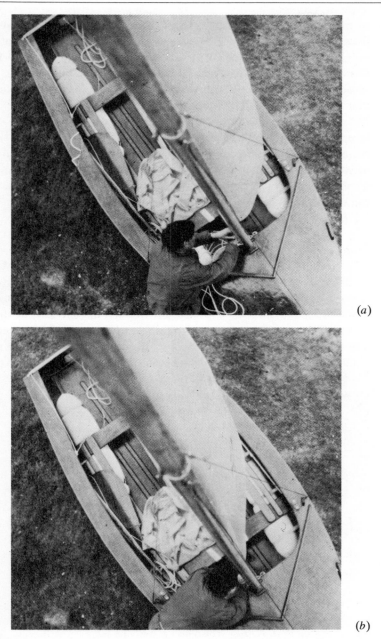

(a)

(b)

Plate 7.1 *Cunningham Hole*   A light weather sail should hoist to its marks without too much tension on the halyard. This *Enterprise* mainsail shows plenty of flow in (*a*); pulling down on the cunningham hole as in (*b*) puts more tension on the luff and draws cloth forward, thereby flattening the sail and increasing the gap in the slot (compare Plate 2.2). (*Author*)

Medium winds

In medium weather (Force $2\frac{1}{2}$ to 4) the mainsail should be hoisted hard enough to draw the flow forward into a fold up the luff of the sail; it will blow back from there as soon as you start sailing. This normally means that the sail has to be right out to its black bands, but some slightly undersized sails may still be half an inch or so short of their marks, particularly in lighter winds (Fig. 2.7 (b)).

Heavy weather

In heavy weather the sail should be pulled right out, and the cunningham hole drawn down if one is fitted. It is important to get the utmost tension on the boltrope or tape, for the strong winds will blow the camber right aft to an inefficient position if given half a chance (Fig. 2.7 (c)).

Cunningham hole

A cunningham hole (named after Briggs Cunningham of the USA who invented it in the 6 metre days) is a means of putting more tension on an adjustable mainsail luff which is already out to its marks and so cannot be pulled farther by its halyard, without breaking the rules, as the sail would stretch beyond the permitted distance. It consists of an eye worked into the luff tabling about 6 to 8 in up from the tack, through which a line is passed so that it can pull down on the hole to add tension to the luff when required, thus drawing the sail's flow farther forward (Fig. 7.1). Besides more pull

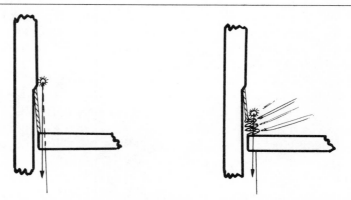

Fig. 7.1 *Cunningham Hole*   The object of the cunningham hole is explained in this chapter. It should be rigged so that it can be pulled down quickly and without too much effort. A permanently rove line is essential, preferably with some sort of jamming cleat. Don't let the resulting wrinkles worry you – they are the lesser of two evils when compared with the alternative of a mainsail with a full after belly.

on the luff, tension on the cunningham will cause a bunch of wrinkles in the tack area, but these are a small price to pay for the benefits gained. Its main use is in light or medium weather sails, which can then be made right up to size for their normal use (and therefore don't have to be set short of the bands as described above) and where the flow can be drawn forward again by use of the cunningham if the wind increases. Equally, a heavy weather mainsail should always have one, so that the effect of really strong winds pushing the belly right aft can be counteracted by harsh use of the device. It can also sometimes give a new lease of life to an old sail where the flow has been blown aft with the passage of time; it is also useful for removing the leech crease caused by bending the mast. The secret of the cunningham is to have a permanently rigged multi-purchase adjusting line operating easily to a jam cleat; it will then be used often.

Foot outhaul

Most of what is contained in the previous four paragraphs can be said about the clew outhaul and foot of a mainsail, though without quite the same emphasis; in particular the effect of a cunningham is not so marked on the foot of a sail. On the other hand, easing the *clew* to add flow to the sail will make a big difference to performance on a reach and run.

Jib Halyard

We have seen how a jib with a wire luff needs to be hoisted at a tension slightly tighter than the forestay, and how you have to rely on the pull of the main sheet transmitted through the mast to the forestay in order to keep a straight luff when you have slack rigging. If that were all there was to it, we could stop this section now. But the control luff jib has changed all that.

The sail is hoisted until the luff wire is at the right tension, and I shall assume that we are talking about the close-hauled condition: the luff wire is accordingly tight. As explained in Chapter 2, the sail itself fits over this luff wire rather like a glove over a finger and it is seized at the head (and sometimes at the tack as well), but the whole of the rest of the luff is loose on the wire and free to float. A line is made fast to an eye in the sail just above the tack, and control of the tension on the luff is exercised in much the same way as a cunningham is used. The basic principles which apply to a mainsail also apply to a jib, but you must remember that there is no tension on the sailcloth at the luff at all from the halyard, which only sets up tension on the wire independently of the sail itself. The control line is thus acting as both halyard and cunningham tensioner as far as induced flow in the cloth is concerned (Fig. 7.2).

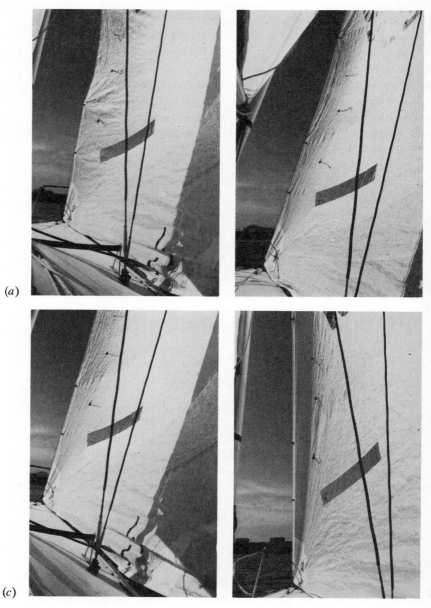

(a)

(b)

(c)

(d)

Plate 7.2 *Jib Halyard*   An overslack jib halyard will cause the luff of a hanked jib to become scalloped between the hanks (*a*). There is still not enough tension in (*b*), as revealed by slight creases arching between the hanks. When the tension is correct (*c*), the sail's camber smooths out and the wind tallies stream nicely. Too much halyard tension will cause distortion (*d*), and even a film laminate sail will show a furrow, with danger of delamination between the sail and the luff tape. (*Chris Howard-Williams*)

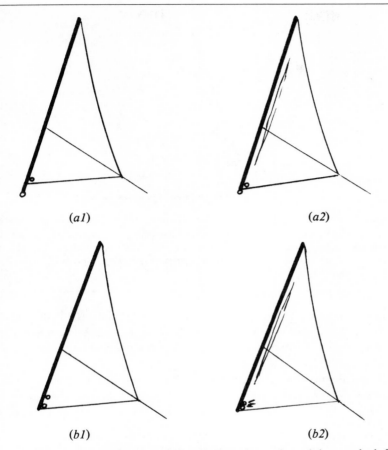

(a1)   (a2)

(b1)   (b2)

Fig. 7.2 *Control Luff Jib*   A control luff jib can be made to slide over the luff
wire, so that it stops short of the tack by a few inches when slack (*a1*) and has to
be pulled down when further tension is wanted (*a2*). Alternatively, it is made full
size and seized to the tack in the usual way, but with little tension on the cloth
(*b1*); it then has a cunningham for adjusting tension just like a mainsail (*b2*).

One of the objections to this system is that you can't roll the jib
without expensive equipment if you have the control lines leading
aft. There are jib rollers on the market on which you can pass the line
down through the drum, but if you can't afford the price of one of
these there is a cheap way round. Sew one of the smaller jam cleats to
the luff of the jib itself, as shown in Fig 7.3, and you can have your
cake and eat it – control and roll.

Talking of having and eating your cake, if you have a woven jib
which has a fully adjustable rope luff, you get the best of all worlds –
the sail is held to a straight luff by a tight forestay, you can adjust the
flow by means of the halyard, and the rust-proof rope coils for

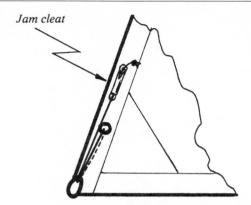

Jam cleat

Fig. 7.3 *Control Luff Roller Jib*   The system shown in Fig. 7.2 will not work with a jib roller unless special equipment is used, because the control line has to pass down the centre of the drum. Use of a jam cleat sewn to the sail itself is a cheap way of overcoming this problem, although it means that remote control is not possible.

stowage more easily than a wire. Much of what has already been said about the mainsail applies here; see also my remarks about keeping an open slot, without too much camber in the jib leech to backwind the mainsail (Fig. 6.8).

The most common mistake with control luff jibs is to put too little tension on the halyard.

Mainsail Twist

As soon as a boat comes off the close hauled condition she is said to be on a close reach. This is one of the fastest points of sailing because not only are you pointing exactly where you want to go and the sails are giving more forward and less sideways drive than when beating to windward, but your own speed through the water adds to the speed of the wind to make you go faster. It is, however, important to keep the power developed by the sails pushing you forward as much as possible and sideways as little as possible. Besides trimming the boom and jib sheet to do this (Figs 1.12 and 1.13), you must give some thought to mainsail twist.

First, what is twist? It is the different angle at the head of a sail when compared with that at the foot: the sail actually twists as it nears the top (Fig. 7.4 (*a*)). You get the same effect from a jib which is sheeted too far inboard or aft. This means that the top of the sail is at a finer angle to the wind than the rest and will lift first. Or put the other way, to stop the top of the sail lifting, the foot has to be quite a long way inside its best angle and the lower half of the sail thus produces a lot of unnecessary sideways force. If we can reduce twist the lower half of the sail can be eased off and will be pushing forward as much as the upper part, so we shall have a more efficient boat.

Fortunately it is relatively easy to cut down twist: all you have to do is to stop the boom rising as it is freed off. This can be done in two ways: the main sheet and the kicking strap (Fig. 7.4). Some twist is desirable, however, especially if the boat has fractional rig; because the upper part of the mainsail is not covered by the jib, it is working in a wind which is at a wider angle than the airflow lower down, where it is deflected by the headsail. A jib can be twisted as well as a mainsail and, as explained in Chapter 9 under *Twist*, this is controlled largely by fore and aft movement of the sheet fairlead, though it is also slightly affected by forestay sag.

Jib Sheet Lead

You should already have decided the fore and aft position of your jib sheet leads, but it may be that some minor adjustment will be

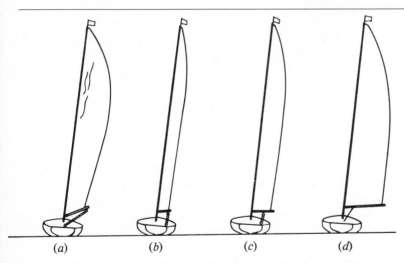

(a)   (b)   (c)   (d)

Fig. 7.4 *Mainsail Twist*   If the boom is allowed to rise, the top of the mainsail will twist and be at a finer angle to the wind than the lower half (*a*). To keep the head of the sail full of wind, therefore, the boom has to be further in than the foot of the sail would otherwise require.

Use of a full width transom main sheet traveller allows the boom to be freed off to the extent of the traveller, yet still pulled down to stop twist (*b*). If the traveller is under the centre of the boom instead of on the boat's transom, the boom can be eased further still before it starts to rise (*c*).

When the sheeting point on the boom is eased beyond the traveller end, the kicking strap takes over the job of holding it down to keep out twist. It has less purchase, so greater tension is required to make it work (*d*).

Plate 7.3 *Kicking Strap*   The kicking strap on this *Tasar* makes use of a multi-purchase pulley to produce power on the vang. (*Author*)

necessary as the result of competition sailing. If the lead is taken forward you will cut down twist, tighten up the leech and add more flow to the foot. A lead farther aft will tighten the foot, free the leech, and increase twist. The former may increase any tendency to back-wind shown by the mainsail as, of course, it will if the fairlead is brought more inboard in an attempt to get the boat to point higher.

Sheet Trimming

The effect of the sheet differs from mainsail to jib. A main sheet, apart from its influence on mast bend and twist when close-hauled, only allows the sail to free off to leeward when it is further eased and does not let the clew go forward to give the sail more belly. The jib sheet, on the other hand, increases flow by letting the clew forward as it is eased from the hard-in position; it then allows the sail to free off to leeward as it is eased further. Conversely, as the sheet is pulled in the last few inches it flattens the jib both at the luff and the leech – which does not happen in the case of the mainsail. There might be a case here for experimenting with a main sheet attached directly to the clew outhaul in order to give extra flow automatically as the boom is eased off.

Close-hauled: jib

In recent years jibs on racing dinghies have tended to become fuller further aft and, so that the luff angle of attack remains the same, to be sheeted closer to the centre line when beating to windward. In strong winds, the sheet is led well aft to ease the leech and open the slot (in some classes the lead is so far aft in really fresh conditions that it is almost in line with the foot). As the wind goes lighter, so the sheet is taken forward and eased so that the foot has plenty of flow; this will tighten the leech so beware of backwinding the mainsail. The slot is well open at the top and parallel all the way down.

Close-hauled: mainsail

Mainsails made for this sort of sheeting arrangement have a fine entry, with the powerpoint at midway; the resulting tight leech is controlled by the kicker and cunningham. In light airs the boom is kept amidships, or even up to windward. As the wind increases, so it will get hold of the leech, giving the boat weather helm and slowing her down; the boom should be eased to allow the wind to escape more easily, and the kicker and cunningham hardened to cut down twist and free the leech. The degree and timing of these adjustments will depend not only on wind conditions but also on crew weight: with a heavy crew and a trapeze, the boom can be kept amidships with advantage in stronger weather.

Reaching: mainsail

To allow the mainsail to pull as far forward as possible on a reach, the traveller should be eased down to leeward, the lee shroud slackened if levers are fitted, and the sheet freed off to the point just before the luff of the sail starts to lift. It is important to see that maximum power is achieved as forward thrust and minimum as heeling force. The kicking strap should be fairly tight to keep down twist but not so tight that the boom drags along in the water half the time. The harm caused by wind pushing the belly or flow aft into the sail when beating to windward ceases when sailing free, because a full sail with powerpoint even aft of the mid-way point is the best shape off the wind. If, therefore, you have strapped down your cunningham hole and gooseneck as hard as they will go (for beating to windward in strong winds) you should ease them both at once – and the clew outhaul too, if possible. You now require a sail with plenty of belly and no hard folds in it. Similarly, unzip the foot, if applicable.

Reaching: jib

When close-hauled, the sheet of a low-cut jib such as a genoa pulls relatively well aft and along the foot. As soon as it is freed on a reach the rearward tension is eased and the clew goes forward, thus giving more flow to the sail. This tends to keep the leech closed, so the fairlead should be moved aft and outboard if possible when the wind comes free, in order to open the slot a bit. If, on the other hand, the jib is tall and narrow with a fairly high-cut foot, the close-hauled lead is usually more down the leech than along the foot. The clew of such a sail rises as soon as the sheet is first eased, when instead we want it to go forward so that more flow is given to the sail. This is particularly true where the clew is some way from the fairlead. To overcome this the brothers Manning and Merritt Barber of California developed the system of adjustment on their International Lightning class boat in 1963 which has been named Barber Hauler after them. In its simplest form, this is an eye or thimble free to run along the sheet between the fairlead and jib clew, which can be drawn downwards by a line running through the deck a short distance forward of the

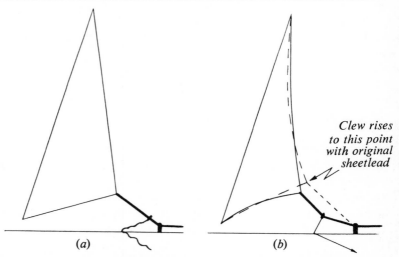

*Clew rises
to this point
with original
sheetlead*

(a)   (b)

Fig. 7.5 *Barber Hauler*   A Barber Hauler offers a means of adjusting the jib fairlead to a more forward position. When close hauled, a jib cut low like a genoa usually has more tension along the foot than down the leech. When the sheet is eased on a reach, the clew goes forward and the sail achieves more belly. The reverse is the case with a narrow high-cut sail, however, and the clew tends to rise too much as the sheet is eased and relaxes tension down the leech. The Barber Hauler should then be tightened to lead the sheet down more, and so allow the clew to go forward and give the sail greater fullness on the reach. Shifting the effective fairlead forward pulls down on the leech and reduces twist, while the opposite occurs as you move it aft (see also Fig 6.22).

fixed fairlead. When the sheet is eased the Barber Hauler is tightened so that the thimble is drawn below the usual line of the sheet; this leads it more downward and allows the clew to ease forward as the sheet is first freed, thus achieving more flow in the sail (Fig. 7.5). It is an adjustable fairlead, so check that your rules allow it before you fit one. Twinning lines on the spinnaker guy are another form of the same thing.

The Broach

No section on trim and handling would be complete without a few words on broaching. The problem is a manifestation of too much

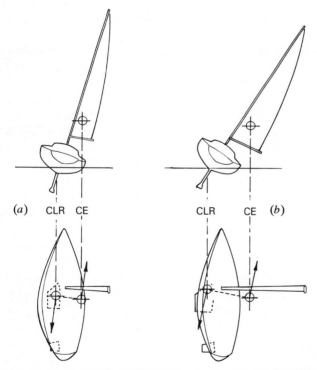

Fig. 7.6 *The Broach*   Much detail has been omitted from this figure for the sake of simplicity. When a boat heels less than 20° (*a*), CE and CLR are not usually separated so much that the rudder cannot control the situation. When she heels more than 30° (*b*), CE is displaced well to leeward and CLR slightly to windward (and often forward, if the bow digs in a bit). The result is a force couple which it is impossible to control by rudder alone, especially if half of it is out of the water. The solution is to stop her heeling so much, mainly by letting the kicking strap or boom vang run with a rush. The boom will sky and wind will be dumped from the head of the sail (see text).

weather helm, and it arises because the moment between the Centre of Effort of the sails and the Centre of Lateral Resistance (or Plane) of the hull becomes more than the rudder can counter.

Figure 7.6 shows diagrammatically what happens. The most usual case is shown in (a), where a slight displacement of force lines produces a small moment which is easily countered by a small amount of rudder. If, however, the wind is strong, then the moment would increase even if the distance between the forces (the arm of the force couple) were to remain short; more rudder is needed. In practice, extra wind usually means that the boat heels more, which increases the moment arm (because the C of E moves to leeward while the CLR moves slightly to windward (b)); the force couple becomes stronger, and still more rudder is needed. Part of the rudder also comes out of the water, so that yet more helm is needed if the remainder is to hold the course. Finally, the rudder is hard over, it is largely out of the water, and round she goes...

There are three ways of tackling the problem (apart from moving the mast forward). First, a bellied mainsail leech will heel the boat and push her round to windward; pull any woven sail as hard on the luff as you can (halyard and cunningham) and bend the mast. Secondly, shift weight aft and to windward, so that the rudder stays in the water and the bow is not buried (which would make extra wetted area forward and move the CLR forward, thus increasing the moment arm and aggravating matters). Thirdly, dump wind from the top of the mainsail by letting the kicking strap or vang and main sheet run with a rush, so that the boom skies (if you try letting go the mainsheet only, the boom won't ease off enough because it will almost certainly be dragging in the water). If you have a pivoting centreboard, raising it slightly will move the CLR aft as shown in Fig 6.18, thereby reducing the moment arm and thus the force couple.

If conditions favour broaching, keep one hand on the kicker and one on the mainsheet because, if you want to avoid a spectacular gyration, speedy action is crucial.

Power Sailing

Power sailing is the art of sailing to windward by freeing the boat just enough to improve speed so that you go upwind faster than the boat which is pointing higher by sailing conventionally close-hauled, in the same way that the latter usually goes better than one which is pointing higher still, but pinching. You will fall off to leeward, so sheer speed will decide whether it pays or not (Fig 7.7). To make it work, three factors have to be right: sails, angle off the wind, and wind conditions.

Sails

As the name implies, the technique depends on developing more power. To do this sails should be fairly full and, as in the case of those Merlin Rocket dinghies which have been using it with success in England, a large 'free' roach area in the foot of the jib (say, 8 to 10 in) should not be barred by the rules. This roach won't set when beating to windward normally, but will do so if the boat is freed a little and

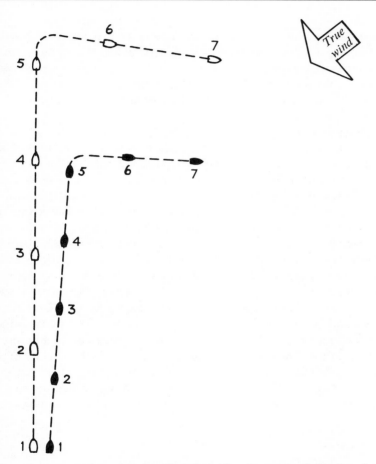

Fig. 7.7 *Power Sailing*   Power sailing depends on extra speed. If a boat frees off from the close hauled course by about 3° to 4°, full sails with deep roaches will generate more power than those of a boat beating normally to windward. If the balance of angle off and speed is correctly adjusted, the extra speed of the boat power sailing (white boat in this drawing) will more than compensate for the distance gained to windward by the conventional boat (black boat). But, if either speed gain is not enough or the angle off too great, the technique will not pay.

the sheet eased slightly. This freer wind also allows the mainsail clew and tack to be eased and zippers undone. My remarks, a few pages back under *Sheet Trimming*, about the different effects of main and jib sheets, apply here. It is more belly which is wanted, not a greater sheeting angle, so you do not ease the mainsheet, only the main clew. The extra area in the foot of the jib is also used to advantage and you will gain a significant amount of fullness and power over the close-hauled boat.

Angle

You will soon find by trial and error whether you can make power sailing pay with your boat. If you have to bear away from the normal close-hauled course by more than 3° to 4° to make the sails develop their full power, you will probably lose more ground to leeward than you will be able to make up in speed through the water.

Wind conditions

The technique only seems to pay in light or in strong conditions. Full sails are needed, anyway, for light winds and smooth water; the extra area gained from the jib foot seems to give the edge on those who are conventionally close-hauled, but the amount you free off is critical and needs careful watching if it is to pay. In strong winds the water is often choppy, when it pays to ramp the boat off a bit and push her through it; fuller sails will help this. If, in addition, marginal planing conditions exist and the extra power makes just the difference in getting up on the step, then the advantages are obvious. There seems to be a gap between light and strong conditions where no profit can be derived, and how wide this gap is will depend on your own boat, sails, and technique. In the stronger winds the boat is of course harder to keep upright because not only are you developing more forward thrust but also a lot more heeling force. With a bendy mast and a good heavy crew, however, you can control these heeling forces and take full advantage of the extra power generated to get greater speed – even more so if the crew has a trapeze or a sliding seat.

Trim Tips

Assuming that other factors such as sail shape, boat tuning, and technique are all satisfactory, the following suggestions are offered as ways of altering speed through use of sails alone.

Note that I say *altering* speed, not *increasing* it: if you have a particular aspect of sail trim correctly set already, then any alteration can but decrease your speed. We have all, however, raced neck and neck alongside a rival without gaining or losing an inch, and longed for another yard or two of speed (and that's all you need over a couple of hundred yards). The ideas in this section are not necessarily in any particular order, although I suggest that the first ones are more likely to have the desired effect than the later ones. Please don't go blaming me if they lose you a coveted cup – you should try them in practice first, or in less important races, and not wait for the grand occasion before experimenting. Above all, don't be prejudiced by knowing that what you have always done is right – conditions may be different today.

First of all bear in mind the general principles of sail shape:

Wide sheeting base	Full mainsail ⎫ not at the same time
	Strong winds ⎭
	Reaching conditions
	More speed, less point
Narrow sheeting base	High point, less speed
	Backwinding
	Flat mainsail ⎫ not at the same time
	Light winds ⎭

Jib halyard
This is often too slack, especially with tight rigging and wire luff sails. Get another inch or two up on it.

Jib sheet
A boat is generally more sensitive to the jib sheet than to the main sheet. Try easing the jib an inch or two on the beat, particularly in the lighter winds.

Jib fairlead
This affects the curve of the jib in both planes and thus has a marked bearing on performance. Movement outboard will give more speed and less backwinding but will stop you pointing so high; movement inboard has the opposite effect. There is some merit in a narrow jib angle on faster boats (of the scow type, for example) to help you point really high. This is directly contrary to the concept of power sailing and you will have to decide for yourself which technique suits your boat best. Putting the fairlead forward gives more flow to the jib and tightens the leech (more speed and less point, with a greater risk of backwinding the mainsail), while movement backwards will flatten the foot and slack off the leech with opposite effect. See also Chapter 9 (*Twist*).

Kicking strap or boom vang
Almost everybody realises the importance of a kicker these days, and I nearly didn't bother to include it here. But it is *just* possible that you

Plate 7.4 *Mainsail Twist*   The Jeanneau Fun does not have a mainsheet traveller, so it is important to have a good kicking strap to control twist. The
horizontal creases at the mast reveal that the halyard is lightly tensioned in order
to achieve maximum flow in the all-woven mainsail in the light conditions
prevailing. (*Chris Howard-Williams*)

don't have one and, if so, your troubles are virtually over – this is the
way to pass the fellow in front. So great will be the difference in boat
handling and speed with the installation of a properly trimmed
kicker, that you can start clearing space at home for the silverware as
soon as you have fitted one. A three- or four-part pulley, with or
without a system of cranks, is cheap and effective, while a wheel
tensioner like a glorified turnbuckle is more positive but more expensive. Broadly speaking it is, of course, used to hold down the boom in
order to reduce twist; this in turn allows you to ease the main sheet,
thus directing the sail's thrust less sideways and more in the direction
you are pointing (which gives less weather helm and more speed).

Cunningham hole

Much the same comment goes for a cunningham, about which we have already had some discussion. It gives greater flexibility to a woven sail by drawing the draft forward when it has been blown aft by heavy winds. This flattens the sail again, lets the wind slide off the leech more easily and thus knocks the boat down less. This is turn means less weather helm, less braking effect from the rudder and greater speed. But take the trouble to fit a permanent control line, operating through a system of pulleys to a handy quick acting clam cleat; in this way the device will be used regularly and will soon pay its way.

Tell-tales or streamers

These are lengths of dark wool or nylon sewn to a sail so that you can tell whether you are enjoying laminar flow over the surface in question; if you are not, the sail is locally stalled and thus not in high gear. Fit them to the luff of the jib first and find out how you get on with them, before trying them on the mainsail; they are particularly useful on a fully battened sail, which doesn't lift so obviously to give warning that you are starting to point too high or to ease sheets too much. Use contrasting thread or wool; mohair is good, because its light weight combined with bulk reacts well and shows clearly, while it sheds water quickly (even narrow ribbon is better than nothing).

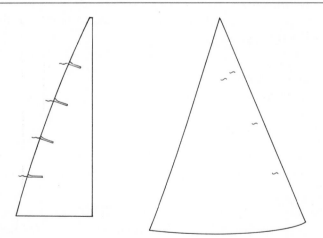

Fig. 7.8 *Tell-Tales*   Tell-tales should be about 6 in (15 cm) long and of dark wool or nylon (mohair is good, being bulky yet light; it sheds water well). Make sure that jib tell-tales cannot quite reach the luff, or they will catch on it in light winds; they will even snag on the stitching of a seam if allowed to. The second tally at the genoa head should be at about the mid-chord position, to act as a twist indicator (see Chapter 9, *Twist*).

Fix your tell-tales in the positions shown in Fig. 7.8, so that 10–15 cm (4–6 in) hangs down each side; knot close to the canvas so that it does not slip. Place one pair at quarter height, one halfway and one at three-quarter height. Make sure that each streamer is situated so that its free end is clear of the luff, piston hanks, or even a seam in the sail, otherwise sooner or later it will get snagged, particularly in light winds. To maintain an unstalled laminar flow, with all tell-tales streaming neatly aft along the sail, you watch for one to get out of line. As soon as it starts to wobble and lift, airflow is disturbed in the region and either the tiller must be moved or the sheet trimmed. The basic rule is trim towards an erratic streamer or turn the boat away from it; thus if a leeward tell-tale lifts you should either ease the sheet or luff up, conversely, sheet in or bear away if it is a windward tally which lifts. That is the simplified method, and you won't go far wrong if you adopt it; see Chapter 9 for more detailed advice on the finer points. The mnemonic for the forgetful is TASTES: Turn Away or Sheet Towards Erratic Streamers.

Mainsail clew
Easing the clew will give the mainsail more flow low down where it does most good and where any attendant increase in heeling force will do least harm. This is worth a try, even in the stronger wind ranges, particularly if you have a wide mainsheet traveller.

Mainsheet traveller
You may be easing it off too soon or too late (probably the former): change the rhythm.

Spinnaker sheet
If it is too tight it will kill the boat. Ease it all you can (but watch out for rhythmic rolling downwind; harden the sheet a little to prevent oscillation).

Spinnaker pole angle
Try changing the pole angle: an inch aft first, then an inch forward if that doesn't work. If you don't already have them, fit twinning lines.

Spinnaker pole height
Move it up or down a few inches and watch for results. If necessary, on a reach, try it hard down on the stem head to straighten the luff of the spinnaker, or poked well up into the sky to flatten the head and disengage the luff from the jib if both are being carried at once.

Spinnaker halyard
Try easing the halyard about 6 in when on a reach. This will disengage the head of the spinnaker from the disturbed airflow near the mast.

Plate 7.5 *Tell-Tales* This unusual shot of Bryan Taylor and Robin Pascal, the 1985 British national 470 champions, reveals that they have eased their jib enough on the reach to maintain nicely streaming leeward tell-tales. (*Julia Claxton*)

8 SPINNAKERS

Spinnaker Cloth

Not until nylon was developed did spinnakers enjoy a change of material from the light cotton which was used for so long. Dacron and Terylene made everyone think twice in the 1950s, but bulging spinnakers need a certain amount of stretch if they are to take up their shape, and nylon is better for this. It has been shown repeatedly that spinnaker cloth should not allow air to pass through the material or loss of thrust will result as the pressure equalises on each side of the sail[15].

Homogeneous film offers a light and completely non-porous cloth, which can be reinforced by a polyester or Kevlar mesh stuck on in the form of widely spaced rip-stop material. The result is a transparent sail, and the reinforcement prevents any tear developing too far, because its threads are merely pushed aside for a very short distance without breaking. But the cloth lacks the inherent springiness necessary to absorb the shock loads inseparable from most spinnakers, so nylon still seems to be the best answer at present, mainly falling short in its rot-proof qualities. Spinnaker requirements include:

Porosity. I have already mentioned the importance of low porosity. A porous nylon cloth can have its airtightness improved by the addition of fillers in the finishing stage in the same way as Terylene or Dacron. But, also in the same way, the chemicals will eventually break down to leave the original slack weave. This will allow air to pass through and the sail will lose drive.

Lightness. At the sizes we are considering, a cloth of 25 to 60 gm/m² is needed, so that the sail hasn't too much weight to lift and fill in the relatively low wind speeds which often exist when the boat is running away from the wind, thus cutting down apparent wind speed.

Strength. When a boat is not running but sailing across or into the wind and thereby increasing its force, the relatively large area of a spinnaker means that is has a good deal of weight in it. For those who may be interested, pressure in a sail under given wind conditions can be roughly calculated by using a formula which reads

$W=0.004V^2A$, where W is the total weight of wind in the sail in lb, V is the relative wind speed in mph, and A is the sail area in sq ft (or $W=0.1\times V^2A$ where $W=$kg, $V=$m/sec, and $A=$m²). Thus a spinnaker of 225 ft² in a 25 mph relative reaching wind (which need be no more than 15 mph true) will have over a quarter of a ton in it.

Power to repel water. It is useful if the spinnaker will not absorb a lot of water and will dry quickly when it is wet.

Rot proof. The cloth should not be too badly affected by heat, cold, dryness, industrial smoke, sunlight, or water.

Low stretch. A certain amount of stretch is useful to help the sail develop its shape in the wind, but not so much that it distorts permanently; once distorted, the cloth should recover its original shape when the load is taken off.

Tests
You can test spinnaker cloth by crumpling it in your hand and looking for crazing of the fillers in much the same way as for other

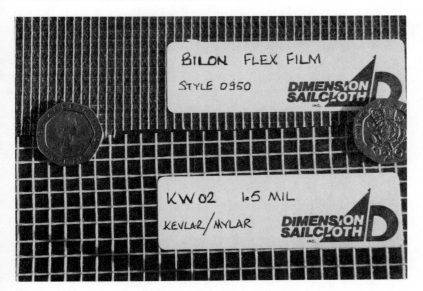

Plate 8.1 *Spinnaker Fabric* The upper cloth is a lightweight material comparable with most ¾ oz ripstop nylons; Dimension Sailcloth recommend that it should be taped or folded at the seams. The lower cloth is stouter, and would appear to be suitable for much heavier use. There are many combinations of film (thicknesses) and reinforcement (nylon, polyester or aramid fibres, with accent variable between warp and weft or fill), not to mention use of different adhesives, so be guided by your sailmaker. (*Author*)

sailcloth. You can also learn a good deal about its porosity by trying to breathe through it. A little experience will soon tell you which is a good tight weave and which is loose. Try the 'breathalyser' test both before and after crumpling the sample; you may be surprised at the difference.

One final point to remember about nylon: it largely obeys the same laws of physical behaviour as Dacron and Terylene. Moreover, because we are dealing with a light material the effects are greater, particularly as regards bias stretch and sunlight deterioration.

Outline Design

As with mainsails and jibs, outline design of a spinnaker is the job of the naval architect, who decides the basic size to make the sail. This in turn is sometimes dictated by an already existing rule but, when dealing with a new one-design class, it may be more a matter for the designer's personal decision made in the light of his expert know-ledge and experience, much as the lines of the boat are the fruit of his training and skill. The spinnakers of boats which race under JOG or IOR regulations are usually restricted to maximum dimensions related to their I and J measurements; see Fig. 9.1. The result is a sail of slightly high aspect ratio for boats which are masthead rigged, whereas a fractional rig lowers the AR to give a spinnaker which is rather more stable. There is nothing you or I can do to alter a particular sailplan even if we wanted to, so we need not concern ourselves here with how it was reached.

Flow Design

In considering flow design (the amount and position of belly) of a spinnaker we have to consider what happens to the wind in the sail. On a reach the airflow behaves very much as in a jib in that it blows from luff to leech; as the boat frees further, so the airflow is directed increasingly downward (and out at the sides), until this virtually takes over when the boat is dead before the wind.

Figure 8.1 shows how a spinnaker with a deep 'nose' is not only more inefficient on a reach but also loses out on a run to a sail which is cut flatter in the head, because dead air collects in the deep part of the sail and disturbs the airflow.

The sailmaker must keep stretch in the sail within set limits. To do this he tries to arrange the cloth panels in the sail so that stress lines run along the threadlines of the cloth and not on the bias. But directions of stress in a spinnaker are many and varied, and this sometimes results in sails which have more cloths in them than a patchwork quilt.

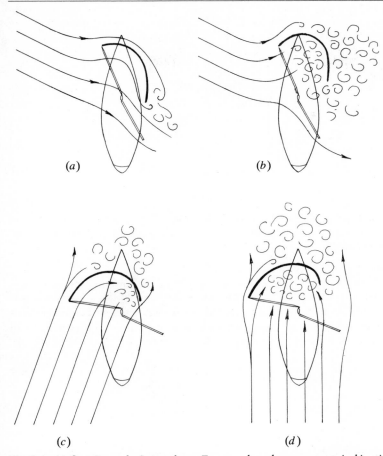

(a)   (b)

(c)   (d)

Fig. 8.1 *Airflow Round a Spinnaker*   Except when the apparent wind is within 10–15° of dead aft, airflow over a spinnaker is from luff to leech, as with a genoa. In (*a*) the streamlines pass smoothly over a fairly flat reaching sail. If the spinnaker is too full for reaching, with a so-called 'Roman nose' which encourages a pocket of dead air in the middle, a lot of separated flow results (*b*). When the wind is some 20° on the weather quarter (*c*), there is still some attempt at airflow from luff to leech. But when the wind is dead aft (*d*), it enters both sides of the spinnaker and flows out at the foot and head, with danger of a pocket of dead air in the middle.

Dinghies

A dinghy spinnaker seldom exceeds 20 m² (±200 sq ft), which is not big enough to need more than three or four short horizontal cloths, or to warrant fussing too much about radial stress lines. It is thus usually best to adopt a simple construction such as that offered by the horizontal cut; see Fig. 8.2 (*a*).

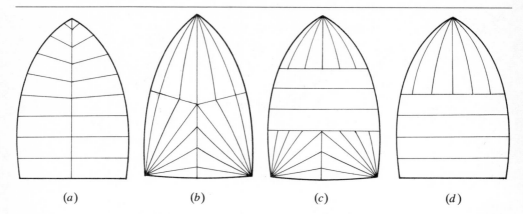

(a) (b) (c) (d)

Fig. 8.2 *Spinnaker Cuts* There are some fairly exotic (and some old fashioned) spinnaker cuts. The most usual for small boats, however, are as follows (see also Table 3).

(a) Horizontal cut for general purpose use.

(b) The starcut is an expensive sail, originally developed for specialist reaching purposes. Note how the panel layout at the corners follows the stress lines.

(c) The tri-radial spinnaker also radiates from the corners, but has horizontal cloths in the middle to allow the sail to develop some flow. It is cheaper than the starcut but, being best suited to reaching, it is still a specialist sail for the racing boat.

(d) The radial head cut is the modern general purpose spinnaker. It is less expensive than either of the two specialist reaching sails, but modern cloth is stable enough to allow it to stay reasonably flat in section.

Starcut

When the spinnaker approaches 25 m² (±250 sq ft), loadings start to become a more significant factor and, indeed, the sail is large enough to need more than three or four cloths in its construction. Because the principal loadings radiate from the three corners, there are sensible grounds for the cloths doing the same, so that the warp yarns can take the strain – hence the starcut originated by Bruce Banks in the 1960s; see Fig 8.2 (b)[10]. It is a cut which is rather prodigal of cloth and time, but makes an excellent close reaching spinnaker because distortion is kept low – the sail holds its shape well under pressure (this needs a slightly revised approach to trim, which is dealt with later in this chapter).

Tri-radial

Because of the starcut's specialist nature (and cost), the tri-radial was evolved; Fig 8.2 (c). This uses most of the same thinking and technology as the former, but has a centre section of horizontal panels to simplify construction and to help spread the sail under load. It is still predominantly a reaching spinnaker, however, and doesn't develop a really full shape down wind, so it is a racing sail which should not normally find room on a boat which does not already have a more general purpose spinnaker in the locker.

Radial head

Still considering areas greater than about 25 m², the most practical cut for all-round use is a radial upper part, with horizontal panels for the remainder; Fig 8.2 (*d*). This takes care of stresses radiating from the head, and ensures that the lower warp yarns run parallel to a horizontal airflow.

Spinnaker wardrobe

We thus have the following suggested complement of spinnakers.

Table 3 Spinnaker wardrobe. The starcut is seldom seen these days; its low stretch makes it a good cut for heavy weather use.

Class	Horizontal	Radial head	Tri-Radial	Starcut
Dinghy	*			
Mini-cruiser		*		
Light displacement cruiser/racer	Alternate to radial head	* (running)	* (reaching)	Alternative to tri-radial

Airflow

The thing to remember about spinnakers is that for most of their active careers they have the wind blowing *across* them from luff to leech, just like a jib. They do not, however, have the advantage of a jib's straight luff and flat leech. Nevertheless, the same basic principles apply, including slot effect, backwinding, and a need for maximum forward thrust and minimum heeling force.

Only when the wind is within about 10° either side of dead aft is the object of a spinnaker to present the greatest area of sail to the wind so that most drag is achieved and the boat blown downwind. Even here there are other factors such as getting the sail into undisturbed wind, ensuring that the thrust is forward and not angled off to one side, and seeing that the spinnaker sits symmetrically with clew and tack evenly balanced.

The spinnaker can thus be likened to an extra large jib which has the advantage (for the initiated), or the disadvantage (for the not so fortunate), of an adjustable tack as well as an adjustable clew. Its setting and trim would take up a book on their own, so I propose to limit my remarks here to some points of theory followed by a few

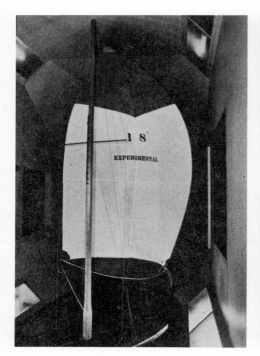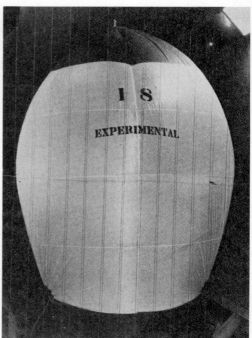

Plate 8.2 *Your Spinnaker* (left) is nearly always a flat-chested and spindly weakling, while. . . .

His Spinnaker is a well-stacked high-busted beauty. In fact, these two photographs are of the same sail in the Ratsey & Lapthorn wind tunnel at Cowes, viewed from astern and ahead. (*Ratsey & Lapthorn Ltd*)

general observations; see *Sails*[9] if you want a fuller discussion.

The way in which the wind travels across both spinnaker and jib on a reach is shown in Fig 8.3 (*a*) and (*b*). Subject to certain considerations, therefore, the larger sail will exert the greater total force for any given wind and boat speed. The spinnaker's main advantage over a jib is thus one of size.

But you should remember that not only will a spinnaker give more forward thrust than a jib, it will also give more heeling force. The time comes on a close reach when the larger sail may fill and draw, but it is so closely strapped alongside that a decent-sized jib would be more efficient. This moment depends not only on the wind conditions and how flat the spinnaker is, but also mainly on how much bigger it is than the jib which would be put on instead.

In light and medium winds, of course, both spinnaker and jib can often be used together if the one does not interfere with the free air of the other. This depends largely on the angle of the relative wind (they usually set happily together with the wind within an arc 15° either side of the beam) and also on the way the sails are cut, and trimmed to avoid taking each other's wind. But in reaching conditions where the two sails are not used together, a rule of thumb can be stated that a properly cut dinghy spinnaker will pay with the apparent wind 5° forward of the beam for each amount by which the spinnaker is larger than the jib which would otherwise be used. Thus if the spinnaker is five times bigger than the jib (as large a difference as is

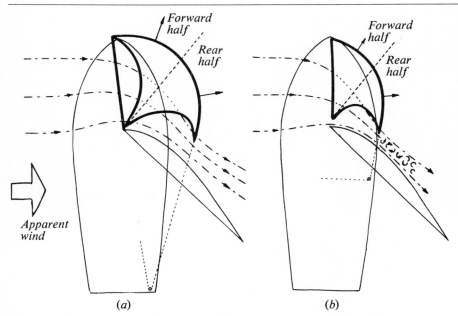

Forward half / Rear half / Apparent wind   (a)

Forward half / Rear half   (b)

Fig. 8.3 *Comparison of Spinnaker and Jib on a Reach*   A spinnaker has greater area than a jib, so it pays to reach with it if that area can be made to do useful work. Remember that, if a spinnaker has more area pulling forwards, it often has the same superiority pulling sideways as well. It is a good idea to divide the spinnaker mentally down the middle, and ask yourself what the rear half is doing. If it is pulling aft, you need to consider very carefully whether this is causing so much heel and brake effect that it is cancelling out the foward pull. The rear half of a jib seldom pulls aft at all (unless it has been blown out of shape, so that the flow is nearer the leech than the luff), therefore that part of the sail only adds to heel effect without actually braking the boat; this ensures that the efforts of the front half of a jib are not cancelled out as they can be in a spinnaker close reaching.

   This explains why it is important at all times, and particularly on a reach, to keep as much spinnaker pulling forwards as possible: you are, in effect, keeping as little of it pulling sideways and backwards as possible. Whether a spinnaker or a jib is better on a particular reach, therefore, depends not only on the relative sizes of the two sails and the closeness of the reach, but also on how the spinnaker can be set and sheeted on the boat to reduce pull rearward.

normally met in dinghies) the larger sail will have the advantage with the apparent wind 25° forward of the beam. The more usual area ratio of three or four to one brings the angle down to 15° to 20°: anything more and the jib is big enough to drive her better. Don't forget that this is a generalisation for use in winds around Force 3 to 4; whether it over- or understates the situation will vary not only with wind strength and class but also from helmsman to helmsman as things get down to the final crunch: skill.

To Spi or Not to Spi

One of the first decisions, therefore, is often whether to set a spinnaker at all. I am not concerned here with tactics nor with psychological warfare but, even if it is agreed that the wind is in the right direction, you may think that it is blowing too hard. The boat is pretty near her maximum speed anyway, so why bother with the thing? The point to realise is that there are moments in even the strongest blow when a boat under main and jib alone would fall below top speed. It is for these infrequent lulls that you must hoist the kite if you want to keep motoring flat out all the time. Other things being favourable, therefore, it usually pays to use a spinnaker if control of the boat can be maintained.

Once you have decided to use the sail you should lose no time in hoisting it. You can sometimes gain several places by slick drill on rounding the weather mark in close company with other boats who are slow to break out their kites. Equally you should hang on to it until the last moment when approaching a leeward mark. It is here that a spinnaker chute will pay dividends.

Pole Angle

As one of the objects is to keep the spinnaker away from the disturbed airflow round the mainsail, the tack should be as far away from the mast in both the horizontal and vertical planes as possible. This means that the spinnaker pole should be at right angles to both the mast and the wind (Fig. 8.4).

There are exceptions to this rather bald rule, but you won't go far wrong if you stick pretty close to it. In light winds the pole can be about 10° to 15° farther aft to stop the head of the sail falling away too much. In heavy weather you should let it go forward a bit and trim the sheet harder in order to reduce any tendency to roll and to aid in control: it may not always be possible in gusty conditions to trim the sheet quickly enough to stop the sail collapsing, so a little in hand will help. You will see from Fig. 8.4 (*a*) that you won't lose much offset if the pole is up to 15° off the right angle.

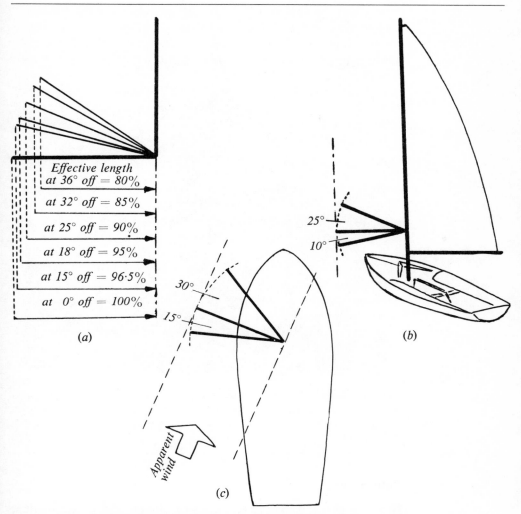

Fig. 8.4 *Effective Spinnaker Pole Length According to Angle*   The outer end of the spinnaker pole, with the tack of the sail attached to it, is farthest from the nearest point on the mast (and thus from the disturbing influence of the mainsail) when the pole is at right angles to the mast. This distance will reduce as the pole is allowed to stray from 90° and, for the mathematically inclined, it varies with the cosine of the angle by which it strays. You can see the precise effect from (*a*): the loss is only 5 per cent of length at 18° off, but the amount then goes up rapidly, so that 20 per cent is lost with the pole only twice as far from its proper line.

I have drawn the pole both horizontally (*b*) and vertically (*c*) with typical angles to show the effect, because the same principles apply when looking down on the boat. The aim here is to get the sail spread across the wind as much as possible, and the pole should be at or near right angles to the apparent wind to achieve this maximum coverage.

Plate 8.3 *Pole Height*   A good illustration of how too high a spinnaker pole produces too much sideways thrust. The 5-o-5 astern has a better trimmed pole giving more forward thrust; my guess is that she is overhauling the leader. (*Eileen Ramsay*)

Pole Height

Dinghies don't always have means of altering the height of their spinnaker poles at the mast end. The following remarks, therefore, may have to be read with the idea in mind that it is only the outer end of the pole which can be altered. Another glance at Fig. 8.4 (*a*) will show that the pole has to be more than 18° off the right angle in the vertical or the fore and aft planes before more than a 5 per cent reduction in its effective length takes place.

The basic aim in deciding pole height is to see that the tack and clew of the spinnaker are the same height above the water; this will ensure that the sail, being symmetrical, is not twisted into a poor aerodynamic shape. The outer end of the pole should be positioned so that the tack will be level with the clew, and then the pole is squared to the apparent wind. When the sheet has been trimmed so that the sail is on the point of falling in at the luff, the height of the clew and tack should be compared and any further minor adjustment made. If the tack is higher than the clew the leech will tend to fall inwards, close the slot and backwind the mainsail.

In light weather the pole should be moderately low to straighten the luff and reduce the amount of sail which has to be lifted before it fills; it may then slowly be raised as the sail fills and the free clew lifts. In these circumstances aerodynamic shape of the sail takes second place to getting it to fill at all. As the wind increases to Force 2 so the pole can be raised to normal height. In medium winds and stronger it sometimes pays when reaching with both spinnaker and jib to raise the pole above the usual angle until it is at right angles to the jib luff. This gets the sail a little farther away from the luff of the jib, thus helping to get it into undisturbed air.

When the wind is well aft, the downflow of air will force the sail up; this tends to draw the leeches together and give the sail more belly. Easing the sheet and raising the tack will help spread the upper part again and flatten the centre section. On a reach, aft tension exerted on the clew by the sheet will flatten the belly low in the sail, but the basic fullness of a general purpose spinnaker will be exaggerated slightly if there is downward tension on the lower corners, so once again the pole and clew should not be carried too low. Dinghies and light displacement boats are fortunate in that they can often be kept almost upright by crew weight, so that the dynamic stability of the plane will help to hold the boat steady; a heavy displacement boat will often tend to roll in brisk conditions, shifting the airflow alternately upwards and across the sail, which will exaggerate the rolling motion.

Horizontal and radial head spinnakers
A wind of given force has a greater apparent strength on a reach than on a run. The horizontal panels of a general purpose spinnaker will usually distort under increased load, inducing further camber. But a reach is just when you don't want a deeply bellied sail, so the average horizontal or radial head spinnaker is not at its best when reaching in anything other than light winds (when the camber is hardly affected). The sailmaker, of course, is aware of this, and usually cuts one of these spinnakers as a compromise – slightly too flat for the ideal running sail, which becomes slightly too full for the ideal reacher. Raising the pole on a reach will keep the spinnaker in the air, spread the leeches to flatten it, and make the whole thing look right for a reach – high, wide and handsome.

Starcut and tri-radial spinnakers
Because cloth distortion is resisted by the starcut and tri-radial cuts, the sail's camber does not increase so much as the general purpose

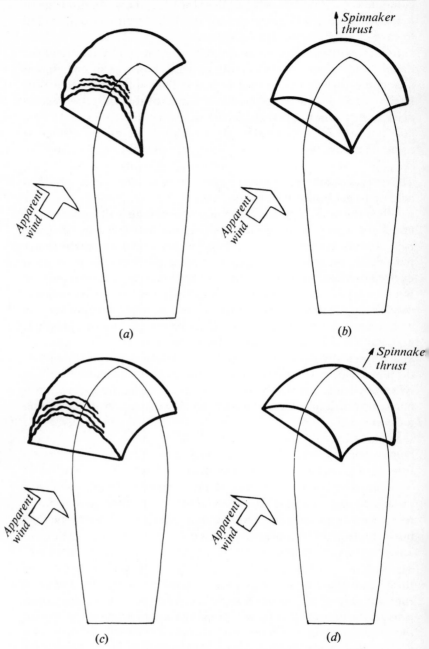

Fig. 8.5 *Spinnaker Sheet Adjustment*   The object of spinnaker sheet adjustment is to get the sail pulling forwards and not sideways, as we have already seen in Fig. 8.3. If the sheet is eased too much, as in (*a*), the luff will fall in and the whole sail will collapse if it is not corrected. Proper trim on a broad reach should

spinnaker in strong reaching winds, but pole height is important. If it is allowed to be too high, the sail will flatten too much, so it is normal to carry it rather lower with one of these specialist racing sails, with the sheet lead brought forward to keep the clew in line. This straightens the luff, but the low clew allows some flow to develop in the sail so that forward thrust can be maintained. If the boat starts to become overpowered, allow the pole to creep up slightly, thus opening the leech and spilling wind through the slot to reduce heel.

Sheet

Once the pole has been settled, the spinnaker is in basic trim and further adjustments must be made on the sheet.

The sail should be evenly balanced so that tack and clew are both about the same height (and also the same distance aft of the bow on a run). Bearing in mind that every bit that the sail can be angled to give forward thrust cuts down the damaging heeling force, the sheet must usually be eased as much as possible. In practice, the first sign that the sheet is being eased off too much is that the luff of the sail collapses as the wind gets behind it; the object ideally is to keep the luff on the quiver and you are then sure that as much of the sail as possible is pulling forward in driving force. Figure 8.5 helps show the reasoning behind this, and proper application to the task requires the sheet to be repeatedly eased and hardened as the crew feels for the first tremble of the luff and then stops full collapse taking place by hardening in again. This control is by no means always possible in gusty conditions, so a more settled trim then has to be adopted which will be closer sheeted than the optimum in order to avoid unexpected and sudden collapse of the sail. It should be checked for any possible freeing of the wind from time to time.

When using a flat cut reaching spinnaker with the wind abeam, try taking the sheet fairlead forward – until it is a prolongation of the centre panel of a radial cut clew; this will give the sail a bit of belly it might not otherwise develop.

---

enable the whole sail to pull forward efficiently as in (b) but if, with the sheet trimmed correctly, the pole is then squared too far aft, the sail will collapse again as in (c).

The most common fault in spinnaker sheet trim is to sheet the sail too hard as in (d); even though the pole is correctly square to the wind, the drive of the sail is partly sideways so loss of speed must result. You can often tell this is happening because the foot of the spinnaker starts to bear on the forestay; if you can't ease the sheet and keep the sail full, the pole is probably too far aft and must also go forward.

It is in light to medium weather that correct spinnaker trim pays the greatest dividends. When the wind is really blowing, your boat soon reaches her maximum hull speed, so the finer points are wasted, unless they are critical for planing.

The Cruising Chute

Like some other sails, the cruising chute owes its origins to racing; it is a direct descendant of the big boy or blooper. The latter was designed to restore aerodynamic balance to a boat sailing down wind, with a large spinnaker out to one side and a relatively small mainsail the other. It was such an easy sail to set and douse, that it quickly became enlarged and adapted as the principal down wind sail on short-handed cruising boats.

The cruising chute is a single-luffed spinnaker, which tacks to the stemhead and is sheeted to the quarter; the leech is shorter than the luff, and the sail tapers fairly sharply towards the head; the width is usually somewhere near $1.7 \times J$ (as opposed to the full spinnaker, which is $1.8 \times J$ under the IOR). These reduced dimensions, and the lack of full shoulders at the head, keep the cruising chute smaller than the spinnaker by some 30–35 per cent, a large part of which is lost aloft, where it would cause the most heeling moment. If the sail is allowed to become too small, it fails to add the extra power expected of it in light winds; if it is too big, it becomes unwieldy and defeats the object. Different sailmakers and boatbuilders work out the area in different ways. I suggest that a spinnaker proper can be assessed as luff×max width, with nothing taken off for the taper at the head, because of the fullness in the high busty top half; a cruising chute can be assessed as luff×max width (which is usually slightly narrower than that of the spinnaker) ×0.75 to allow for the loss of area through the leech being shorter than the luff, as well as the fairly sharp taper of the sail towards the head. Figure 8.6 shows comparative shapes and sizes of the two sails and a No 1 genoa.

As far as mini-cruisers are concerned, a full-scale spinnaker is still small enough to be handled fairly easily, so the main reason for the cruising chute does not exist. If you decide to go for one, it sets without a pole at any angle from its closest to the apparent wind (say, 60° off the bow), round to a quartering wind (40° off the stern); under these conditions, the sail will set on the same side as the mainsail. When the wind goes nearer dead aft (in the arc 30° off the stern to zero), the cruising chute may be set opposite to the mainsail and boomed out to windward with a whisker pole.

Because the sail is tacked down to the bows, the entire foot length has to be set to weather, unlike a spinnaker which sets across the boat. This means that a normal spinnaker pole (which is the same

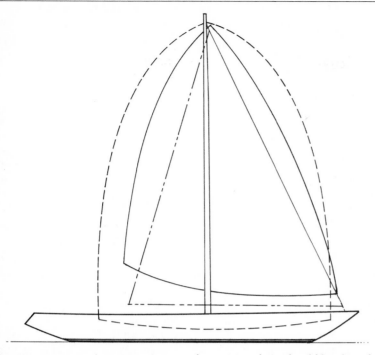

Fig. 8.6 *Cruising Chute Size*   In area, the cruising chute should be about half way between the genoa and the spinnaker. This should give the boat a good performance off the wind in light airs, without causing her to heel too much on a reach or roll too much down wind. Note how the cruising chute is narrower than the spinnaker, and loses more area still by tapering fairly sharply towards the head. Owners can, of course, place more emphasis on greater area for extra speed (and a possibly unruly sail), or a smaller sail and a quiet life – but less speed in the lighter winds.

length as the J dimension) is rather too short to push it right out. A cruising chute pole needs ideally to be $1.5 \times J$ in length; because the stresses are less, the pole may be lighter, and it doesn't need all the control lines of the spinnaker pole proper. Such a length makes it difficult to stow, so get one which is telescopic.

The cruising chute should always be set with an adjustable tack pennant – ideally one which is brought right back to the cockpit. From here it can be eased as the boat comes off the wind, while the same happens to the halyard; this allows the sail to fly well out to one side. As you luff closer to the apparent wind, so should tack pennant and halyard be progressively hardened, until they are both as tight as they will go; this straightens the luff as much as possible, and enables you to point as high as you can effectively carry the sail (60° off).

The cruising chute does not measure to the IOR, because it has a half-height cross-measurement of more than half the foot length (so it is not a jib), and because it is asymmetrical (so it is not a spinnaker)[17], but some clubs allow them to race, for the very sensible reason that they are smaller and less efficient than spinnakers, so that no advantage is gained by using them.

Spee Squeezer®

The spinnaker squeezer or dowser was invented by Chris Hall of Cowes, and works equally well with spinnaker or cruising chute; it makes life a lot easier, especially for a weak crew. It is a long nylon sheath, which usually has a ring or plastic funnel of some sort at the lower end. The sail is fed into it with cleared leeches, and attached to a ring inside at the top; once loaded, you should not have to attend to it again. When you want to fly the spinnaker or cruising chute, hoist the whole thing on the spinnaker halyard as a kind of sausage in the fore-triangle (don't believe those who say that you can use the genoa halyard, because the inevitable sideways pull at the head will chafe the wire or rope on the side of the exit to the sheave box). The funnel is then hoisted on its own halyard (which comes as part of the squeezer package), to compress the sheath into a concertina of nylon at the top of the sail which, as the funnel rises, fills from the bottom so that snarl-ups tend to unwind on the head swivel. The sail is doused

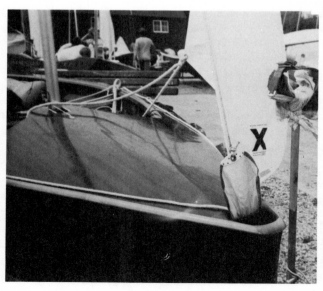

Plate 8.4 *Dinghy Spinnaker Tube*   A neat arrangement on a Merlin Rocket. (*Author*)

Plate 8.5 *Keelboat Spinnaker Tube* One of the first light displacement keel-boats to use a spinnaker launching tube was *Quarto*. The rings on the hatch-cover guide the sail to the tubes proper, which extend each side of the boat to the cockpit (so that any water taken in at the bows drains out of the stern). (*Author*)

by the reverse process of pulling down the funnel (its own halyard is an endless line attached for this purpose), to bring the sheath back down over the de-powered sail. It can even be used in the half-way position as a form of reefing.

The down wind sails we are considering are really too small to warrant its use at all, but it can be very useful for single-handed cruisers both large and small.

Spinnaker Chute

The easiest way to hoist and recover a spinnaker is by means of a chute, in the form of a long flexible tube into which the sail is drawn and from which it is re-hoisted. The mouth is near the bows and is rigid, either bell-shaped or with a roller to facilitate passage of the

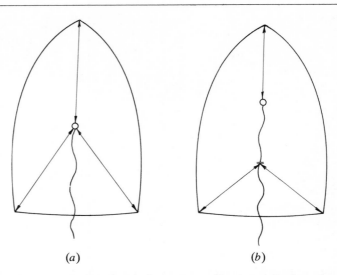

(a)   (b)

Fig. 8.7 *Recovery Lines*   In (a) the recovery line is attached so that it is
equidistant from all three corners of the spinnaker. For a faster stow, the line is
taken through a fairlead to an attachment point further up the sail (b); from
clews to fairlead and from patch to head need to be the same distance. Recovery
lines used with a spinnaker chute are rather harsh on the sail; when used on the
open foredeck of an offshore boat, they can save snags.

sail. A light cord is attached to a small loop on a reinforcing patch in
the centre of the spinnaker and then passed down the chute, so that it
may be pulled to collapse the sail and draw it into the chute as the
halyard, sheet and guy are eased. It is important for this recovery line
to be attached equidistant from the head and both clews so that when
the sail is lowered these finish side by side just clear of the bell mouth,
where their respective ropes may be clipped and unclipped if required
(Fig. 8.7).

The tube needs to be anchored at its aft end to hold it steady as the
sail is pulled forward on hoisting, and must be long enough to hold
the spinnaker when it is folded from its centrepoint. It is a good idea
to make the tripping line into an extension of the halyard tail, so that
neither is allowed to run free, but see that it is light line so as not to
disturb the set of the sail by its weight; detach it altogether in very
light weather.

9 LIGHT DISPLACEMENT CRUISER RACERS

I remember seeing a number of French 16-footers arrive at Cowes in the early 1960s. They were little more than sailing dinghies with lids on, but they had raced 100 miles across the Channel, and their two-man crews (some were two-woman, some were mixed) were then sleeping and cooking aboard. We thought they were mad, but they were the advance guard of a movement which has increased with the years.

Improvements in design and construction methods have enabled slightly larger mini-cruisers to evolve within the genre, so that boats up to about 7–8 m (at 23–26 ft, a good deal larger than the official mini-tonners) are sailed like dinghies, with crews sitting out as they plane along. Most of what has already been said in this book applies to these light displacement craft, but they also have one or two aspects of their own which will repay examination. What follows may seem to relate largely to the racing owner at times, but efficient sailing should know no frontiers because a boat doesn't know whether it is being raced or cruised, and it will always obey certain laws. It can be just as important for a family on holiday to save their tide at a particular headland, as it might be for a boat to beat a particular rival to the weather mark. So these pages affect you, whether you race or cruise.

Sail Handling

Sail areas on mini-cruisers are usually small enough not to need powerful winches (racing boats may have 2-speed winches, but they don't have to be all that hefty), even the biggest sails should be within the scope of the average husband and wife team. In addition, modern equipment means that many sail drills on cruisers can be effected from the cockpit, so that forays to the foredeck are limited to sail changing and anchoring; cruising sails can often be effectively changed from the cockpit, especially since the introduction of headsail roller reefing systems and spinnaker dowsers.

Correct co-ordination of forestay, mast, sheet, rudder and crew weight is a major factor in boat-speed – particularly when the helmsman understands the importance of positioning the boat cor-

Plate 9.1 *Light Displacement*   The similarity between the underwater lines of a modern light displacement keelboat and many planing dinghies is evident from this view of a *Sonata* being craned. (*David Thomas*)

rectly in the wave system. The improvement in speed due to one minor adjustment may not be readily discernible without a sensitive speed-log, but the cumulative effect of several such adjustments will be considerable by the end of a race (or may make the difference between just making or just missing bar closing time). One of the pleasures to be gained from racing these small cruisers, is this interplay of go-fast factors, as the helmsman and trimmer strive to get, and stay, in the groove. The crew which profits from each and every opportunity, be it wind speed or direction, change in wave formation, or eddies in the current, will not only gain satisfaction from putting their skill to work, they will be a long way ahead of any rival who is content merely to 'set it and forget it'.

It is not my province to tell you how to sail, but even the cruising owner doesn't want to waste unnecessary time getting from A to B, and you won't be giving your sails a fair chance if you do no more than steer adequately to windward. We must start with the assumption that you are a reasonably competent performer with the tiller, or you would not be indulging in this book. Forgive me, however, if I run over a few basic hull parameters, but we must start from an efficient platform.

Keep the boat upright, because wetted hull shape changes considerably as you heel, usually resulting in less speed if only due to excessive weather helm. I must also warn against forgetting fore and aft trim; in general, light displacement craft don't like sailing with either bow or stern too low. An exception is very light weather, when raising the stern can sometimes result in better speed due to the relatively large reduction in wetted area. Equally, moving weight aft on a brisk reach can help reduce weather helm by immersing more lateral resistance aft of the centre of effort. But in general terms, it pays not only to have the boat level both athwartships and in the pitching place, but also to keep the weight out of the ends, so that she is dynamically more stable.

Plate 9.2 *Class Racing* The *Sonata* is a British national class, and offers close racing in the dinghy tradition. In the situation shown here, only K.8008 would dare to gybe; the question of contrary current aside, any of the other boats would put herself into a vulnerable port/starboard situation if she were to change to port tack. (*David Thomas*)

Plate 9.3 *Boat Trim*   Light displacement cruiser/racers like this *Eygthene 24* should be sailed bolt upright like dinghies whenever possible. (*Author*)

The Mainsail

When I showed this new chapter to a friend with experience in J.24s, he felt that mainsails had been neglected and that they needed as much attention as I give to the genoa. But the genoa is a new sail to this book, and I hope I have already said enough in Chapter 7 to show that the mainsail is a crucial part of a boat's sail system; it forms the aft end of the aerofoil and, as such, controls the upwash onto the leading edge of the genoa. In this chapter I shall content myself with stressing the importance of a flat mainsail leech, in order to ensure a clean run off to the wind without unnecessary side pressure. See also Chapter 6 for discussion of bendy spars to flatten the mainsail.

The Genoa

When going to windward, most of us know that the headsail provides the major driving force in a boat. Many of us know that this is because (a) there is no mast at the leading edge to disturb the airflow, and (b) the presence of the mainsail, downstream in the airflow, creates an upwash round the luff of the jib, so that the local apparent wind frees the headsail by an extra 5–7 degrees (see also Chapter 1). Nearly all of us pay lip-service to these facts, but not so many give the headsail the priority care and attention it thus deserves – whether it

Plate 9.4 *The Slot* David Thomas designed the 22 ft (7 m) *Intro* as an introduction to keel boats for dinghy sailors. Gerry Stillman had the first fibreglass hull, and is seen here crewing for the designer's son. The IOR only allows battens in headsails if they are not longer than 0.08 J, and provided they reach forward of the mast; this effectively restricts them to working jibs and smaller. Note that this headsail reaches to the top of the fore-triangle (so that the maximum amount of the mainsail can benefit from the slot, even at the expense of some mutual interference at the head); this rig will be an effective reduction in area from the full size genoa as the wind increases. (*Gerry Stillman*)

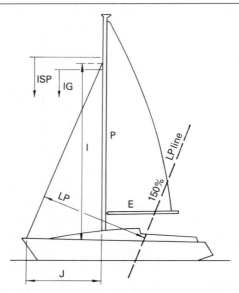

Fig. 9.1 *IOR Sail Parameters*   The principal IOR sail parameters are:

P=mainsail hoist.

E=foot of mainsail.

I=height of foretriangle; forestay at mast to deck sheerline (IC is I corrected for any penalties; IG is height of genoa halyard; ISP is height of spinnaker halyard).

J=base of foretriangle (JC is J corrected for any penalties).

LP=longest perpendicular of headsail.

Spinnaker	Max luff	$=0.95\sqrt{I^2+J^2}$. (95% of the fore-triangle hypotenuse.)
	Max width	$=1.8\times J$.
Genoa	Max luff	$=\sqrt{IG^2+J^2}$. In practice the luff is limited by the length of the forestay, but this rule prevents a longer luff being set flying (i.e. not hanked on).
	Max LP	$=1.5\times J$. When *any* headsail is set on its proper stay and trimmed along a parallel to the yacht's centreline, its clew may not fall aft of this so-called LP line without penalty; this holds good for staysails set on an inner stay. Any headsail may have a high or low clew, provided it falls on or in front of the 150% LP line.
Storm Jib	Max area	$=0.05\times IG^2$.
Trysail	Max area	$=0.175P\times E$; this is slightly small when compared with the maximum size storm jib.

Rating   If a fractional rig yacht wishes to lower her rating by a small percentage through altering sails alone (perhaps to fall into a lower rating bracket), reducing the I measurement gives the greatest rating reduction for the smallest loss of area; reducing J comes second. Other factors also come into play, however, such as efficiency of the area given up, and economy; it may therefore be better to reduce P. Lowering and raising the rating, through sail parameters only, are more fully discussed with graphs and examples, in my other book *Sails*.

be a one-design working jib or an overlapping genoa. Matching the genoa to the conditions (weather, mainsail, mast, and available adjustments) is crucial to optimum performance; matching the available adjustments to the selected genoa is then equally crucial.

Setting aside the working jib of a one-design dinghy for the moment (where luff, leech and foot lengths are laid down, overlap is usually small, and there is no larger or smaller headsail available), the measurements controlling an overlapping genoa are luff length and the shortest distance from the clew to the luff (the longest perpendicular, or LP, in the International Offshore Rule); clew height can then be adjusted up or down the LP line so that the sail sheets nicely to the fairlead; Fig. 9.1. In turn, the IOR allows within the rating, any headsail with an LP up to $1.5 \times J$ (J=the distance between the front of the mast and the forestay on deck); this is known as the 150 per cent genoa. A 100 per cent genoa would be one which had an LP exactly equal to the J measurement; other sizes vary in between (see Nos 2 and 3 genoas in Table 4).

Maximum genoa area within the IOR rating is obviously obtained by having as long a luff length as possible, coupled with an LP of the full $1.5 \times J$. In Chapter 1 we saw the importance of the leading edge of our combined aerofoil, so that most Nos 2 and 3 genoas these days are nearly full length in the luff (at wind speeds over Force 4, there is something to be said for a slightly shorter luff in order to allow some separation from the mainsail at the head, where the slot is smallest, thus reducing blockage and turbulence in this constricted area; it also lowers the Centre of Effort).

In order to hold a light displacement boat at or near the optimum heeling angle (zero degrees), we have to keep the heeling moment to something which we can counteract by crew weight. In this connection, it should be remembered that a displacement boat has a heavy keel helping to achieve this, so the latter can tolerate greater heeling moments than the former. In the more tender lightweight vessel, it is doubly important to reduce sail at higher wind speeds (see also my remarks about angle of heel at the start of this chapter).

What is equally important is slot size. The large overlap of a No 1 genoa means a tight slot, which can only accept so much air at any one time; as soon as the wind speed increases beyond a given value, more air is trying to get through than can smoothly pass. The result is blockage and turbulence. So a wider slot is needed in the higher wind strengths – another reason for a smaller sail, and incidentally a reason for having plenty of leech hollow in a No 2 or a No 3 genoa, even if the area is already reduced. Table 4 gives a general guide to genoa selection, but individual choice must in the final analysis depend on hull shape, crew weight and height of foretriangle (a boat with a bigger I measurement will have a greater in-built heeling moment).

Table 4 Genoa selection for light displacement boats.

Apparent wind (kts)	Sail	Beaufort scale (true)
0 – 6	Ghoster	0 – 1
4 – 15	Light No 1	1 – 3
12 – 20	Heavy No 1	3 – 4
17 – 25	No 2 (135% J)	4 – 5
23 – 28	No 3 (110% J)	5 – 6

Plate 9.5 *Fore-triangle Height*   The *Sonata* was the result of smoothing the chines of *Intro* (Plate 9.4), and laying out the deck for series production. It will be noted that David Thomas reduced the I measurement to give a ¾ rig, rather than the ⅞ths of the earlier design. The *Sonata* is so easily driven, that the loss of area has a negligible effect on performance, while the gain in rating is significant. See also my remarks in this chapter on the stiffer qualities conferred by a lower AR rig, as compared with the greater tenderness of a masthead fore-triangle. (*Yachting World*)

Fractional v. Masthead Rig

In the 5th edition of my larger book *Sails*, there is an analysis of the pros and cons of fractional versus masthead rig. Suffice it to say here that both theory and practice show that the fractional rig is better for light displacement boats: the lower aspect ratio mainsail gives better results on a reach; there should be less heeling moment; and the smaller spinnaker is easier to control. The masthead rig points slightly better to windward, and profits from its larger spinnaker down wind in light airs. The advantage is the other way round for heavy displacement boats. See below under *Twist* for reasons why the mainsail of a fractional rig boat should be allowed about 5° of twist at the head.

Genoa Tune

Chord angle

Setting up the genoa is basic to getting the most from any sailing boat, and it is particularly important in racing a light displacement craft. The chord angle of the genoa to the boat's centreline (not the same as the angle of incidence, which is the angle of the chord to the apparent wind) is crucial, and it is controlled by the distance inboard or outboard of the sheet fairlead. We have already seen that the genoa operates in the upwash created by the mainsail (Fig. 1.6), so that the apparent wind frees the headsail by some 5–7 degrees more than the mainsail. Representative close-hauled angles of incidence are shown in Fig. 1.1 (chord angle=apparent wind angle−angle of incidence); if conditions are right (smooth water, Force 2, possibly with a contrary current or tidal stream which can just be lee-bowed by pointing very high), the genoa may be trimmed further inboard, to enable the boat to sail slightly closer to the wind. Under those circumstances, the main boom should also be trimmed to the

Table 5 Chord angle; cause and effect.

	Fairlead inboard	*Fairlead outboard*
Boat tune	Low drag boat. Main traveller amidships, or to windward.	High drag boat. Main traveller to leeward.
Conditions	Light winds. Smooth water.	Strong winds. Choppy seas, or big swell.
Effect	High pointing. Less speed.	High speed. Less pointing.

centreline – even barber-hauled to windward – so that the slot
remains open and there is no backwinding of the main. Watch that
you don't get so hooked on pointing high, that the boat drops out of
the groove and makes excessive leeway as she slows down.

Twist

Because the airflow over the head of a fractional rig mainsail is not
deflected through an angle by the genoa, the apparent wind has a
greater angle of incidence aloft than down on the deck; such a
mainsail should be allowed some 5° of twist to prevent premature
stall at the head. A genoa also needs a small amount of twist, in order
to meet the slightly more favourably angled wind aloft; this is due to
wind sheer caused by the gradient which, it must be said, is only
of marginal effect with headsails which reach little more than
20 ft above the water (see also Chapter 7); Fig. 9.2. Fore and aft
movement of the fairlead is the controlling factor here – move it
forward to pull more down on the leech, to reduce twist and to
increase depth of camber near the foot; forestay sag also has a small
effect (see Table 6). Check your setting by close-hauling and then

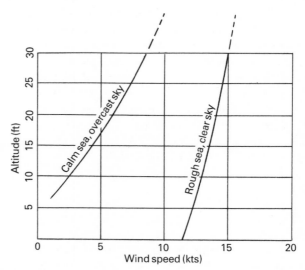

Fig. 9.2 *Wind Gradient*   Due to friction caused by a rough sea or earth surface, wind speed increases with altitude; it reaches its true speed at about 100 ft.
The curves above show the change low down of a representative wind of 20
knots true speed (the proportions hold good up to about Force 5 or 6). The
gradient also depends partly on temperature. On the left are the values when the
sea is calm and the sky overcast (low temperature change). To the right is the
curve with an average sea and winds up to Force 6. Fog or drizzle (which allow
considerable temperature loss) would shift the curve even further to the right.

Plate 9.6 *Crew Strength* A crew of three can handle most of these light displacement cruiser/racers in light conditions (they can cruise with two); a fourth member is useful in heavier weather, not only to help with sail handling, but also to keep the boat more upright. Chris Ratsey is here racing *Quarto*, one of the first keelboats capable of true planing to go into series production in the UK. (*Yachting World*)

watching the tell-tales as you luff slowly towards the wind; all streamers should lift at the same time from head to tack. If the top one breaks first, there is too much twist so move the fairlead forward; and vice versa. Fine tuning of twist can be obtained through use of the extra tell-tale which I normally recommend at the head of a genoa (see below under *Tell-tales*).

Forestay sag
Forestay sag is another factor in correct genoa tune; this in its turn is affected by backstay tension. The effect of sag is to increase flow forward in the genoa – it is one of the few ways of altering the flow in a film laminate headsail; Fig 9.3. A secondary effect is to straighten up some of the twist in the head of the sail: sag reduces twist slightly. So, when you need more flow in the headsail (to get more speed, at the expense of pointing ability – for example in light winds and choppy water, when you need to keep her moving), ease off the running backstay *very slightly*. But forestay sag is bad news when going to windward in stronger conditions, because the effect will be

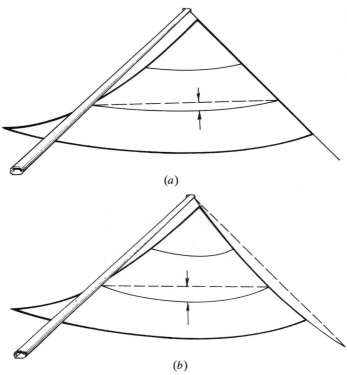

(a)

(b)

Fig. 9.3 *Forestay Sag*   A tight forestay(*a*) lets the headsail develop only that flow which has been designed into the sail. If the stay is allowed to sag (*b*), the headsail luff moves aft towards the leech and increases the sail's camber. This is about the only way in which the flow in a film laminate jib can be controlled.

exaggerated by the higher forces involved, and the boat will fail to point; in addition, the extra fullness aloft will make her heel more. This is the kind of basic tuning tip which will be as helpful to the cruising boat trying to cross a harbour bar before the tide falls too low, as it will be to the racer struggling for inside berth at a mark.

Camber

The powerpoint in a genoa should be somewhere between 35 per cent and 50 per cent aft of the luff, depending on conditions. Flow forward is typical of strong winds and associated sea conditions – the wind will blow it aft in an all-woven sail anyway, so firm tension on halyard and cunningham will be needed to keep it forward. The boat will need to be sailed a degree or two more free in these conditions (the groove is wider), and forward flow will give extra power to push through any chop. With the halyard eased on a control luff sail in light winds, so that the powerpoint is at 45 per cent or even 50 per

Table 6 Forestay sag and its effect. Note that reducing sag in the forestay may be what we seek in strong winds, but it has the effect of narrowing the groove just when it is most difficult to keep within it; luff tension should be increased in line with Table 7 below. Conversely, a fuller genoa may be what is wanted in light winds, but in these conditions a fine entry sail with a narrow groove will point very high, so ease up on the halyard as well, to get a finer entry.

Boat tune	Backstay tight. Forestay straight.	Backstay slightly eased. Forestay sags.
Genoa	Flatter, with fine entry. Powerpoint 45–50%. More twist (upper slot more open).	Fuller, with round entry. Powerpoint 35%. Less twist (upper slot more closed).
Conditions	Force 3+.	Force 1–2, with chop or swell (power needed).
Effect	Higher pointing. Less heel (more speed).	More heel. Less point (more speed).

cent, the entry will be finer and the boat will point slightly higher – but the fine entry will be more demanding of the helmsman, and will need a smoother sea with less wind if this rather narrow groove is to be maintained.

Sheet
The genoa sheet is the most obvious trimming device, and the one which is (rightly) used most often. If I were to be asked which is the most common fault with trimming sails to windward, I would have to answer 'over-sheeting'. Most of us know that on a reach the sheet should be played to take advantage of minor wind shifts, so as to angle the thrust as much forward as possible. Equally, we know that,

Table 7 Effect of halyard and cunningham on the position of the powerpoint in an all-woven sail.

Halyard/cunningham	Tight	Slack
Powerpoint	35–40%. Round entry.	45–50%. Fine entry.
Conditions	Force 3+. Smooth or choppy.	Force 1–2. Smooth water.
Effect	More speed. Wider groove.	High point. Narrow groove.

Plate 9.7 *Planing*   This American J.24 is planing down wind – a sure sign that she is no marginal performer. Note how upright she is, and how the spinnaker is trimmed to pull directly forward. (*J Boats Inc*)

going to windward, these minor wind shifts don't go away, but it is the helmsman who should take advantage of them by playing the tiller. But how many of us have thought the thing through to its proper conclusion? If the genoa is sheeted too hard in the first place, potential forward thrust is being thrown away all the time, and is being converted into heeling moment. There is no inherent merit in getting the genoa as flat as a board; if you are having trouble going to windward properly in light to medium winds, and you've checked on boat tune, the best single piece of advice I can offer is: 'Try easing the genoa sheet'. This should restore flow to a flat sail, and give the boat back some forward power – even if it is at the expense of pointing high. High point+low speed=leeway; it is no good whatever *pointing* high if you don't *foot it* high.

Wind gusts, of course, alter the tension in the weave of an all-woven cloth, and they also increase forestay sag. In broad terms, this means that flow moves aft in a sail, flattening the entry and forcing open the slot. A good guide to basic genoa sheet trim is provided by the spreader ends. I know that the pundits are quick to point out that the relationship of genoa leech to spreader end will vary from boat to boat, depending on the length of spreader and its position up and down the mast. Nevertheless, thousands use this as a yardstick for genoa trim, and it works. If I had to make a generalisation, I would say that, in high winds, the genoa leech should usually be on, or not more than an inch or two from touching, the spreader end; in light airs this gap may increase to 4–6 in (10–15 cm). If this results in the foot of the genoa bearing too hard on the main shroud, you either have very short spreaders (so that the genoa is trimmed too hard) or, more likely, the sheet lead is too far aft (thus overtightening the foot and easing the upper leech too much). Learn your own boat's preference, and keep it constantly in mind (and notice how the gap widens in the puffs, so that you should harden the sheet momentarily).

Tell-tales
Once basic sheeting is established, watch the tell-tales (Fig. 7.8). We have already seen that these should all lift at the same time; the sheet trimmer's job is to see that they don't lift at all on the lee side; the same holds good for the windward tell-tales as a generalisation. The experts will tell you to sail with the windward tallies starting to lift towards the vertical – the more they lift, the higher you are pointing (or pinching), so stream them aft if you want boat speed (in a chop, or just after tacking) and let them edge upwards if you want to feather the sail or grab a few yards to windward. But you won't go far wrong if you keep everything streaming – the finer points can come later; it is particularly important that the leeward tell-tales keep streaming, because it is here that separation starts, leading to the stall

and loss of thrust. I have long used the mnemonic TASTES, which stands for 'Turn Away or Sheet Towards Erratic Streamers'. If the leeward streamers start to lift, the trimmer can react immediately, so he should ease the sheet and tell the helmsman, who should then luff gently while the trimmer hardens sheet again; this sequence is particularly important in light winds, when sudden movement of the tiller could stall the rudder and/or keel (remember, there's no point in pointing high if you don't foot it high; see also under *Ghosting* below). The windward tell-tales reveal when you are pinching; they will start to lift as you get towards the windward end of the groove sector, and they will point straight up as the sail luff verges on lifting. I advocate a streamer near the head in the half-chord position, as well

Plate 9.8 *The Extreme Dinghy*   Nearly 28 ft (8.5 m) overall, *Buoy Racer* is a Half-Tonner, where David Thomas has paid great attention to weight. The boat will accordingly plane as opposed to surf, and all the dinghy skills are needed to keep her upright and moving to best advantage. I do not belong to the school of thought which advocates leaving the genoa partly hoisted to catch more wind when reaching like this; airflow down from the foot of the spinnaker will be directed into the lee of the mess on the foredeck, and this can only serve to slow the boat. (*Patrick Roach*)

as at the luff. This acts as a twist warner – if the windward half-chord tell-tale starts to lift before its companion right at the luff, the head of the sail is twisted too much and needs attention to the backstay or sheet fairlead as outlined above.

The Groove

We have talked a lot about the groove: what is it? The groove is that combination of tune and trim when close-hauled, which brings the boat alive; she eats her way to windward because everything is right. Flow is correctly positioned in both sails, which are correctly angled to the boat and to the wind so that the slot is right all the way; the helmsman steers the boat so that advantage is taken of every lift; the sail trimmer is in constant communication with the helmsman, so that sheet, backstay, kicking-strap, cunningham, traveller and out-haul are all under constant review – but above all, sheet and traveller.

The groove has a sector, outside of which the helmsman should never stray, and which can be either narrow or wide. In brisk winds with a lumpy sea, the groove needs to be fairly wide, because it is not possible under those conditions to keep within narrow margins; thus the sails should be reasonably forgiving, even at the expense of optimum efficiency. When the boat is pointing high in the groove, some power goes out of the rig, so that the forestay (relieved of some of its load) straightens, genoa fullness moves aft, and the finer entry accepts the lower angle of incidence. When the boat is pointing low in a wide groove, the greater power in the genoa causes greater luff sag, which in turn increases fullness forward, enabling the genoa to absorb the increased angle of incidence without flow separation.

In smooth waters and light winds, you can accept a more demand-ing shape, if that shape will give improved performance – in other words, a narrower groove of higher potential. A narrow groove has less latitude, and the helmsman and trimmer have to keep the forces on the rig more constant. If the angle of incidence strays by more than a degree or so, the genoa's finer entry will be in danger of suffering flow separation. The easiest and most obvious indicators of the groove are luff tell-tales, as described above. Keep them streaming aft and you won't go far wrong – provided the basic tune has first been set up correctly.

Ghosting

Being so light, mini-cruisers will usually go quite well in light weather. But most of us have experienced the frustration of condi-tions so light that we are unable to move, while a rival ghosts along, seemingly powered by a private wind.

Plate 9.9 *Ghosting*   In common with most of the cruiser/racers we are considering, the Jeanneau *Fun* is a good performer in light weather. But the size of the crew in this shot shows that my son's *Moonshine* is obviously cruising in these ghosting conditions on Lake Annecy – a task for which she is as well suited as for racing. (*Chris Howard-Williams*)

The reason is almost certainly nothing to do with the cut of his or your sails, and can be explained in one short sentence: your keel is stalled, while his is not. Flow separation can occur with a foil immersed in water, in just the same way that it can with an aerofoil in air. When this occurs, lift from the keel breaks down, and there is no force to oppose any aerodynamic lift emanating from the sails; if she moves at all, the boat goes sideways or round in circles (evidence that the rudder is also stalled).

The cure is to sail on a broad reach, even if it is nearly opposite to the way you want to go, re-establish attached flow over the keel and rudder, and then gently bring the boat back onto course. Once you get her going again, avoid large rudder angles and too much movement on board or you will stall it again.

Furling Headsails

The racing owner is apt to think that the world revolves round competitive sailing. The fact is that cruising owners outnumber the racing fraternity by about ten to one, so it was with considerable acclaim that Major Wykeham-Martin's furling headsail was turned into a reefing headsail by the advent of ball races capable of withstanding sufficiently high thrust loadings. There is thus far less sail changing on a wet foredeck as the wind increases, and the lockers are not filled with a mass of supplementary jibs of differing sizes. It also means that the sail can be rolled on its foil when the boat is at anchor, thus avoiding the inconvenience of bagging and stowing when the day's sailing is over.

Plate 9.10 *Jib Roller* The halyard on the smallest Rotostay furling gear has to be cut to length, so that it can return down the foil beside the sail luff and be made fast at the drum; it then rolls with the sail. (*Rotomarine Ltd*)

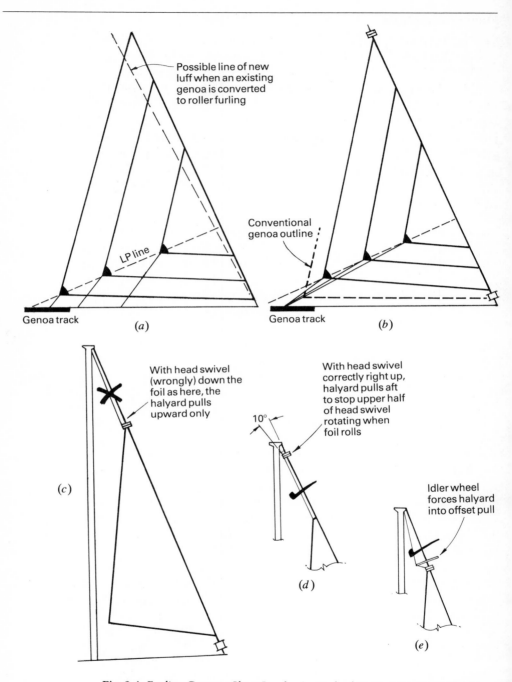

Fig. 9.4 *Furling Genoa – Sheet Lead*   A standard No 1 genoa normally sheets below the LP line, along which the clew would travel if the sail were rolled on the luff; this requires the fairlead to be moved progressively forward (*a*). Raising the

UV degradation

As we know, polyester is weakened by prolonged exposure to the ultraviolet rays of the sun and, indeed, to some industrial smoke. If a genoa is left furled on its stay for any length of time, the exposed part of the sail (a strip down the leech and another along the foot) will be weakened to the point where it will eventually tear like paper. To guard against this, either special sacrificial strips of cloth may be sewn to the outside of the leech and foot, or else the whole sail may be made of UV resistant cloth. The former offers better protection, because the latter is not completely UV proof – in any event, the sewing thread is the same and, though also resistant to UV rays, will eventually weaken. If you sail in the tropics, or if the sail will be left furled in the open for weeks on end even in temperate climates, sacrificial strips offer a better protective barrier (and are cheaper to replace than the whole sail). UV strips do, however, mean extra weight at the leech, so a furling sail made totally of UV resistant cloth is preferred by some; in this case the sail may well be cut with vertical panels, to avoid having a multiplicity of seams with their vulnerable stitching exposed when rolled. The vertical cut does not lend itself to having sacrificial strips, because the leech offers no seams for adjustment and will almost certainly curl under the extra layer of cloth along its length; a complete sheath, preferably of UV resistant cloth, which is put on round the rolled sail is the answer in this case.

Cloth weight

A furling genoa will be used in the part-rolled condition as a reefed sail when the wind increases. Its cloth should therefore be heavy enough to withstand this, so it should be nearer that of the boat's working jib rather than its genoa, or it will get blown out of shape when part-rolled, i.e. 200 gm/m² rather than 150 gm/m² for the average mini-cruiser. The use of two cloth weights, so that the leech is heavier than the luff, is not suitable for sails of the small size we are considering, because they don't have enough panels to make it a practical proposition.

---

clew brings the sheet lead more nearly onto the right angle, but it would usually also take the fairlead aft of the existing genoa track, so the clew has to be moved slightly forward to bring it back on again (*b*). Even then, the lead is normally slightly below the 90° line, but this improves as the sail is rolled.

Halyard Wrap   The halyard can wrap round the forestay during the furling process if the head swivel is as little as 6 in (15 cm) below the halyard sheave box. This is because the pull would then be virtually fully in tension, which can cause the two parts of the swivel to lock together when the sail rolls. Either (*d*) or (*e*) gives a pull slightly in shear, so that this problem is avoided.

Sheet lead

If the sheet lead is to remain constant as the sail is progressively rolled on its foil, it should be at right angles to the luff; the clew will always roll directly up this 90° line. A low-clewed genoa of conventional proportions will, however, have its sheet lead below this imaginary optimum line, so that its fairlead would need to be taken forward as the sail is rolled. If the clew were raised, as in Fig. 9.4 (*b*), the sheet lead would be better, but it would probably need to be taken aft, off the rear end of the fairlead track; the most common solution is to raise the clew and then to take it forward slightly in order to re-establish the lead from the same position as the standard genoa. This gives a sheet angle which is probably just below the 90° line, but not so much that it precludes leaving the fairlead unaltered during the furling process. The practical effect is that the average furling genoa will have an LP of somewhere around $1.4 \times J$ (140 per cent) instead of the 150 per cent of the normal No 1, and with a slightly high clew.

Luff length

The luff length of a furling genoa will be reduced by the amount of room taken up by the drum at the tack and the halyard swivel at the head. This is usually somewhere between 0.5–1.0 m (2–3 ft), depending on the furling system and, to a lesser extent, on the angle of the forestay at the masthead (which, if it is very acute, can restrict the final travel of the head swivel); see Fig. 9.5.

Area

Because both LP and luff length are reduced slightly, the area of a furling genoa is some 10 per cent less than that of a conventional IOR No 1 genoa for the same boat. Typical figures for a fractional rig boat of 7 m (23 ft) LOA are 16.5 m² and 18.5 m² (180 and 200 ft²) respectively; if you want to go bigger, you must be prepared to extend your jibsheet fairlead track further aft.

Halyard wrap

If the halyard pulls straight up from the head swivel when the sail is fully hoisted, friction between the two halves of the swivel can sometimes cause both parts to rotate together when the sail rolls; this wraps the halyard round the foil, to the attendant danger of them both. When the head swivel comes to within 10–15 cm (4–6 in) of the halyard exit box at the masthead, the pull will be angled enough aft to avoid this problem (as little as 10° is sufficient, because the top part of the swivel will be pulled against the lower part slightly in shear rather than entirely in tension; some gears include a small bullseye fairlead to fit a short way down the mast from the exit box,

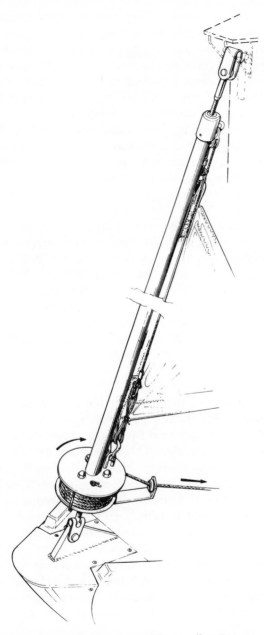

Fig. 9.5 *Rotostay Furling Gear*   The smallest Rotostay gear has no sliding head swivel, because the jib halyard comes down the luff of the sail next to the foil. The wire is cut to length so that it makes fast near the tack by means of a lashing, and the sail rolls round both the foil and the halyard fall. Toggles top and bottom are essential to absorb deflexions.

in order to achieve the same effect). The sail should thus have a luff which is within 15 cm (6 in) of the maximum length which the particular installation can accept, or else there should be an equalising pennant attached to the head of the sail in order to allow the swivel to travel its full distance up the foil; see Fig. 9.4 (d). Some furling gears fit a large diameter spacer wheel immediately above the swivel, to force the halyard out of line and achieve the same effect; Fig. 9.4 (e). Others have the halyard returning down the luff, inside or outside the foil, so that the sail rolls round it; the smallest Roto-stay® uses a wire halyard cut to exact length, with a rope tail which can be removed after hoisting, so that the wire can be lashed down to the drum neatly out of the way; see Fig. 9.5.

Sail draft
The extra cloth which forms the draft in a furling headsail can cause inefficient bags and wrinkles as it rolls. This can best be avoided by having shaped padding of some sort built into the sail immediately behind the luff (it need be no more than a second, fatter, bolt rope tapered at top and bottom); this enlarges the diameter of the roll along the middle half of the luff, so that more cloth is removed from the camber at each turn of the foil (the device must not be extended too near to the head and tack, or any UV strips will enlarge the roll again and cause exactly the opposite effect).

The furling gear
Having selected the make of furling gear that you want, check whether its drum will fit over the turnbuckle or rigging screw at the lower end of your forestay; if it won't (and many don't), you will need to discard the offending fitting. This will involve replacing the existing forestay with a longer one which is all wire, so check whether one is included in the furling package you are buying; it should, of course, be the same diameter as (or larger than) the one you are taking off. In some cases the replacement stay has a long shaft screw terminal, so that it is still possible to tension your forestay directly (the Rotostay is one), but in others there will be little or no adjustment, and you will henceforth be dependent on the backstay for a tight or slack forestay. This is no insuperable problem, but a correct length for the new stay, and a suitable tensioning device on the backstay, are essential if you are ever going to get to windward properly.

Ordering a Furling Headsail

The sailmaker needs to know certain details before a furling genoa can be made for a particular boat.

Dimensions
Luff, leech and foot lengths are obviously basic to the task. Even so-called standard boats vary quite widely – apart from variations such as short or tall rigs, some boats of the same class are masthead and some fractional, some just have their forestay set at a different height from all the others, some furling gears take up more room on the forestay than others (so that the sail luff must be slightly shorter), and some boats which are otherwise identical have their sheet leads in a different place to others. The luff length is critical so, if in doubt, hoist a tape measure on the genoa halyard and measure from head eye to tack eye (send up a light downhaul line with it, if you don't want to risk breaking your tape as you pull it down again); if you fit the gear yourself, measure the distance available when it is cut to length and laid out on the ground before installation.

Luff groove
Different gears use a luff groove of different size, usually somewhere between 3–8 mm diameter ($\frac{3}{8}$–1 in circ); this may sound small, but the load is shared over the full length of the luff. The sailmaker will hold details for most of the more common furling gears, so it should be enough to specify the make and model of gear; if in doubt, a sample strip of taped rope can be tested.

Sail specification
The sailmaker will advise on cloth weight which, as stated above, should be the same as the working jib (about 200 gm/m² for the average mini-cruiser) rather than the genoa. He will want to know whether to use standard cloth, with or without UV strips (and which side of the sail to place the strips, so that they are on the outside of the roll), or UV impregnated cloth; film laminate is still a non-starter because it is too hard, though great strides are being made to soften it so, some time in the near future, I may be proved wrong in this respect. Some sailmakers offer a de luxe version of the sail, complete with various trimmings such as camber stripes, clew trim line, tell-tales, luff flattener, and extra reinforcement patches in approximately the working jib position (to help absorb the stresses when the sail is part-rolled).

Converting an Existing Genoa

It is easy enough to convert an existing headsail to suit a furling gear. The luff rope or wire is removed complete with its hanks, and the appropriate smaller rope-in-tape is put on instead, open-ended at the head so as to feed into the foil. If the existing sail is a full sized genoa, the luff length may have to be shortened to fit into the available distance on the foil (we have seen that this is shorter than the full forestay length); the clew can be raised at this time to give a better lead as discussed above under *Sheet lead* (see Fig. 9.4 (*a*)).

The principal snag stems from the fact that most hanked No 1 genoas are made of a lighter cloth than the boat's working jib (probably 150 gm/m² in our particular case), so the result may blow out of shape when it is used part-furled in the higher wind strengths. If the old sail is in good heart, however, the saving is usually enough to make the conversion a sensible one – if nothing else, you will know exactly what you want in a season or two when the time comes to order a sail specially made.

Storm Jib

Use of a storm jib with a furling gear poses problems of its own. There are four options.

1. The furling genoa is considered adequate if enough of it is rolled away, provided the gear is utterly reliable.

2. A storm jib is made with a grooved luff to set on the foil. This means that, when the wind increases and the genoa is progressively reefed on the roller, there comes a time to switch to the storm jib. The part-rolled genoa must then be completely unrolled and lowered (in Force 7–8!), before the storm jib can be hoisted.

3. The storm jib is set flying (i.e. without being hanked to a stay or set on the foil) alongside or just aft of the rolled genoa. This will work all right off the wind, but is not aerodynamically efficient and will not take the boat to windward very well, just when it may be important to get off a lee shore.

4. The most seamanlike solution is to have a second stay on a strongpoint, which is either permanently established as an inner stay some way aft of the forestay (not very practical on small boats – think of the problems of chafe every time you tack), or else is movable. The inner stay should then normally be kept stowed up and down the mast, and can be set up on a special fitting when required; it will need some means of tensioning (Highfield lever or wheel). The furling genoa is then completely rolled, the inner stay set up, and the storm jib hanked to it in the usual way before being hoisted on its own halyard.

If the boat rarely goes outside estuarial waters, you can probably get away with rolling the genoa down to a tiny area, or perhaps having a storm jib which is set flying (options 1 or 3). But the furling gear may fail (Murphy's Law will see to it that it does this in your first gale), and any serious sailing offshore demands a separate storm jib which hanks to a stay (the IOR insists on a storm jib for their category 1 and 2 races[18]); the last option is the one to go for if you value your safety. You can always have the storm jib made so as either to run in a groove (in case you are ever tempted to set out from port in a gale, when the genoa can first be removed from the foil in comfort), or to hank to its own collapsible stay as well.

Jiffy Reefing

All this talk of storm jibs leads naturally to mainsail reefing. Those who feel that jiffy reefing involves too much modification to the boom to bother about, should look at Fig. 9.6. This shows how the same result can be achieved without resorting to bee-blocks and fairleads on the side of the boom; it can be incorporated in any existing mainsail with the minimum of fuss (or expense).

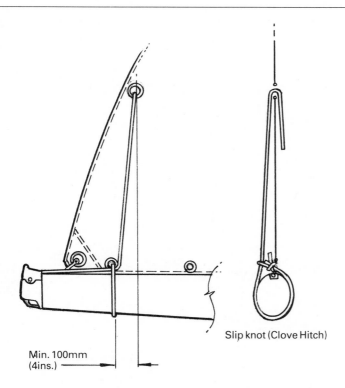

Slip knot (Clove Hitch)

Min. 100mm
(4ins.)

Fig. 9.6 *Jiffy Reefing – 1*   If your boom doesn't have bee blocks (fairleads) attached for jiffy reefing lines, the sail itself can be made to do the job. An eye or eyes worked into the foot tabling enable the reefing line to be tied round the boom, before being taken up through the reef cringle and back again under the round turn; it then either goes aft into the boom end or forward to be cleated near the gooseneck. (Based on a sketch by *Kemp Masts*.)

The Spinnaker

See Chapter 8 for a full discussion of the spinnaker; in this chapter I propose to limit my remarks to one or two points of special relevance to light displacement cruiser/racers as opposed to dinghies. Unlike the average dinghy, the former will have a spinnaker just large enough to profit from radial cutting. The loading is sufficient to cause distortion to a sail with horizontal panels in the head, so the stress-absorbing radial head cut gives a better setting sail for general use.

Tri-radial

If a racing owner already has a radial head spinnaker, he or she may consider the addition of a tri-radial sail for close reaching. As we saw in the previous chapter, this is a specialist sail which is time-absorbing to make and somewhat wasteful of cloth, so it is expensive, but there is no doubt that it keeps a flatter section and thus will let the boat point higher to advantage. If the competition is hot, and

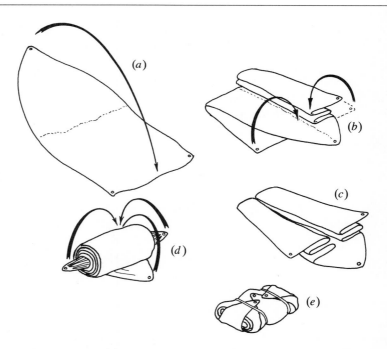

Fig. 9.7 *Spinnaker Fold-and-Hold*   If you lose your spinnaker launcher overboard, all is not lost. Folded in the manner shown, the sail can still enjoy a hassle-free hoist. Even if elastic bands are not available for the final parcel in (*e*), it can be held by one of the crew if conditions aren't too brisk (but don't spend too long on the foredeck, if you don't want to be passed by half the fleet).

you have the money, this will help keep you near the front in marginal spinnaker conditions (angle off) when once you have mastered the tricks of trimming it. In general terms, you should keep a fairly low pole and clew on the reach, in order to maintain some shape, and be prepared to hang on in the gusts (see Chapter 7 under *The Broach*).

Launching and Recovery

Slick or slack drill in setting and recovering a spinnaker, gains or loses as much ground in light displacement boats as it does in dinghies. The sail is just that much bigger, so it offers just that much more opportunity for foul-ups.

Spinnaker chute
As I have already suggested, this is the easiest way to hoist and dowse the sail.

Turtle
When Philip Benson invented the spinnaker turtle in the early 1950s[19], he did a great service to foredeck crews. If you don't have any special launching device, try the Soling fold-and-hold method shown in Fig. 9.7; this was first published in *Yachting World* (June 1978), and Guy Gurney admits that it is somewhat complicated, and best first packed ashore.

Spee squeezer
The principle of Chris Hall's similarly labour-saving invention was explained in Chapter 8. The spinnakers we are dealing with are really too small to warrant its use, but if you consistently make a hash of your spinnaker or cruising chute drill, or if you do a lot of single-handed sailing, try a squeezer and you will never look back.

10 DINGHY CRUISING

There is a lot of fun to be had from cruising in a dinghy, and there are some good books on how to do it. It is not my province to tell you to choose a boat with good floorboards if you want to keep dry, with a pivoting centreplate rather than an awkward dagger board if you want to minimise damage on grounding, or to try out the bottom for full-length lying before committing yourself to purchase (you'll be happier sleeping aboard, rather than in a tent ashore, after you have once had to drag the boat across two or three hundred yards of foreshore, on return to her at low water after your comfortable night in a tent ashore).

Boom tent
Having made sure that you can stretch out properly each side of the centreplate housing, and that you will stay dry even if there is an inch or two of water aboard, the next thing is to organise from your sailmaker (or your own hands if you have the skill) a good boom tent. First prop the boom to the horizontal by means of a rigid horse (the topping lift will allow too much swing and play); this can either be the traditional scissors-type crutch, or else a single stick with padded jaws in a socket. The latter is preferable because it stows more easily, cannot trap fingers (having no moving parts), and also collapses in use less readily than the scissors type.

You will need lashing points round the gunwale, and some care is needed in siting these, so that the tent can be erected easily from on board. The forward end should come right down to the deck, to provide full protection from head winds, and it is open to consideration whether to design it so that it may be rigged on its own in order to provide a spray shield when under sail (more easily achieved if there is a small foredeck). Flaps or doors at the aft end are not usually necessary, as the boat will often be windrode at anchor, so that the wind comes from ahead; if you are a cold person, perhaps opening flaps should nevertheless be included.

Battens across the boom can make a lot of difference to headroom and little difference to price or complication. Finally, some form of airvent is necessary if you are going to have the back closed off by flaps.

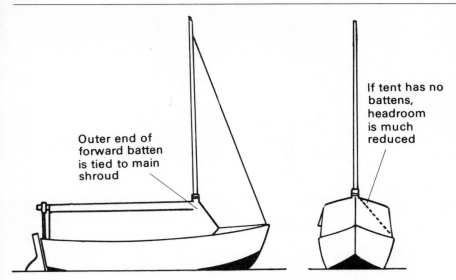

Outer end of
forward batten
is tied to main
shroud

If tent has no
battens,
headroom
is much
reduced

Fig. 10.1 *Boom Tent*   Battens built into the roof of the tent will greatly increase headroom; the outer ends of the forward batten should be tied to the main shrouds for support. There should be a collar to wrap securely round the mast.

Design of the Rig

One of the first points to be considered is heavy weather conditions. The need to avoid capsizing if at all possible is obvious (as is the need to be able to right the boat again, if the worst should happen). Given reasonable freeboard and beam, you will do more to prevent capsize by intelligent sailplan design than by incorporating wide side-decks. Once a dinghy is heeled to the point where water is coming over the gunwale, you are in trouble anyway; side-decks may postpone the evil moment, they won't prevent it – they will only reduce the usable space in the boat.

Mainsail reefing
Easy and efficient mainsail reefing is important; this virtually means points or lacing reefs, for you can hardly be expected to remove the boom from the gooseneck to roll the sail in a Force 5, and mechanical roller gears have a nasty habit of going wrong at the critical moment – not too worrying in a river, but uncomfortable if out of sight of land. The jiffy system used on keelboats may be incorporated with advantage on dinghies which go into open water regularly. The halyard is lowered so that the luff reef cringle can be engaged in a stout hook on the boom near the tack. The leech reef cringle is then

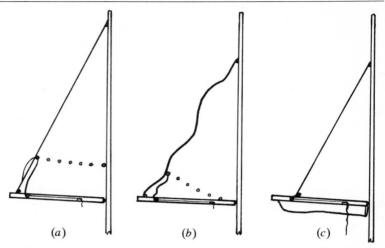

Fig. 10.2 *Jiffy Reefing – 2* The leech reefing line should be permanently rove (*a*). Lower the main halyard until the luff reef earring or cringle will fit over the hook on the boom near the gooseneck (*b*). Hold the boom level by hand and pull on the permanent leech reefing line to bring the leech reef earring down to the reef cleat or fairlead on the boom; it should also exert tension aft along the foot (*c*). The intermediate reef eyelets or points may then be secured if necessary.

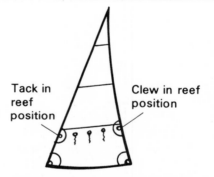

Fig. 10.3 *Jib Reef* It is not essential to have the reefed clew on a cloth or mitre seam, providing there is a stout patch to help take the strain.

pulled down by a line permanently rove from the boom, up through the cringle and back to a fairlead on the boom on the other side. The position of this fairlead should be such that it is about 2 in aft of the leech reef cringle when the latter is pulled down; this means that there is a good pull aft on the sail to keep the foot taut, as well as downwards. Individual reef points may then be tied down to tidy up the spare canvas, but they are by no means essential. The whole exercise takes no longer to perform than it does to read this description.

Jib reefing

Dinghies being what they are, there will probably be no room for a special heavy weather headsail, so have a reef fitted to your jib. The reef position tack eye goes on the tack fitting and the sheet is made fast to a new clew eye some way up the leech, due regard being paid to sheeting angle. A jib roller is strong enough these days to act as a reefing gear, and it makes stowing easy; sails are weakened by long exposure to the elements, so don't leave the jib rolled while on the moorings, unless fitted with UV strips.

Clew height

The mainsail should not be cut so that the boom lies unduly low. Apart from being a danger to unwary heads in a seaway, and reducing visibility to leeward, the boom may tend to drag in the water on a brisk reach if it rides too low. The same generalisation holds good for the jib which, if low in the clew, restricts the view forward and is also liable to pick up water in a chop and throw it into the boat. If you are having reefs put into the sails, it is an easy and relatively cheap modification to have them cut higher in the clew at the same time (Fig. 10.4).

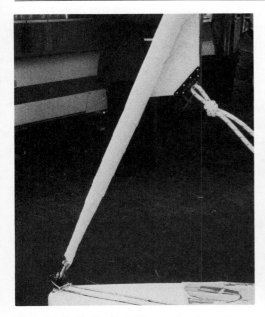

Plate 10.1 *Jib Furling Gear – 1*   A very neat and unobtrusive system on a *Tasar* at Southampton Boat Show. (*Author*)

Plate 10.2 *Jib Furling Gear – 2*   A Barton roller gear fitted to a Hawk *Surfcat*. The drum is clipped to a wire span between the hulls. (*Author*)

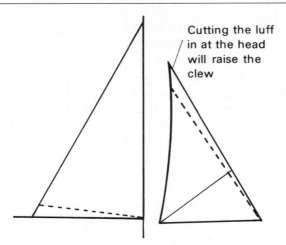

Cutting the luff
in at the head
will raise the
clew

Fig. 10.4 *Raising the Clew*   A mainsail may be cut up at the foot without endangering the set of the sail. It is best to cut a jib in along the luff at the head; this leaves the foot and leech undisturbed (thus avoiding excess cloth bias which would cause flutter), and also leaves the clew on the mitre seam.

Luff slides

An unfortunate fault is for the mainsail not to come smoothly down when it is lowered in an emergency. If the luff is fitted with sail slides, make sure that they run easily. External claw type slides should have a light coating of vaseline or similar grease which will not mark the sails too badly, and the width of the jaws should be checked for correct size; make sure that the mast track is smooth and even, with no protruding screw heads. Internal slides should preferably be made of nylon, which needs no lubrication; if they are metal, greasing will unfortunately be necessary. If you have a mainsail which runs in a groove in the mast, you should seriously consider the unseamanlike nature of this arrangement for offshore work. When the sail is lowered it has to come off the mast, with the attendant risk of being blown out of control all over the boat. Fit slug slides, which are designed to run in a mast groove and will enable you to keep the sail under control when it is partly lowered to reef or, indeed, fully down for any reason.

The careful owner will fit a downhaul on his jib, from the head to a pulley near the tack and then aft to a point near the halyard (also sited well within the boat for ease of access). A reluctant sail can then be pulled down (and held down) despite all that the wind can do to hold it aloft while it slats heavily from side to side.

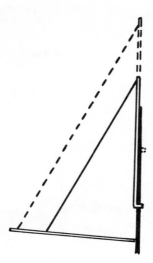

Fig. 10.5 *Gunter Rig*   The gunter comes down with the reef, thus lowering the centre of gravity with the centre of effort.

Gunter rig

If you are buying a dinghy with the specific intention of cruising long distances, you should consider the advantages of the gunter and standing lug rigs. Reefing the mainsail also 'reefs' the mast, as the yard comes down with the sail, thus lowering the centre of gravity and windage to advantage. A further useful spin-off is that the spars are usually designed so that they all fit within the boat, thus making stowage and trailing easier.

Leech roach

Don't forget what I said in Chapter 4 about doing away with roach (and thus with battens) and headboard. This applies with particular force on any dinghy which will spend a good deal of time in open water. The problems connected with battens which break and then force their splintered ends through the sail are not worth putting up with just for the sake of a few extra square feet of sail area; the same holds good to a lesser extent regarding the headboard. The whole argument is reinforced a hundredfold if the boat already carries too much weather helm; reduction in mainsail area by removal of the roach may completely cure the problem – and incidentally possibly make the boat faster at the same time, due to the removal of the braking effect of the rudder which no longer has to be held over to keep her straight.

Plate 10.3 *The Lugsail*   This is the standard lugsail as fitted to the West Wight Scow, and has the same area as the crab claw sail shown in Plate 1.4. The picture shows my great-aunt, Miss Ida Gibson, winning a single-handed race at Newtown, Isle of Wight, on her 80th birthday (the amiable connivance of her competitors was, I may say, by no means necessary). (*Author*)

Light weather

If you don't have room for a special heavy weather or storm jib, you certainly can't find space to stow any light weather sails. Most dinghies carry more than enough canvas for light winds, and will sail well in the gentlest of breezes. Don't bother with special sails for light weather.

Down wind

A spinnaker is not a seamanlike sail for a cruising dinghy, and you will be better off without the hassle, gear, problems, and expense of such a sail. If you must have one (or, more likely, the boat already has one and you don't want to see it go unused), see that it is cut very flat in the head. This will make it easier to set, work better on a reach and make it less likely to knock the boat down. You could also have the foot cut slightly hollow with advantage; besides reducing area to cater for strong winds, it will also improve forward visibility. If you think you are going to do a lot of downwind sailing (in which case you have probably never heard of Sod's Law which says 'the wind is always on the nose for all cruising'), then just possibly you might invest in a large lightweight jib and a whisker pole to boom it out, so that you may goosewing into the setting sun... This will also be usable to windward as a light weather jib, so now we have managed to find room for one after all. There are those who advocate that such a sail is best made without hanks, on the grounds of simplicity. I would not go against this advice, and would be prepared to accept the slightly reduced efficiency in exchange for ease of setting and taking down. Indeed, the lack of hanks would be an incentive to take in the sail as the wind increased when using it beating and close reaching; its efficiency would be so poor that it would *have* to come in, which is what should happen to a light weather sail in Force 3, but which all too often does not, to the permanent ruination of the lightweight canvas.

11 SAILBOARDS

Sail Development

The invention of the sailboard marks a milestone in sailing comparable with the introduction of synthetic sailcloth or the switch to fibreglass hulls. All three developments have in common the fact that they have not invalidated any basic principles, but they have opened the path to some radical changes. A sailing vessel still moves through the water for the same reasons, whether she is made of fibreglass or wood (or steel, or concrete); her sails still provide power according to the same laws of physics, regardless of the material they are made of (cotton, polyester, film laminate or, indeed, coconut matting); books on aerodynamics and hydrodynamics have not been outdated overnight. A sailboard therefore responds normally to the forces of lift and drag, despite the fact that its mast is movable in relation to the hull – in terms of aerodynamics, this merely means that the Centre of Effort can be moved about at will, causing the craft to turn into or away from the wind, as we saw in Chapter 6.

But as with many inventions, once established, sailboards and their sails have evolved rapidly. Initially, development was slow, as board sailors experimented with new ideas and techniques. Recent years, however, have been characterised by more rapid change, as expansion took place and fresh minds were spurred on by the impetus of competition, particular attention being paid to the sailplan.

Sail Area ·

Different sailmakers seem to follow their own methods of working out sail area. The Association of British Sailmakers has proposed a standard formula but, as most board sails in the world are made abroad, the Association is a lone voice crying in the wilderness. Discrepancies are unlikely to be due to ignorance, so where a sail is patently over or under the area claimed, I can only suggest that it is due to a desire to get it into a particular category. A true area can only be established by breaking up any roach into its component triangles or rectangles, and adding them to the area of the basic triangle; see

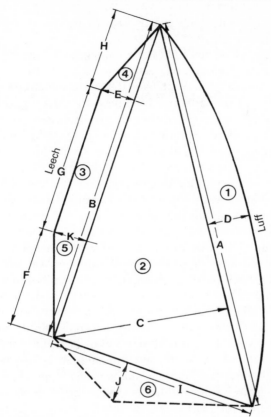

Fig. 11.1 *Board Sail Area*   Accurate area calculation of any fully battened sail has to take account of the various roaches involved. The Association of British Sailmakers is considering board sails, and the above proposal is one way of solving it. The various sub-areas would be calculated as follows:

$$\text{Sub-area } 1 = A \times \frac{2D}{3} \qquad\qquad 4 = H \times \frac{E}{2}$$

$$2 = A \times \frac{C}{2} \qquad\qquad 5 = F \times \frac{K}{2}$$

$$3 = G \times \frac{E+K}{2} \qquad\qquad 6 = I \times \frac{J}{2} \text{ (if applicable)}$$

It is difficult to draw up hard and fast rules to cover all shapes and sizes; full length battens may number more than two above the boom and one below. Depending on the degree of accuracy required, the solution will probably lie in one of two methods:

(*a*) Breakdown of roaches into component sub-areas, with mathematical calculation of each triangle and rectangle.

(*b*) Use of the two-thirds rule to assess a complete roach as one sub-area (length × ⅔rd width).

Fig. 11.1. Nevertheless, the average owner can reach a near approximation by assessing each roach through the two-thirds rule ($\frac{2}{3}\times$ width$\times$length).

The sailboard started life (as the Windsurfer®) in the form of a surfboard some 3.65 m long, using a sail area of just over 5 m²; the sail sometimes had short battens in the leech, sometimes none at all. The beginner in the sport has little need for anything other than a fairly conservative fun sail without roach or battens, of around 5.0 m², using a standard mast of 4.5–4.7 m long and a boom as short as the particular sail will allow. A short boom, to suit a short luff perpendicular, comes completely out of the water more easily than a long one as the mast is pulled upright when starting, thus avoiding the problem of the wind catching the sail and pivoting the whole rig about the clew stuck in the water. As soon as the basic skills are mastered, however, a more advanced sail will enable the competent learner to enjoy a much wider range of wind and wave conditions. The general purpose rig of the first Windsurfer was thus soon not enough to cater for the ever-widening scope of sailboard use. As with any other sailing vessel, in general terms a high aspect ratio (AR) sail goes best to windward, while a low AR is better down wind. The sailboard was further soon characterised by its ability to negotiate very steep seas – indeed, this kind of sailing is exhilarating and soon became a *forte* of the craft. But the sailplan is so low that the reduction of wind speed in the troughs has an appreciable effect on board speed; this has meant that emphasis has been placed on more area high in the sailplan (the very sharp wind gradient under the

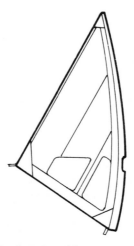

Fig. 11.2 *Fun Sail*   This beginner's sail has a 4.5 m luff and a 2.2 m boom. It has no roach and no battens, so can be economically cut with vertical cloths.

Fig. 11.3 *Advanced Fun Sail* A slightly more advanced sail may turn out easier to handle than the rather wide-clewed beginner's sail in Fig. 11.2. Certainly full length battens and 6 m² will give better power for the average weight sailor (11 stone, or 70 kg) in Force 2–3. I have shown this with a vertical cut radiating from the head, but this is by no means the only way to make it. Basic dimensions 4.8×1.8 m.

specific conditions puts a premium on even a relatively small increase in area aloft). Early attempts to overcome the problem resulted in the so-called fathead sails, with full-length battens in the head to extend the roach in the upper part of the sail; nowadays virtually all sails have this feature to some degree or other. Sails intended for the shorter boards used for wave riding or surfing now have a taller mast of 4.8 m; the chord of these more specialist sails is kept relatively narrow, giving a high aspect ratio, because total area must be restricted to what the average sailor can balance (it is no good having a nice lot of area aloft in order to make good progress in the troughs, if you are overwhelmed as soon as you reach the crest). Given a reasonably competent sailor, total area is dependent on crew weight and conditions, which include board type (wetted area, use of skeg, etc.), CE height, wind speed and sea state, and it usually varies somewhere between 3.0 m² for the smallest storm sails, to as much as 8–9 m² for a 13 stone (80 kg) sailor when fun sailing in light weather; the maximum area for racing under International Board Sailing rules is 6.3 m². An average intermediate sailor will need about 6.0 m² for medium air sailing, and a smaller sail of some 5.0 m² for higher wind speeds (Force 6) – the so-called marginal sail.

The low aspect ratio sail is reserved for steadier conditions, where

Plate 11.1 *Advanced Fun Sail*   This boardsail compares with Fig. 11.3. The owner may think that the sail is made mostly of woven polyester; in fact, the area of reinforcing film in the head and leech, plus the window, is probably larger than the rest of the sail. At all events, the boom is too long, and will be both unwieldy and inefficient. (*Author*)

there is plenty of wind low down to give drive. Low AR means that better control can be maintained, so the sail is best suited for beginners and possibly slalom work. The high AR sail comes into its own not only in steep seas and brisk winds, as already indicated, but also in very light inland conditions where there is a natural wind gradient unaffected by the wave conditions. Over 90 per cent of all board sails have a fairly high AR. The heavier sailors can hold up a bigger area as the wind gets up – and so can the more skilful. Start conservatively (around 5.0 m²) and work up as you improve.

Mast

Most masts are made of fibreglass, and this is certainly what your first board will have; the top will be tapered, and about the only factor which will be variable will be the stiffness ratio. Like sail area

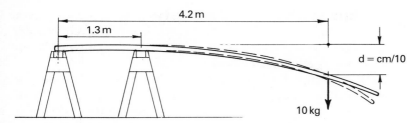

Fig. 11.4 *Mast Stiffness Ratio* I am indebted to Jeremy Evans, Editor of *Boards®* magazine, for the technical details of the German standard test for mast stiffness ratio. It is found by subtracting distance 'd' (in decimetres) from 10, e.g. if the statutory 10 kg weight moves the attachment point through 37 cm, 10−3.7=stiffness ratio 6.3. The illustration shows how it is possible for two masts with different flexibility to have the same figure (don't ask me why the stiffness ratio figure isn't given as 37 or 3.7).

figures, however, this ratio won't tell you much. This is because it relates to the distance which a given force will cause the masthead to move when applied with the mast fixed horizontally. Figure 11.4 shows how two mastheads of different spars will move differently under this test, yet they have the same stiffness ratio because the test datum point moves through the same distance. At best the figure gives a vague idea of a mast's flexibility; at worst, it can be downright misleading.

Fibreglass
Polyester resin reinforcement is too weak to stand up to the flexing loads and general rough treatment of board sailing, so most manufacturers use epoxy reinforcement, which withstands the rough and tumble of wave sailing and learning well.

Aluminium
Light alloy gives good rigidity, so that the mast does not bend too much and open the leech excessively. The material does, however, have a tendency to accept a permanent bend after use in a strong wind. This may take some of the fullness out of the luff, but it makes the leech difficult to control in heavy weather, when it is not always easy to keep a downward pressure on the clew because the sailor is leaning so far to windward. Aluminium masts are used at competitive level by some sailors, who often have a special mast to go with a particular sail.

Boom

You might be tempted to think that a boom is a boom, is a boom, is a boom. Apart from some historical interest, when early attempts were made to get round Hoyle Schweitzer's patents by altering boom shape (trapezoidal instead of curved wishbone – which may have been OK on the water, but was a flop in the courtroom), there are one or two remarks which can be made about booms. To start with, of course, the two arms of the wishbone should have the correct amount of separation, with maximum depth at the right place (about one-third aft), to accept the camber of the sail (we shall see later that some sails have considerably more draft than others, and thus need a wide profile boom); the grip should be comfortable and the whole boom stiff yet light. Secondly, the length of boom is of paramount importance. It should be long enough to allow the clew to be tensioned correctly, but not so long that a length of line is needed between the clew and the boom end (this would allow the clew to move from side to side too much). Sails vary in their luff perpendicular more than their luff length, so that different booms are needed for different sails using the same mast. This is achieved by having adjustable booms, it being more rigid and lighter (but more expensive) to have several end sections of different lengths which can be clipped to the main wishbone, than to have a more convenient telescopic wishbone; the latter may be cheaper, but it is also heavier.

Thus a high AR sail with reduced area will have a short boom (say, 1.5 m), while a fun sail – or even a slalom – will be up to 2.3 m. The greater the mean chord, the further aft will be the clew (and the longer must be the wishbone). Apart from being unwieldy, this means that the CE will be well aft on the board, and makes handling more difficult on short boards (say, less than 3.0 m LOA). Finally, booms should not be too flexible or they will bend in the gusts, thus easing the clew forward and increasing sail flow, just when you need to keep it flat.

The height at which the boom is carried is a matter of preference. Factors affecting this decision are convenience of use, which in turn will vary with height of the sailor and the method of sailing adopted. Before harnesses were introduced, booms were usually carried at about eye level; this meant that the clew was high enough for downward tension to be applied to the leech when required (to eliminate twist to windward, or to tighten the leech if excessive mast bend slackened it too much). Early harnesses were round the chest, and this suited the high boom technique; more recently, however, seat harnesses have been adopted, and booms have tended to be lower. A low wishbone also confers the benefit of a lower CE; some medics say that the lower harness is better for spinal posture. Fashion

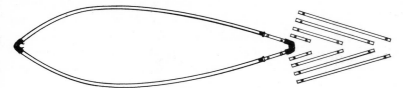

Fig. 11.5 *Adjustable Boom*   A boom may adjust either by means of extension pieces or else through being telescopic. The Shokwave extension boom illustrated above is made of heavy duty aluminium, and its anti-sand device guarantees freedom from jamming when the boom is used properly. There are two basic types, as follows.

	Total Length	
Extension Piece	Wave Type	Slalom Type
15 cm	130 cm	150 cm
35 cm	150 cm	170 cm
55 cm	170 cm	190 cm
65 cm	180 cm	200 cm

The firm also produces a range of booms with multi-extensions (30 cm, 50 cm and 80 cm), which have further micro-telescopic adjustment in 5 cm stages up to 35 cm; this enables them to offer various adjustable booms from 135 cm (shortest wave type) up to 250 cm (longest race type).

has a fairly large say in the matter, so that what is right this year may be old hat next.

Beginners like the low setting largely because it is less tiring. If the truth be told, skilled boardsailors can be found who swear by booms at each and every height. The tyro should not let himself be talked into allowing it to be too low, however, or he will never learn to hang out to windward properly.

Flow

Boardsailing is a young branch of sailing, uninhibited by years of tradition and conservative rules. Enthusiasts have been quick to exploit this freedom, so the various sailboard classes are not so restricted in development as their more senior conventional sisters. So-called exotic sailcloths, sleeved luffs, full-length battens, camber inducers and asymmetrical sails have all been accepted with gusto by the aficionados. We shall examine the pros and cons of these later, when we come to consider various classifications of board sails.

My remarks in the chapter on Theory at the start of this book hold good for sailboards, just as much as for any other kind of sailing boat – even more so in some cases, because lack of displacement means that the board is planing nearly all the time, and there is a low tolerance to incorrect positioning of the CE under these conditions.

So it pays to have an evenly cambered sail, with its powerpoint about 35–40 per cent aft if you race (for windward work), and which is not restricted in developing its camber by the wrong battens or by a mast which bends too much or too little; time spent matching battens to sail will not be wasted. See also Fig. 11.6 below for comments on stability.

Sailcloth

The conflict, as ever with sails, is between durability and boat speed. A sail used only for fun doesn't need the expensive (and sometimes short-lived) materials which are so important if speed is the only object; the fun sail should be able to stand up to the wearing effects of casual use (being left on a sandy beach; being rolled on its mast and carried on a roof rack without being first put into a sausage bag; being stored through the winter in a garden shed – all regular practices of the unthinking owner).

Most board sails are made of all-woven polyester cloth, perhaps with film laminate reinforcement patches; not only is this cheaper, it wears well and any one sail can be set on a wide range of masts. Racing sails get better attention from careful owners, and expensive materials such as Mylar or Melinex, with or without Kevlar reinforcement, are preferred for the extra speed they offer – these may have woven patches for the extra protection they confer. Mylar is less forgiving than Dacron or Terylene in nature, and the luff needs to be set precisely in the same way each outing (unlike the all-woven sail, which will offer a choice of shape through extra tension on the downhaul to draw flow forward in strong winds); the *amount* of camber (rather than its *position*) can be altered in both laminated and all-woven sails, by clew tension – a harder pull gives a flatter sail for heavy weather or windward work; less tension gives a fuller sail for reaching or light weather. *Position* of the powerpoint can be altered by different flexibility of full-length battens (see below).

Handling

It is no good having a fast sail, beautifully made, if it is awkward to handle. The sail should duck-gybe easily, without being difficult to get past. It should be easy to water-start the rig (water should either not penetrate the luff sleeve too readily, or else it should drain out quickly). Batten ends should not catch in foot straps, and they should not snag the sailor when he or she is balanced over the centre of the board (in light weather); battens should also change camber at will. Rotational sails should do just that – easily (it is not practical to buy a sail on sale or return in order that this can be checked on the water, so try to find a friend with a sail like the one you want, and try that one first).

Boardsailors need to remember that in anything above Force 4, the wind can gust sharply. Too little or too much power will have a more dramatic effect on a sailboard than it will on a dinghy, because human reactions are too slow under these conditions to alter the sail's angle of incidence to accommodate a new wind angle; in any case, the sailor's balance depends on keeping the sail full of wind, so there can be no question of spilling too much of it.

Soft sails

Soft sails (those with short battens or none at all) lift at the luff when the wind's angle of incidence gets too low; this upsets the airflow on both sides of the aerofoil and thus depowers the rig. A gust of wind, however, usually frees a boat, and this will cause the flow in an all-woven soft sail to move aft and create greater heeling effect. In general terms, therefore, a soft sail lacks stability in gusty weather because it depowers in headers and won't carry through the lulls, or else distorts under load if it is all-woven. Nevertheless, this very ability to depower is useful when sudden changes in direction are required in brisk weather, such as for wave sailing or slalom work. In light winds, the soft sail's lighter weight means enhanced control.

Hard sails

Full-length battens maintain a sail's aerofoil section more or less regardless of the action of the wind. The depth of camber can be controlled by varying tension on the battens, so that a so-called hard sail can be set up to suit prevailing conditions. Because the luff does not lift, airflow remains attached to the lee side of a hard sail down to a finer angle of incidence, so that more power is generated over a wider wind range. Greater stability and high efficiency make the hard sail useful not only for general purpose, but also in strong winds (better lift for jumping and less backwinding in flight, more stable in gusts, continued power during heading lulls). The extended leech of a fully battened sail, plus the curved upper luff created by a bending mast, produces the highly efficient elliptical planform mentioned at the end of Chapter 1. Full-length battens do, however, cost more than short ones, so efficiency has to be assessed against cost.

Camber

The depth and position of camber in a sail govern its characteristics to a large extent. On a conventional boat, flat sails with forward flow (powerpoint 30–35 per cent back) are needed for heavy winds, and full ones with central flow (40–45 per cent) for medium conditions. But we have just seen that a sailboard can't control its sail's angle of incidence as quickly as if it had a sheet; nor does it want either to depower through letting a large part of its sail spill wind from the luff, or to make too large an angle with the wind so that airflow separation occurs. On a reach, the camber itself must enable the sail to accept a freeing gust without stalling, thereby maintaining thrust (and support for the sailor). In general terms, best stability is offered by fully battened sails (which hold the shape of the luff in a sudden header) with camber well forward (to accept any sudden increase in the angle of incidence); see Fig. 11.6 (*a*). Windward work requires a small angle of incidence, catered for by the fine entry shown in Fig. 11.6 (*b*); if you are a racing owner for whom windward ability is paramount – to the detriment of some stability – this means having the powerpoint around the 40 per cent chord position.

Plate 11.2 *Fully Battened Boardsail*   An all-woven boardsail of simple construction. The lowest batten doesn't confer much extra area, so might, with advantage, be done away with (and the foot slightly hollowed). (*Alpha Sails*)

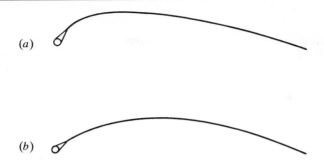

(a)

(b)

Fig. 11.6 *Camber* A powerpoint at 25 per cent chord position (*a*) allows the sail to absorb freeing gusts, so that flow separation does not occur under the sudden wider angle of incidence. The finer entry of (*b*)'s 45 per cent powerpoint will be less stable than (*a*), but it will be more efficient when close-hauled; as such it will be a better racing sail but will require more skill.

Accessories

Window

The point to remember about a window (apart from the prime importance of being able to see through it comfortably while sailing), is that the material cannot be shaped. If it is too big, therefore, it could be the cause of a flat spot in the sail; this is why a window is often split between two or more panels. Modern transparent materials are softer than earlier products, so things are better than they used to be in this respect.

Sailbag

A bag long enough to contain mast, sail and battens is both convenient and good for the sail; it offers protection from dirt and chafe when the rig is being stored or transported. Make sure you keep the inside clean, even if the outside gets a bit tatty.

Battens

Almost all board sails have battens to extend the leech these days, many of them being full length. Some storm sails have a straight or hollow leech, so they don't need the inconvenience of battens; some fun sails (usually those for beginners) avoid them for the same reason, and for economy as well. But the expert usually has them, because they not only help put area where it is wanted, they are useful in controlling flow – and thus power. You can up-grade a sail by using battens with different characteristics from your usual set: more flexibility forward will put flow forward in the sail and make it better in brisk winds; a central bend will give central flow with a fine entry for light airs to windward. It saves time (and mistakes) when rigging if you have marked your battens permanently with a felt tip marker, not only to designate those meant for light or heavy weather, but also which end goes in first.

There are three main kinds of batten – all of them based wholly or partly on fibreglass.

   (a) Extruded
   (b) Foam-filled sandwich
   (c) Heat laminated

Plate 11.3 *Batten Angle* Experiments are continuous in most lofts. Here Alpha Sails of Southampton are checking the effect of aligning all but the top batten with the airflow rather than with the seams. (*Alpha Sails*)

Extruded

Extruded by machine in a uniform thickness and section from resin-impregnated fibreglass, this kind of batten is relatively cheap and reasonably light and durable. Because it is not tapered, it bends in the middle of its length. This is all right for short battens located at the leech only, but full-length battens need to have maximum curve between 30 and 45 per cent from the front end (depending on the flow required), so they should be more flexible one end than the other. If any attempt is made to taper the width or to sand down the thickness, an extruded batten becomes weak and liable to fracture. The fibres are usually uni-directional, so that splintering occurs under these conditions. If you follow the advice I have been giving since my first book *Sails* came out in the days of hickory battens in cotton sails, you will tape them along their length – not so much for reinforcement, but so as to be able to pull out the several pieces of any breakage in one.

Foam-filled sandwich

A high density closed-cell foam is sandwiched between two layers of fibreglass laminate, to form a relatively light batten. By tapering the foam, the batten is made more flexible at its inner end. You thus get a light batten with a pre-determined area of bend, so it is popular with racing enthusiasts, especially in light conditions, because it is often more flexible than other types. The result, however, is rather bulky (it won't go easily into all sail pockets), and it is sometimes prone to delamination. Tape them as you would an extruded batten, and be prepared to buy new ones at fairly regular intervals – particularly if you race on salt water, which they don't like. This kind of batten is not common, probably because the faults tend to outweigh the plus points, so expect to have difficulty in finding them at your regular dealer.

Heat laminated

The heat laminated batten is made by building up layers of dry fibreglass sandwiched in sheet film, which is then heat pressed and from which the battens are cut in strips. The thickness of fibreglass in any sheet can be varied at one end, so that battens can be tailor-made as to taper or thickness, with resulting control in flexibility. The end product is pricey, but it is the one which the serious racer should select. The extra expense will be repaid over the seasons by extra durability, and you can have battens with different bend characteristics for different wind strengths, as discussed at the start of this section.

Types of Board Sail

With development taking place so rapidly, it is not possible in a book to stay abreast of changes – fashions and techniques will arise and die away between galley proofs and the bound copies appearing in the bookshops. All I can do is to point to some trends, and advise you to follow your favourite magazine for up-to-date articles. Or else do as I did – find a helpful sailmaker who knows his stuff, and seek advice from the loft (in my case, this was Ian Henry of Alpha Sails at Southampton, who should nevertheless not be saddled with any opinions I express).

The two broad categories of board sails (soft and hard) each respond to certain requirements, and we shall look at some of these below. There are many other applications with which I shall not deal, largely because they are so specialist that they cater for a small market, but also because they often tend to be ephemeral, disappearing without trace when some newer fashion appears (and make no mistake about it, fashion plays its part in this market just as it does in others).

Soft Sails

We have already seen that the very first board sails were soft sails, which evolved for recreational purposes – what are now called fun sails. It is a general purpose sail of conservative nature, which is aimed at what its name implies.

Beginner's sail

Most beginners start with a fun sail of about 5.0–5.5 m² (Fig. 11.2), made for a fibreglass mast of 4.5–4.7 m and with no fewer and shorter battens than the sail they will progress to later; this is for reasons of economy as much as anything else, in order to keep what might be called the 'starter pack' as cheap as possible. For the same reason, the sail will be made of all-woven polyester (Terylene or Dacron), not the more costly film laminate. It is often made for a boom of over 2 m, which can make for awkward handling. This is not only because 2 m is a bit long for ease of manoeuvre, but also because it tends to leave its clew trailing in the water as the sail is being hauled up, so that the wind fills the rest of it too soon and the whole rig proceeds to pivot on the clew still in the water.

Storm sail

For these reasons, the first move is often to go to the more convenient size of 4.2 m², using the same mast; see Fig. 11.7. This is variously known as a storm sail or a school sail, and it has no battens – indeed,

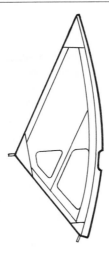

Fig. 11.7 *Storm or School Sail* A much reduced area of 4 m² will cater for 7 or 8 stone (45–50 kg) beginners. This one has the advantage of a short boom for ease of manoeuvre. As skill improves, so can wind strengths be greater, until the competent sailor can cope with Force 6 – even Force 8 if he is over 14 stone (90 kg)! Basic dimensions 4.65×1.8 m.

Plate 11.4 *Storm Sail* This storm sail is horizontally cut with a straight leech and no battens; as such, it approaches Fig. 11.7. The boom is long, so will allow the clew to move about too much; it will also be unnecessarily awkward to handle. In a race, the board could be protested against for not having the numbers on the starboard side of her sail uppermost (IYRU rule 25). (*David Eberlin*)

the leech is often hollow – and the boom is brought well below 2 m (1.8 m is typical), which is much more manageable. A storm sail is essential for every boardsailor who aspires to better things than simply messing about up to Force 4, so such a school sail will come in useful later. The CE and powerpoint should both be well forward (to help stability in high winds) and relatively low down (to reduce the sideways or capsizing moment); the clew should be high for simpler tacking.

Cloth

The fact that cloth such as Dacron or Terylene is cheaper than film laminate (Mylar or Melinex) is a plus point which the all-woven sail has going for it; there is also superiority in wear qualities – not an insignificant factor in a sail which receives casual treatment. It is, however, somewhat of a paradox that a beginner's sail can be *harder* to control in some circumstances than a high-tech product of more advanced design. This is because all-woven cloth allows the flow to move under load (see Chapter 2, Fig. 2.5), so that the powerpoint moves aft in the gusts; a soft sail will also depower through lifting at the luff as we saw earlier in this chapter. So the next step is often towards a shape which stays constant unless sail tension is changed; this usually means film laminate cloth and/or full length battens.

Hard Sails

A soft sail, whether made of all-woven or film laminate cloth, will shiver and collapse up the luff as the rig is pointed too high into the wind. Use of full length battens delays this lifting, and gives the sail the more efficient elliptical planform, and more power at finer angles of incidence. A sailboard is planing nearly all the time, so it is fast; this reduces the angle of incidence of any wind which is forward of the beam, so that anything which improves the airflow at fine angles must be beneficial. These days most board sails are fully battened.

Fathead

The movement started in the early days with so-called fathead sails. These were the result of wanting more area aloft for a given mast and boom, so that a large roach was added at the head, which was held out by full length battens.

Fully battened sails

The logical progression from the fathead is a sail with roach all the way from the clew upwards; the whole of the area above the boom is braced by battens running the full length from luff to leech; Fig. 11.8. All kinds of sail are given this treatment, from storm sails of just over

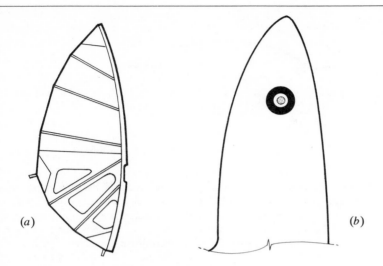

(a)   (b)

Fig. 11.8 *Fully Battened Sail*   An average weight sailor of some 11 stone (70 kg) needs a minimum of 6 m² for Force 2–3. As skill improves, so can greater power be controlled, and this fully battened sail will provide it. It has a radial head, with panels arranged to suit the battens below the boom. Basic dimensions 4.8×1.8 m. The near-ellipse of this board sail (*a*) is much more aerodynamically efficient than the bermudan's triangular planform. The latter promotes trailing vortex drag, and high loading at the head causes local breakdown of the airflow. Compare the Spitfire fighter's excellent wing shape at (*b*), and try to think of any triangular wing with sharp taper ratio in nature (which usually gets it right).

4 m², through wave jumpers and fun sails of 5.0–5.5 m², to racing sails of 6.3 m² (unless the rules don't allow it). Apart from holding their shape in strong winds, these sails can have their depth of camber altered by the tension put on the battens; to a certain extent, the position of the powerpoint can be moved forward or aft by altering the taper of the battens. An extension to this is to make the area below the boom fully battened also, which tends to make handling a bit difficult as it restricts room to duck under the sail; it is important that the leech end of such battens should not stick too far out of the sail or they will catch in toe-straps or clothing – if they do, cut them off to length with a small saw.

Rotating asymmetrical foil
Abbreviated to RAF, this sail-form had a tremendous vogue as soon as it was introduced by Neil Pryde; its principle is shown in Fig. 11.9. There is no doubt that it is not the single answer to all sail problems, but there is equally no doubt that it is aerodynamically efficient. It is

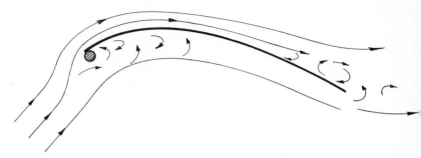

Fig. 11.9 *Rotating Asymmetrical Foil*   The RAF sail has full-length battens which automatically switch to the aerodynamically efficient position to leeward of the mast each time the sail tacks. This maintains the all-important attached flow to leeward, where most thrust is generated. This is not a sail for the beginner but, once it is mastered, it gives great thrust, even if tacking and gybing are subject to surging as the power switches on quickly on the new tack.

Fig. 11.10 *Asymmetric*   By locking the battens to one side of the mast, the more powerful configuration of Fig. 11.9 can be used, say, for working out through waves. When the board is tacked for the ride home, the battens take up the inefficient windward position shown in this figure. Airflow to leeward is poor, with resulting loss of thrust, such as might be required when too much power would be detrimental to control (accelerating down a wave face).

usually fairly full forward, both above and below the boom (which thus needs a wider profile than usual). It has full-length battens, which switch from side to side of the mast automatically, so that they are always to leeward after the sail tacks; it is important to get the battens right for a particular sail, or else they may ease to the centreline of the mast rather than take up a leeward position. A development of the RAF is the asymmetrical sail, where the full length battens are pre-locked to a selected side of the mast; Fig. 11.10. This is so that full power is available for working out through big waves (battens to leeward) but, for the downwind surf back again when too much speed becomes an embarrassment, the battens are on the aerodynamically less efficient position to windward of the mast. This takes power out of the rig and keeps everything controllable (the sail can't be feathered, because it must be kept full in order to balance the sailor).

Camber inducer

One of the snags of all the fully battened sails we have discussed so far, is that the battens are held in sail pockets, and the pressure which is exerted on them lengthways is totally absorbed by the pocket ends at the luff and leech. The camber inducer is a plastic A-frame which fits on the inner end of the batten, and straddles the mast, thus transferring the loading directly to the aft face of the mast; Fig. 11.11. This is much more positive, and gives better control of sail shape. A logical development is to have the batten split at the inner end, so that the same function is achieved.

Double luff sail

The standard luff sleeve which goes over the mast is about 6 in (15 cm) from front to rear. The double luff sail has a much larger sleeve, with the object of forming a symmetrical foil at the leading edge. The idea behind the concept appears at first to be good, but there are several snags. First, the two sides of the sleeve tend to collapse on each other, so that the sail ends by effectively having only one surface. Secondly, such a large sleeve picks up water easily, so that speed of draining becomes a factor (water-starts on short boards are

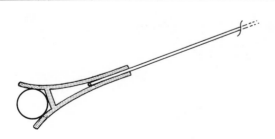

Fig. 11.11 *Camber Inducers*   It has been claimed that a camber inducer cleans up airflow to windward. In fact, the more important side of the sail is to leeward, and it is here that the device is beneficial (compare the poor aerodynamic form of Fig. 11.10). Because the batten end bears on a cloth strip in the inducer, the load on the batten is transferred directly to the mast; this makes for better control of sail shape.

Plate 11.5 *Sleeveless Boardsail*　The attachment points of this vertically cut Alpha sleeveless invention can just be detected at the forward end of each batten; the resulting gap between luff and mast is also visible. An easy sail to use because there is no sleeve to pick up water, it was condemned for aerodynamic inefficiency rather too hastily in my opinion, and may yet make a come-back. (*Alpha Sails*)

difficult). Thirdly, the mast must be matched exactly to the sail, for there is little tolerance if bending characteristics are wrong.

Sleeveless sail

Some time ago, Alpha Sails developed a sail without a luff sleeve; it was attached to the mast by Velcro straps at the batten ends. The result completely by-passed the bogey of a luff sleeve weighed down by water as the exhausted beginner tried to pull it up for the tenth time in as many minutes; it made life a lot easier. But it also suffered from some loss of thrust through the quite large gap between mast and sail, and was rather prematurely panned by some of the critics. I say prematurely, because I have the feeling that its detractors failed to get their priorities right – the beginner needs to find things easy, and is not necessarily as absorbed in total thrust as some might believe.

12 CARE AND MAINTENANCE

Lowering Sail

Always pull sails down by the luff. Dragging at the unsupported leech will cause localised stretching and give rise to fluttering and creases.

Hosing Down

Sails should be hosed down after use where salt water or dirt have got on them. While these will not harm synthetic cloth chemically, salt crystals or particles of dirt will work into the weave and saw away at the fibres causing the finish of the cloth to break down, particularly if it has been reinforced with chemical fillers.

After hosing, sails should be hung by the head and tack to dry. In this way weight is not thrown on the leech, which would cause it to stretch (Fig. 12.1).

Don't let Mylar/Melinex sails flog in the wind unnecessarily, because they will start to delaminate after a fairly short time; this also holds good for those woven board sails which have Mylar or Kevlar reinforcement patches.

Fig. 12.1 *Hanging Sails to Dry* Sails should be hung to dry so that their weight is supported by the luff, which has reinforcement in the shape of a wire, rope, or tape. If the leech is called upon to do the task, it will stretch out of shape.

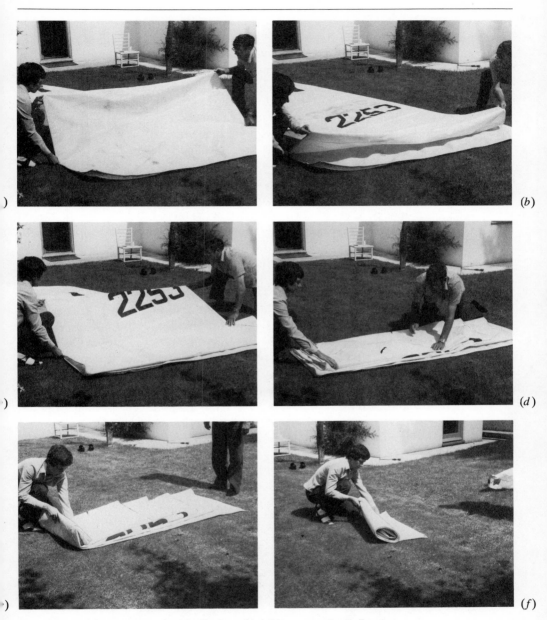

Plate 12.1 *Folding a Mainsail* Ideally the sail is laid out completely flat; in any case the foot must be pulled out straight. One person is at the luff (the lady) and one at the leech (*a*). The first fold is laid down on the foot (*b*), with the luff superimposed upon itself. The second fold (*c*) follows the first, and so on until the head of the sail is reached (*d*). The sail is then rolled from the luff at (*e*) (if it is not film laminate), taking care to avoid creasing any window, until the job is finished at (*f*). (*Author*)

Bagging Sails

Most of you know that synthetic sails should be kept in big bags to avoid the creases which would be caused by crushing into small ones. What many forget, however, is that this crushing can still take place after the sails have been bagged. It's no good having sails gently put into roomy bags if you go and throw the rudder or a couple of boat. chocks on them as they sit in the corner.

Even if you are careful about their bags, sails will eventually crease in the wrong places if they are not rolled or folded before they are put away. All creases in sails are wrong, but it is not possible to avoid them completely. What can be done is to see that haphazard creasing does not take place near the leech, or you can be quite certain that bad permanent creases will settle in the leech tabling – the worst place to have them. This will immediately give rise to 'motorboat-ing', which is doubtless familiar to you and which is so bad for the helmsman's morale due to its unsettling effect.

Folding a mainsail

Figure 12.2 shows two ways of folding a mainsail. It can be argued that the one which gives horizontal creases is the better of the two, because the creases offer less interference to a smooth flow of air across the surface. But I prefer to ring the changes so that creases do not get the chance to settle in one spot. Fastidious owners with plenty of room at home only fold their sails for the journey between home and clubhouse; you should certainly take them from their bags and flake them out (in the guest-room, perhaps?) if you are not going to use them for several weeks. If the sail has a zipper, leave it unzipped

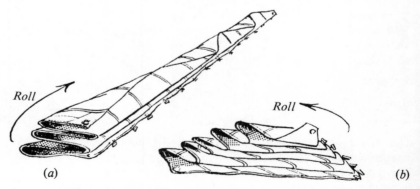

Roll   *Roll*

(a)   (b)

Fig. 12.2 *Mainsail Stowing* A woven mainsail may be folded as here and then rolled for its bag. If it is made of hard cloth or film laminate, roll it round the foot and use a long bag as in Fig. 12.3. Take out the battens first!

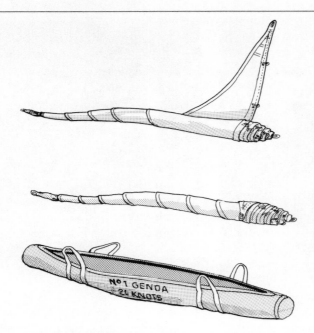

Fig. 12.3 *Genoa Stowing* A sail made from film laminate or hard-finish woven cloth will react badly to poor stowing; even a neat flake will cause unwanted creasing of the cloth. Roll the sail up the luff from the foot and, without folding it further, stow it in a long bag with a Velcro®-closed side opening. If you have a window roll from the head, so that there is a larger diameter when you reach the window; the sailbag will protect it from scratches.

when folding the sail or you risk the teeth disengaging for a short length where it may be bent in a fold. Film laminate sails should preferably be rolled rather than folded, as this offers less risk of delamination; board sails should have a long narrow bag which can take the sail when rolled round the mast.

Folding a jib
Plate 12.2 shows how to fold a jib. Note that the window is carefully placed on the outside of the roll, so that it does not have to be bent round too sharp a corner. The sailbag should protect the window from scratches. It is worth getting long narrow bags with side opening; Mylar jibs can be rolled along the axis of the foot and kept virtually free from creases (Fig. 12.3).

Folding a spinnaker
Spinnaker nylon is so thin that creases quickly blow out. It is therefore not important from this point of view to fold your spinnaker. If

(a)

(b)

(c)

(d)

Plate 12.2 *Folding a Jib*   Roll the sail down the luff from the head (a), adjusting the roll so that any window is not creased (b). When the roll is finished (c), check the window and, if it is not film laminate, fold to finish the job (d). (*Author*)

you have a patent way of setting it from its bag, you may care to see that it is put away all ready for hoisting. A good crew, however, will probably undo it all again at the start of the next day's sailing, to satisfy himself that it has been done properly. So it is probably best not to bother in the first place, it being more important to see that the spinnaker is free from tears and is completely dry, not only from the mildew point of view but so that it will be nice and light for possible ghosting conditions next time out.

Cleaning Sails

Besides the regular hosing down with fresh water which most dinghy sailors give their sails, cleaning off the more stubborn stains will make a suit last longer. A guide to the problem is given in ICI Fibres' pamphlet *Laundering and Dry Cleaning of Terylene*[20], which they kindly allowed me to publish in full in *Sails*. The following are my suggestions for simplified treatment of some of the more usual problems and are given in all good faith, but no responsibility is accepted nor warranty given or implied.

Warning
Normal care in the use of chemicals should be observed, especially as far as fumes, poisoning, burns, and fire are concerned: ensure plenty of fresh air while working; do not smoke (not only because of the fire hazard but also because some chemical cleaners produce poisonous fumes when their vapour is drawn through a burning cigarette); wash any neat chemicals off your body or clothes immediately; avoid naked flames or a lot of heat. Although many of the treatments given here are free from harmful chemicals, some are not, and it is a good idea to get into the habit of always taking these precautions. In addition, you should only use containers made of stainless steel, porcelain, enamel, or polythene, and not galvanised iron or alloy; keep strong chemicals away from galvanised luff wires, thimbles, splices, etc. Finally, always rinse out after cleaning so as to remove the danger of a 'high water mark'.

Washing

Dinghy sails of woven polyester can usually be washed in the bath. Don't be afraid to use a scrubbing brush (a sailmaker will probably have an industrial rotary scrubber) and use water as hot as your hand can bear, with a bar soap (Lifebuoy® is as good as any) or any proprietary liquid detergent such as Stergene®, Quix®, or a similar brand. If this won't shift local areas of general dirt, soak the affected part in neat detergent overnight before washing.

Stains

The following suggestions refer only to white Terylene or Dacron woven sails. Stains on coloured sails should be treated only after specialist advice; the adhesives of some film laminates may react unfavourably to some chemicals, so don't try it.

Adhesive numbers

Many adhesives used with stick-on racing numbers can be dissolved by soaking in benzene; any adhesive remaining on the sail after the numbers have been removed may be rubbed away with a benzene soaked rag, but it can leave a general dark staining, so be careful how you rush into it. Or try one of the biological soap powders.

Blood

Biological cleaners are best for removing blood and other protein stains, but there is a danger that those of them which contain optical brighteners may have an adverse effect on dyestuffs, some special resins, and also on the bolt rope; this is particularly true where the sail is left to soak for longer periods (overnight) for the enzymes to 'digest' the protein. Treat stubborn stains by soaking for an hour before washing out, or soak in a 5 per cent solution of ammonia and water. Keep adhesive numbers out of the solution or they may come off. Pre-soaking overnight in cold water before any other treatment is helpful and harmless.

Mildew

Scrub lightly with a stiff dry brush to remove as much of the mould as possible, then soak for two or three hours in a mixture containing a domestic bleach; one part Domestos® or Clorox® to ten parts of water will do a fair job. Wash well afterwards and repeat if necessary, but be prepared for only partial success because mildew stains are hard to get rid of.

Oil, grease, or wax

These stains may be tackled with a proprietary grease remover not containing carbon tetrachloride – which may be carcinogenic. Or mix one part of liquid detergent with two parts of Polyclens® or similar cleaner and brush well into the fabric. Leave for 15 minutes and then wash off with warm water. These treatments will not remove stains caused by the fine metallic particles which are often associated with lubricants. Such stains have to be tackled with special acid solutions outside the scope of a day-to-day book of this nature (see The Care and Repair of Sails [21] for fuller instructions).

Paint
All paint is difficult to remove unless treated without delay with turpentine, turpentine substitute, or something similar. Avoid using paint strippers based on alkalis (and most of them are); solvents such as chloroform, however, may be successful on dried paint.

Pitch and tar
While these have their own more sophisticated cures beyond the scope of this book, you will find that they respond as well as anything to the same treatment as for oil, grease, and wax stains. Complete cleaning will always be difficult.

Varnish
Polyurethane varnish is hard to remove once it has dried, but you could try chloroform; shellac varnish can be removed with methylated spirits or alcohol. Any varnish which is still wet should respond to turpentine.

Ironing Sails

The best advice about ironing sails is **Don't**. But there are those who do it, and who do it successfully, so I must obviously say some more. Be careful of isolated patches of the sail becoming overheated. This will cause localised melting of the filaments, which will fuse together and distort the cloth and which can never be cured. In addition, a heat of 70° C (160° F) causes uneven shrinkage, so you must be careful even if you are satisfied that you will not actually melt the filaments. Use a heat-controlled iron on the coolest setting and switch it off before starting; do not leave it in contact with one part of the sail for more than one or two seconds.

Reproofing Sails

The chemicals which are put into some synthetic sailcloths will eventually work their way out of the weave, and the sail will be the worse for it. As these fillers have been forced into the material straight from the loom, under pressure between heated rollers, they cannot be put back again once the cloth has been cut and sewn into a sail. There is nothing, therefore, which anyone – professional or amateur – can do to restore resin filling permanently and successfully to a synthetic sail.

Laying Up

When putting away your sails for the winter, besides thoroughly washing and cleaning them, have a good inspection for repairs. A stitch at laying-up time will certainly save nine a week after you start sailing again.

Ancillary items

Check over all *eyes* and *cringles*. The one most likely to give trouble is the jib tack, which supports the full weight of the jib and mast and may be twisted if you have a jib furling gear; it also spends quite a bit of its time under water. In wire eyes, and eyelets worked or punched into the sailcloth, there is usually a metal *thimble* or *turnover* inserted to protect the wire or seizing from the chafing effects of shackles and pins; this protecting piece may distort and start to pull out of the eye. If caught early enough it can often be hammered back again; otherwise it may need replacing by a new one put in with a punch and die. *Piston* or *snap hanks* should be looked at, and a drop or two of oil put on the plunger (not more, if you don't want it to get all over your sails); check their lashings. *Nylon twist hanks* chafe readily on the luff wire and they should be examined carefully. *Wire jib clips* can get bent and weakened. *Zippers* on sails are usually made from nylon so they need little attention save a check to see that the stitching is still good and all the teeth are there. The *slider* itself will probably be metal, however, so it should be checked for corrosion and given a spot of oil or light grease. *Lashings* for clew outhaul or tack fitting should have suspect whippings renewed, as should the ends of *sheets*, which should also be checked for chafe on blocks and jam cleats. *Battens* need attention to see that they don't have jagged edges or splits in the ends; a lick of varnish won't hurt wooden battens, and you can reinforce thin ends by binding with adhesive tape. Look at the *headboard* to see that it is not split or coming away from the sail, and check any *window* for splits or scratches. Finally, see that the *sailbag* itself is in good shape, for it has to protect the sail from dirt and damage for most of its life.

Chafe

Stitching sits on the surface of synthetics instead of bedding in, and likely points of chafe are jib leeches, where they rub on shrouds, spreaders and odd projections on the mast, and mainsail luffs, where they chafe on the shrouds when running; batten pockets can go at both ends, particularly where they rub on shrouds when running. Look carefully at the head of your spinnaker where the swivel is attached, thus giving it play to work from side to side and attack the stitching; the foot of the spinnaker may well chafe on the forestay under certain wind conditions. It goes without saying that you should always try to remove the cause of any recurrent chafing if possible.

Ropes
If the bolt rope is sewn outside the sail along its entire length, check it for security, particularly at the head and clew. If the rope is sleeved into the tabling or tape, check that the seizings at each end are firmly attached and that it has not picked up splinters from wooden spars. A conventional tabling, being made from sailcloth panels with seams where these join, is more likely to pick up splinters than a luff tape; it will also tend to chafe where the rather thick seams rub on the groove. If the luff has a tape (usually with a rope as well), check that the machine stitching is unbroken and that it is firmly attached at head and clew.

Wires
Have a close look at all luff wires. Galvanised wire will rust away unless it has been well protected; stainless steel does not always live up to its name and may cause discolouration of synthetic cloth (which does not necessarily harm the material, but is unsightly and hard to remove). You should pay special attention to the tack, where the protective coating has been disturbed during the splicing or swaging process, and where the wire gets wettest. Jib luff wires are usually hidden inside the tabling so it is difficult to see any damage; bend the wire back and forth, and listen carefully for any cracking or chafing noises which would betray a partly stranded wire, especially in the bottom foot or so of the sail. If your spinnaker has wires in the luff/leeches, check them for the same faults and also measure one against the other for equal length: if one is longer than the other, it is probably broken. If any wire is suspect, its replacement is best done by a sailmaker.

Storing Sails

When synthetic sails are put away for any length of time they should ideally be loosely flaked in a dry storage room; a weatherproof attic is as good as anywhere, provided the sails are not forgotten. They should be turned over once or twice during the winter and checked to see that the attic is indeed dry (don't forget that mildew can form on wet synthetics where dirt is also present) and that rats and mice haven't chewed off bits of them for nest-making purposes.

Where a good airy space is not available for spreading out, the sails may be hung up. Roll the mainsail round its boom to avoid creases and hang it over the rafters in the garage. The jib can hang down against the wall alongside, supported by the head and tack and with the clew hanging free; this keeps the weight off the leech.

The third best alternative is to leave them folded and stow them away in a dry cupboard. Wives please note that I do not actually specify 'in the linen cupboard', although this obviously fits the requirement admirably...

Fitting Out

If you did all that you should have done at the end of the season, you should have few problems when it comes to fitting out. If you did not make a good job of laying up, get out your sails as soon as you can and go through the items listed above. In any event, put a second drop of oil on all hanks, snap hooks, and shackles, and check zippers for ease of operation. Make sure that spar grooves are smooth-running (a light coating of paraffin wax will help here) and that all wire is free from barbed strands, and you are then ready to go.

If you find any repairs which need the attention of your sailmaker, get the sail away as soon as possible, but don't hope for too fast a service if you have left it late.

Film Laminates

The advent of film laminates has not out-dated the general advice on care of sails, but it has altered the emphasis somewhat and added some new points of interest. In the early 'eighties I presented a paper[22] in America on the subject of new sailcloth, and when preparing the new edition of this book, was interested to note that subsequent innovations have not invalidated the principles I then expounded.

Delamination
Delamination is the breakdown of bonding between the film and the substrate. It can start in a number of ways, which includes overloading (hoisting too hard), point loading (hoisting a hanked jib too slackly), rips or tears and, above all, flogging head to wind.

Yield point
Using any sail in winds above its designed range is bad for it; with film laminates it is usually destructive. Like metal, polyester film has a yield point and, if you stretch it beyond that point, it will never recover. Make sure that your sailmaker marks your sails with their top *apparent* wind speed, and then invest in a good anemometer which all crew members should be encouraged to use.

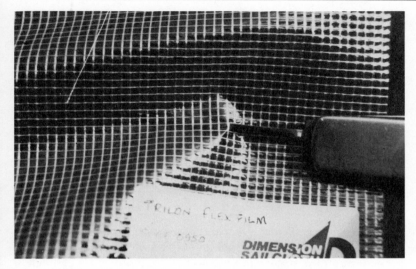

Plate 12.3 *Tear Strength*   The reinforcing mesh of a spinnaker laminate is clearly shown here to be doing its job – tension on the spike is causing a fold in the very thin cloth, but the tear does not run. Dimension Sailcloth point out that the cloth does not distort with point loading (for instance, through finger pressure as the sail is pulled down), as well as offering high tear strength. (*Author*)

Flogging

If laminated sails are allowed to flog head to wind, possibly aback on the rigging, they will respond by chafing (as will any all-woven sails) and delaminating. This not only demands care in use, but also not hoisting them by the tack to dry so that they flap in the wind (if you want to dry them, take them sailing in a light breeze or spread them on the lawn). A good deal of wear and tear can be avoided by fitting a tacking line. This is just over a foot (30–35 cm) of rope spliced into an eye halfway along the foot of the genoa; a crew member can then help the sail forward at each tack.

Point loading

Even if you are careful not to overload your sails in strong winds, you can still cause point loading if you hoist them wrongly. If you have a Mylar or Melinex sail fitted with hanks or slides and you hoist it too slackly, each fitting will pull a crease from the luff as the sail strains unevenly; equally, there is a danger of the luff tape being overstressed and causing delamination if the sail is hoisted too hard on the winch. Haul them up, therefore, until the small wrinkles at the luff are pulled out, and then don't haul any more, or you may get local delamination.

Flexing

Flexing does not cause quite the damage you might imagine, unless carbon fibres are involved (which weaken dramatically through repeated flexing), because the film will blow back into shape in use, and the substrate is so light that it does not take up permanent creases easily. This is not to say that Mylar and Melinex should be stuffed into sailbags willy-nilly, because repeated creasing will eventually cause problems. It has been said that laminate sails are like omelettes – they are better folded than scrambled. If sails are rolled as described in Figs 12.2 and 12.3, creasing will be kept to a minimum not only as they are bagged, but also while they remain stowed and later get dragged on deck for use.

Tearing

There are enough spectacular tears each season to make every owner nervous of this problem with laminated sails. But not only have tears been made a rarer occurrence by modern technology, the problem is also not as bad as it may at first seem, because most tears usually start as the result of thoughtlessness. It is important to ensure that all snags and sharp points are removed or fitted with anti-chafe tape or boots. The sails themselves should be protected from permanent snags such as spreader ends or shrouds, by incorporation of sacrificial patches; these are often best fitted after the new sail has been hoisted and the danger area identified and marked with a pencil. Any hole should be patched immediately with repair tape, and then returned to the loft for permanent repair depending on size: anything under quarter of an inch (6 mm) may be safely left, providing there is no delamination and the repair tape is adhering well (it sticks better to the film rather than the substrate).

Owners should be aware that film does not adjust itself round any hole, in the way that woven cloth tends to. Therefore any puncture will remain open, and this extends to those holes caused by a sewing machine. Too much sewing with close-spaced stitches will therefore result in a weakness somewhat similar to the perforations on a breakfast cereal packet, where one is exhorted to 'tear along the dotted line'. It is sometimes better to be content with iron-on sticky tape in preference to sewing.

Seams can give trouble for the same reason. This is especially true where, as in the leech, they are subjected to extra stress without the support of a bolt rope or webbing tape. This is why you will sometimes see mainsails with taped seams for some distance inside the leech (enlargement of stitch holes is further discussed at the beginning of Chapter 3). This is largely a matter for the sailmaker, but it is also something an owner may add for himself.

In addition to the above few paragraphs, which are a distillation of

(b)

Plate 12.4 *Reinforcement Patches* This Jeanneau *Fun* shows fan cut patches at the leech reef cringles of her all-woven mainsail (*a*). Any part of a film laminate sail which is liable to high stress or constant chafe, should be well taped or reinforced, like *Smokey Bear's* (*b*). (*Chris Howard-Williams*)

the experience of myself plus that of other users, ICI Fibres and ICI Films have been kind enough to send me some general guidance on the care of Melinex laminated sails. This is offered in good faith but without warranty; freedom from patent rights must not be assumed.

Melinex, being chemically identical to Terylene, resists attack by the same wide range of chemicals, including weak acids, and it withstands long term exposure to sea-water well. It is, however, affected by ultra-violet light which, over a period of months or years depending on the length of exposure to sunlight, will cause the film to lose tensile strength. When not in use, therefore, ICI recommend that a film laminate sail should be rolled and stored in a light-proof bag.

Stains
Warm water plus a mild detergent will remove most soiling from Melinex but, if a particularly stubborn mark offends, of the various

stain removers, carbon tetrachloride is now suspected of being car-cinogenic so is not advised; white spirit or methylated spirits should be tried instead. Carbon tet fumes are very dangerous if there is any alcohol in the body.

Board Sails

Besides all the problems which any sail is heir to, board sails have one or two of their own. To start with, they get wet from top to bottom every time they are taken out – even on fairly calm days. Secondly, at the end of sailing there is a temptation to roll it round the mast, put it on the car roof rack, and drive home regardless of the ensuing buffeting.

Washing
Rinse out all salt from the sail by hosing down with fresh water. Too much scrubbing and detergent may affect some modern materials, so don't worry too much about the odd individual stain.

Stowing
Anyone who races at all seriously will be advised to keep his or her racing sail for racing days. This will be removed from the mast, the battens taken out, and then rolled horizontally (with due regard for the large window), and preferably stowed in some sort of long bag or plastic piping of 6 in (15 cm) diameter, such as that used by plumbers; this protects the leech and batten pockets in particular and, as with any film laminate sail, should preferably be light-proof. A board sail for leisure use may, indeed, be rolled round the mast but, if it is transported on top of the car, you should keep the whole thing in a special stocking.

Chafe
Keep an eye on the top of the luff sleeve, where the mast head bears against it. Remember that camber inducers not only chafe the sail adjacent to them, they also wear the mast itself where they rotate against the same place.

13 FAULTS AND ALTERATIONS

Examining for Faults

When examining a sail for faults, there are some basic rules to follow if you want the most accurate results:

1. A sail will often only show its faults when set on the boat with its matching mainsail or jib and using its normal spars. Examine it afloat first, therefore, and then look at it ashore, either in the marina, the dinghy park or on a static test rig. Many sailmakers have a horizontal rig inside the loft, and it can sometimes be most useful to walk all round a sail set in this manner. You can examine at close quarters those parts of the sail which are suspected of giving trouble; you can try the effect of pinching or pulling the cloth in various places and you can usually bend the test mast at will.

2. When sailing, always sight up the mast to see that it is behaving normally *on both tacks* before checking the sail.

3. See that all leech lines are slack or you will get a wrong impression of the sail.

4. Look at the sail from off your boat if possible; at any rate get to leeward and in front of it, for it will often show its faults better from this angle.

5. Write down the faults you find, even marking the positions of creases in pencil on the sail; you will be surprised how inaccurate your memory can be when the sailmaker wants exact details later.

As class competition becomes hotter, special needs require special attention, and minor alterations to new sails are often necessary to get a perfect fit. Give them a chance to settle down first, then let your sailmaker 'breathe' on them to add that touch of greatness which marks the champion. Also, and this is important, do not maltreat your sails and then return them to the loft blaming the sailmaker for faults of your own creation.

A full list of possible faults and the cures for them takes up much more room than we have in this small book. I shall content myself with listing the chief faults and only giving those cures which it is in your power to effect yourself. You will then be able to take action in many cases, and also to observe intelligently those problems which are beyond a limited do-it-yourself capability. I refer the reader anxious to undertake more than routine tasks, to the fuller information in my specialist book on the subject, *The Care and Repair of Sails*.

Mainsail Faults

The chief faults which affect all-woven mainsails are:

> *Leeches:* slack (motorboating or falling away) or tight.
> *Creases:* wrinkles and hard spots other than in the leech.
> *Fullness:* too flat or too full; fullness in the wrong place; backwinding.
> *Size:* too small or too large.

Slack mainsail leech
A slack leech is caused by cloth which has stretched locally too much at the leech of the sail. This can be caused by such simple acts as pulling the sail down by the leech instead of by the luff, by treading

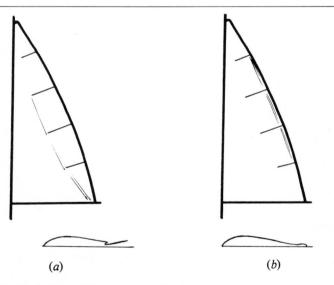

(a)   (b)

Fig. 13.1 *Slack Mainsail Leech*   A leech which is slack right into the sail for a good way, will reveal itself by a crease running along the ends of the battens as in (*a*). The inner ends of the battens tend to poke up to windward, and the sail falls away to leeward from there out to the leech.

If the last 3 or 4 in only are slack, as in (*b*), it is possible that the leech may vibrate in the wind, causing the characteristic drumming noise known as motorboating. The sail may be quite all right apart from this, but there is a danger to morale so get the trouble seen to by your sailmaker.

awkwardly on the sail, or by factors outside your control, such as the sailmaker laying the cloths too much on the bias. Controlled use of a leech line or drawstring can steady a motorboating leech, but avoid overdoing it or you will hook it to windward. The trouble is best cured in the sail loft, and the job of the leech line is to restore the morale of the helmsman by quietening the drumming noise, which can be so distracting. A lot depends on how far in from the leech the sail has stretched. Thus, if the whole leech falls away from the inner ends of the battens, it may either be because the leech cloths have been set by the sailmaker too much on the bias, the sail has too big a roach, or possibly because the sail is not hoisted up hard enough: if there is not enough tension on the luff, there won't be enough on the leech. Before sending the sail back to its maker, try hoisting it a bit harder. If the sail is already out to its marks, a pull down on the cunningham hole will soon tell you if a tighter luff will cure the problem; if it does, you must get your sailmaker to shorten the luff, so you can get more tension on it within the black band distances (Fig. 13.1).

Tight mainsail leech
This is most probably caused in the sail loft by laying the cloths with too little bias at the leech, or by building too much flow too far aft in the sail. It can, however, also be caused by maltreatment by the owner: if you use the sail continuously in hard weather, the flow will be blown aft. In any event, it is a matter for the sailmaker, but before you send the sail back, just make sure that you have not been looking at it all the time with the leech line tight...

Mainsail creases
Wrinkles, pleats, and hard spots can come from headboard, eyelets, seams unevenly sewn, a mast which bends too much for a fairly flat sail (Fig. 13.2), or a dozen other reasons. Many of these faults can be laid at the door of the sailmaker, but synthetic cloth takes a little time to settle down, so always use a new sail for a few hours before complaining; you may find that variation of halyard and outhaul tension will work wonders. Also, before you go rushing off to your sailmaker triumphantly quoting these pages as authority for heaping blame on him willy-nilly, be advised that there are more creases caused by owners than by sailmakers, through maltreatment, wrong setting of the sail, wrong rigging of the spars, wrong information on mast bend before the sails were made, and so on. Finally, creases in synthetics are sometimes almost impossible to avoid, particularly at the clew.

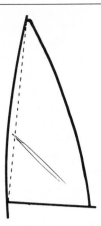

Fig. 13.2 *Flat Sail on a Bendy Mast*   If a bendy mast is used with a sail which hasn't got enough cloth built into the luff to allow full movement, mast bend will be restricted. In any case, the mast will remove all flow from the sail as it tries to bend fully, and a crease will run from the clew to the point on the luff where the shortage of cloth is most acute. The cure is to use a stiffer mast, and give your sailmaker accurate offsets next time he makes a mainsail for your bendy mast.

Mainsail fullness

A sail may have the wrong fullness because, when ordering, you did not compare the fullness you required with that of another suit by the same sailmaker; his idea of flat may be what you mean by medium. Fullness too far forward or aft can be for the same reason. It is easy for a sailmaker to pleat out fullness forward (and the stitching can always be released again if it doesn't do the trick, with no more damage than a few small holes up the luff), and harsh use of a cunningham hole may draw forward again some of the fullness which has shifted aft. On the other hand, too flat a sail is hard to cure and may be expensive.

Mainsail backwinding

A mainsail which lifts along the luff whenever you are sailing close hauled is said to be backwinded. This is very often not because the sail is too full forward but because the jib has a curling or bellied leech which is directing wind into the lee side of the mainsail (Figs 1.8, 1.9 and 1.10), so don't rush off and have the mainsail flattened before you have looked at the jib leech pretty hard.

Mainsail size

When a mainsail is spread on the floor without being pulled out along the luff and foot, it will almost certainly measure under size.

This is because the cloth is gathered on the rope or tape, which has to be pulled *with just sufficient tension to remove wrinkles across the line of the measurement being taken* (to quote from the IYRU *Sail Measurement Instructions*[23]) before a true picture can be obtained. When failure to pull a sail properly is coupled with the wide variety of methods of getting particular measurements (and take my word for it, some class rules still lay down some pretty silly ways of taking certain measurements), you can see how mistakes can occur. Legality of a mainsail can sometimes turn on a nice point of rule writing. For instance, when some class rules were drawn up, instead of including as a requirement that sails should be measured in accordance with (the current) IYRU Sail Measurement Instructions, they specified that, say, the 1973 or the 1975 issue should be used (because these were current at the time). This has had the effect of requiring that particular issue to be used, regardless of any subsequent revision. Among other amendments since those dates, the datum points for determining mainsail half-height cross-measurement were radically altered between the 1973 and the 1975 issues – and one method might clear a particular sail, whereas the other might make it illegal[24]. Don't, therefore, jump to conclusions when deciding sail size, but call in an expert.

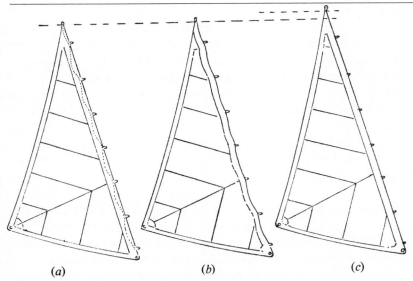

(a)   (b)   (c)

Fig. 13.3 *Jib Luff Measurement* In jib (a) the luff is not pulled enough to stretch the cloth, and the luff wire is loose inside the tabling (except where it is seized by the hanks). The sail appears short, but the dotted line shows the wire. Jib (b) is similar, but the luff is seized to the luff wire along its length, so easily shows the kinks. Jib (c) shows both the previous sails pulled hard out to straighten the wire and get full length, thus also inducing flow in the luff.

Jib Faults

A jib suffers from much the same faults as a mainsail, and I shall save space if I don't run through them all again. It is worth mentioning the question of size, however, because of a slightly different problem brought on by the luff wire. Here again the sail has to be pulled to its full length on the luff before the measurement is taken. Reference to Fig. 13.3 will show how a woven sail can appear fully stretched, but only by feel can you tell that the luff wire is snaking inside the luff tabling and is not taut, and therefore the canvas on the luff is not pulled to full length. The mistake is more obvious with control luff jibs, but take care to remove all wrinkles when stretching the luff for measurement.

Spinnaker Faults

Spinnakers are usually made of nylon, and the elastic nature of the thin canvas (don't forget that all sailcloth is canvas: flax, cotton, duck, polyester, or nylon) means that it can absorb a good many wrinkles in everything but the lightest winds.

Nearly all spinnakers suffer from being too narrow in the head. What looks like a narrow-gutted, spiky affair when viewed from behind in your own boat, however, appears to your rival as a high-breasted beauty bursting with power when seen from in front as, indeed, his sail looks to you. The cure for this universal problem is to get off your own boat once in a while and look at your spinnaker through somebody else's eyes just to revive your morale. If you really do have a narrow-gutted sail, console yourself with the thought that it should set well on a reach and have a low knock-down effect due to its smaller area aloft (Fig. 8.2).

Apart from this overriding defect, spinnaker faults can be fairly evenly divided into three categories.

Head girts
These stem from an attempt to cram too much cloth into the sail in order to get the biggest area within the rule. After allowing a decent interval for the sail to settle down and solve its own problems, the cure lies in cutting away some of the surplus cloth in the head: this is a matter for the expert. It is interesting that ultra-light weather spinnakers are often made fairly narrow in the head, especially for bigger boats, when you might think that every square inch of area would be crucial. Spinnakers with more area, however, also have more weight to lift in ghosting conditions, and they do not fill as quickly as smaller sails.

Fig. 13.4 *Curling Spinnaker Stays* If the tapes on the edges of a spinnaker become shorter than the length of cloth, the stays (luff and leech) will curl inwards to give a poor aerodynamic shape. You can also recognise this fault by a lot of tiny wrinkles running out from the tapes for an inch or so into the sail, where the nylon is gathered along the stays.

Tight stays
Stay is another word for the luff/leech of a spinnaker; if they are tight they curl and offer a poor aerodynamic shape when reaching (Fig. 13.4). The trouble is usually caused by the cloth just inside the edge of the sail stretching, while the tape running the length of the stay remains constant. Cure is a matter for the sailmaker.

Porosity
Spinnaker nylon is very thin and has to be of high quality if it is to stop air passing through it too quickly. Chemical fillers (resins) often dress an otherwise indifferent cloth to a passable stage in its early life, but these will eventually break down (according to care, quality, and amount of use) and the sail will lose a good deal of drive through too much porosity. The cure lies in selecting a good cloth when you buy a sail.

Alterations

Alterations which can be made to sails cover such a wide range that I shall reluctantly have to skim the surface and only touch on those aspects which have most bearing on the alteration of second-hand sails to fit another boat. A 470 or J.24 mainsail is made to the same stretched sizes the world over and, since I assume that an owner would not go outside his class for second-hand sails, alterations to one-design sails do not really apply (unless they were made to the wrong sizes, when minor surgery will usually bring them into line). Interest in this part of the book, therefore, will be limited to those classes like the JOG or the Flying Dutchman which can vary the size of sails within their rule, and also to owners of knockabout dinghies who are keen to add cheaply to their wardrobe.

Mainsails
If a mainsail needs enlarging, a great deal depends not only on how much bigger it has to be made but also which cut has been used to

make it: horizontal, mitre, radial, or vertical. Generally speaking, enlargements are neither easy nor cheap, and any saving which you may enjoy through buying second-hand will be more than swallowed up by the alterations. Reductions, however, can more easily be done, but care has to be taken when re-cutting the leech not to leave the unsupported cloth too much on the bias or it will distort.

Mainsail foot
The foot can sometimes be shortened by cutting in at the clew and fairing to the first or second batten pocket, depending on how much is taken off (Fig 13.5). The least that can be taken off is about an inch, to a point just inside the clew eye, because anything less would cut through the middle of the eye and leave a gap at the leech.

Mainsail half height
The half height can easily be reduced by half an inch or so through pleating the luff (which will draw in the leech), but remember that this will also flatten the sail; if more is required, it will have to be cut off the leech, which will then have to be faired above and below the half height, possibly for most of the length of the leech (Fig. 13.6). The foot will probably also have to be shortened if the half height is too much, so you can count on the whole leech being altered; this means taking off and replacing all batten pockets, besides remaking the leech itself.

Fig. 13.5 *Shortening the Mainsail Foot*   It is a fairly simple matter to chop an inch or so off the length of the foot at the clew. How high up the leech the sail will have to be faired off will depend on how much is taken off and also on the amount of roach on the leech.

Fig. 13.6 *Reducing the Mainsail Half-height Width*   If the sail is trimmed off at the leech to reduce the cross measurement, the amount of reduction will determine how far up and down the sail the leech will have to be faired. In any event, at least two batten pockets will have to be lifted and put back again. A cheaper alternative is to pleat the luff – but this will flatten the sail.

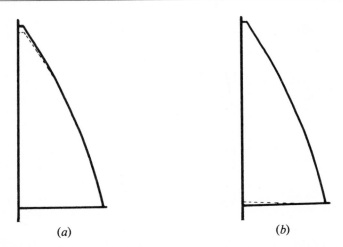

(a)   (b)

Fig. 13.7 *Shortening the Mainsail Luff*   A mainsail luff may be shortened by cutting a piece off at the head (a) or tack (b). If the head is cut, the leech will also be shortened and the clew will be lifted the same amount as the luff is shortened – usually a good thing. If the tack is cut, the leech stays the same, and the boom will then droop. If system (a) is used to shorten the luff by a lot, care must be taken that the cloths won't then meet the re-cut upper leech at too great an angle; if they do, this part of the sail slackens and it would be better to find another way to make the alteration.

Mainsail luff
Reducing the luff usually means taking off the top foot or so of rope
and the headboard, cutting off the appropriate amount of luff, and
replacing the headboard and rope. Unless a wider headboard can be
fitted lower down to fill the larger gap from luff to leech, without
infringing class rules, the leech also has to be attended to, as a glance
at Fig. 13.7 (*a*) will show. The job can also be done by cutting up at
the tack as in Fig. 13.7 (*b*), but this means that the boom will droop
more, because the leech is undisturbed and remains its original length
despite the shorter luff. In addition, the whole rope has to come off
for this method, so it is much more expensive. A quicker way
altogether, where only an inch or so is involved, is to oversew the bolt
rope by hand for its entire length; the action of pulling the stitches
tight will cause the rope to shorten and take the sail with it.

Bendy/stiff mast
A sail which was made for a bendy mast can have some of the convex
round trimmed or pleated out of the luff, to adapt it for a stiffer spar.

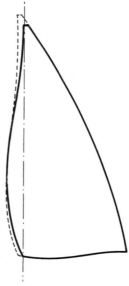

Fig. 13.8 *Making a Mainsail Fuller*   It is not easy to add extra cloth to a sail in
order to make it fuller – neither easy nor cheap. A fair job can be done if slightly
smaller overall dimensions are acceptable. Cut the upper luff back from the
dotted line, and more luff round will result – at the expense of luff and leech
lengths. If the foot were also to be shortened slightly at the tack, there would be
further scope for adding round to the lower luff. With luck, this modification
will only require the headboard to be refitted, while batten pockets and sail
numbers may remain.

Fig. 13.9 *Shortening a Jib Foot*   It is not as hard a job as it may seem, to take the luff wire out of a jib, cut the sail as shown in this drawing and then replace the wire; this shortens the foot and leaves the leech undisturbed. The alternative is to cut the sail at the clew, which runs the risk of spoiling the leech, as it has to be faired almost all the way to the head.

Fig. 13.10 *Shortening a Jib on both Luff and Leech*   If the luff is cut in at the head, rather than the tack, the leech will be shortened at the same time as the luff. The resulting sail will have a higher clew, because the angle of the luff will be altered.

To alter the sail the other way means adding cloth to the luff, and is not possible without major expense and risk of failure; about the only practical way is shown in Fig. 13.8, where all three principal dimensions have to be slightly reduced.

Jibs
The most important part of the jib is the leech. If this is flat and without a curl at the tabling, you are 90 per cent of the way towards a good sail. Any alteration to such a jib, therefore, should leave this

(a)   (b)

Fig. 13.11 *Shortening a Jib Luff*   If it is important to leave the clew at the same place when shortening a jib luff, the sail must be cut as in (*a*), with all the dangers attached to altering a leech. Cutting up at the tack as in (*b*) will lower the clew, but present small danger to the set of the sail. This latter alteration can often be done with little loss of area if the opportunity is taken to put a lot of round, or roach, on the foot (dotted line).

vulnerable part undisturbed if possible. You can see from Figs 13.9 and 13.10 how the foot can be shortened and how the luff and leech can be shortened together, both safe alterations as far as not disturbing the leech is concerned; both are fairly cheap, but note that both leave the jib at a different angle on the forestay, so your sheet lead position will have to change. If you want to shorten the luff, you may cut in at the head or tack as shown in Fig. 13.11 (*a*) and (*b*); the first method disturbs the leech (which can be all right if it is not excessive, but is always a risk) and the second lowers the clew nearer to the deck. Almost all other alterations to a jib are either costly or dangerous, or both.

Spinnakers
The most common alteration to a spinnaker is to cut down a fairly old sail for use in heavy weather. The sail can be split down the middle and made narrower and flatter, particularly in the head, as in Fig. 13.12; it can also be taken apart at the first cloth above the foot for something to be taken off the length of the stays (Fig. 13.13). Both these alterations leave the stays undisturbed except for length and don't mean making new clews. They are, therefore, fairly safe and cheap. Even a spherical spinnaker (one with no vertical seam) can be safely split down the middle in this way, provided you don't mind having a vertical centre seam when the job is done; the alternative is the more costly one of taking half the reduction off each side and fitting new luff/leech tapes and new clews.

Second-hand Sails

Talk of alteration leads naturally to thoughts about second-hand sails. As I said above, you should be careful when buying sails which were not made for your sizes, because you may wind up paying enough for the alterations to have enabled you to buy new sails in the first place.

The first question to ask when buying second-hand sails is why they are being sold. If there is no convincing reason, the suspicion must be that they do not set very well; perhaps they look all right to the untutored eye, but the flow may have been blown aft to an inefficient place through persistent use in strong winds.

Next, examine the sail as though for laying up as suggested in Chapter 12. Then look for pleats and empty stitch holes. A pleat will

Fig. 13.12 *Making a Spinnaker Narrower and Flatter*   If the centre seam of a spinnaker is undone, the sail will then be in two halves, and making it narrower is simply a question of trimming the right amount from the middle and joining the two halves again to remake the centre seam. Taking rather more cloth from the upper half will flatten the head.

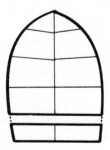

Fig. 13.13 *Shortening a Spinnaker on the Stays*   Similarly, if the first horizontal seam above the foot is undone, a parallel piece can be taken out to shorten the height of the sail. This means that the two clews are left undisturbed and don't have to be undone and remade, so it is a fairly economical alteration.

show that the sail has been flattened, while empty stitch holes, particularly at the leech, betray alterations which may mean that the set of the sail is suspect.

The sail should now be set on your own boat and taken afloat for a trial. If it fits, examine it for creases and fullness as listed at the beginning of this chapter – and make sure that you have a look at it in both light and strong winds. If it doesn't fit, don't take the word of the seller (or the evidence of this book) that the alteration will be easy and cheap, but take the sail to a sailmaker and ask him for a quotation for the job.

New Sails

If, after reading this book, you decide that nothing less than a new suit of sails will please you, yet you have never ordered such a thing before, how do you go about it?

First, select your sailmaker. Questions of price and quality, specialisation and location will all play their part in this. Ask around the clubhouse, have a look at other people's sails, and consult your bank account. Remember that a loft near at hand can help a lot if you think you will want after-sales service. If you already have a sailmaker, it should take a lot to make you decide to leave him; the devil you know ...

When you have made your choice, be content to put yourself in his hands. He has dealt with all sorts of customers before, and it is unlikely that you can surprise him. Besides basic information on fullness required and any cloth preferences you have, accurate details of your spars are crucial for a good fit, and information on crew weight will reveal how much power you can expect to control. If your class of boat is not well known, it is worth asking if he has all the latest amendments to the rules (some class secretaries are bad at circulating sailmakers with rule alterations affecting sails). Ask for a sample of the cloth the sailmaker proposes using, and tell him of any extras you want: window, racing number, boat's name on the sail-bag, special set of battens for light weather, and so on.

Like tailors, sailmakers do not always have the best reputation for prompt delivery, but if you order in plenty of time and allow a small margin on the promise you get, you should not often be disappointed – especially if you drop him a reminder just before the sails are due. Ordering in the off season not only ensures that you have your new sails by the spring, but also often gets you the benefit of seasonal discounts.

While new synthetic sails do not need breaking in as cotton ones did, they will be the better for careful use during the first three or four hours of their life. You may hoist and race with them straight away, but try at least to get half an hour cruising up and down on a reach before the gun goes. I always advise against reefing new sails in their first four hours of sailing. Despite all these warnings, you can misuse synthetics for limited periods and they won't let you down, but if you consistently neglect them you will pay for it in the long run.

Once again, sails are the power unit of a sailing boat, which wouldn't get far without them. Look after them and they will repay your attention.

REFERENCES

1 *Wind Tunnel Technique* R. C. Pankhurst and D. W. Holder (1932).
2 *Aero-Hydrodynamics of Sailing* C. A. Marchaj (Adlard Coles Ltd and Dodd Mead & Co USA. 1979) pp. 175 et seq.
3 *Sailing Theory and Practice 2nd Ed* C. A. Marchaj (Adlard Coles Ltd and Dodd Mead & Co USA. 1982) p. 49.
4 *Ibid*[3] pp. 47–51.
5 *The Best of Sail Trim* Arvil Gentry (Adlard Coles Ltd and Sail Books Inc USA. 1975) pp. 247–50.
6 *A Preliminary Note on the Results of Rigid Sail Tests in the Unheeled Position* C. A. Marchaj and A. Q. Chapleo (Southampton University Yacht Research Paper No 6. 1961) p. 9.
7 *Wind Tunnel Tests of a 1/3rd Scale Model of an X One-Design Yacht's Sails* C. A. Marchaj (Southampton University Yacht Research Paper No 11. 1962) p. 93.
8 *Design Factors Affecting Sail Power* (MacAlister Elliott & Partners, Lymington. 1985).
9 *Sails 6th Ed* J. Howard-Williams (Adlard Coles Ltd and John de Graff USA. 1988) p. 13.
10 *Looking at Sails* Bruce Banks and Dick Kenny (United Nautical Publishers. 1979) pp. 130–31.
11 *Sail Measurement Instructions* (IYRU. 1985) Section III, 1.
12 *International Offshore Rules* (Offshore Racing Council. 1987) Rule 802.
13 *International Yacht Racing Rules* (IYRU. 1985–88) Rule 25.
14 *Ibid*[12] Rule 851.
15 *Spinnaker* R. R. King (Adlard Coles Ltd and Sail Books USA. 1981) p. 28.
16 *Ibid*[9] Chapters 12, 13 and 14.
17 *Ibid*[12] Rules 816 and 817.
18 *Special Regulations Governing Minimum Equipment and Accommodations Standards* (Offshore Racing Council. 1987) Section 10.21.2.
19 *Ibid*[9] p. 258.
20 *Laundering and Dry Cleaning of Terylene Sails* (ICI Fibres).
21 *The Care and Repair of Sails 2nd Ed* J. Howard-Williams (Adlard Coles Ltd and Hearst Marine Books USA. 1985) Chapter 3.
22 *The Ancient Interface XII – Proceedings of the 12th AIAA Symposium on the Aero/Hydronautics of Sailing* (American Institute of Aeronautics and Astronautics. 1982) Paper by J. Howard-Williams pp. 224–8.
23 *Ibid*[11] Section III, 4.
24 *Ibid*[11] Appendices A and B.

INDEX